MAN AS AN END

Other books by
ALBERTO MORAVIA

THE WOMAN OF ROME
THE CONFORMIST
TWO ADOLESCENTS
(*Agostino* and *Disobedience*)
THE FANCY DRESS PARTY
THE TIME OF INDIFFERENCE
CONJUGAL LOVE
ROMAN TALES
A GHOST AT NOON
BITTER HONEYMOON
TWO WOMEN
THE WAYWARD WIFE
THE EMPTY CANVAS
MORE ROMAN TALES
THE FETISH

ALBERTO MORAVIA

MAN AS AN END

A Defense of Humanism

LITERARY, SOCIAL AND POLITICAL ESSAYS

Translated from the Italian by
BERNARD WALL

FARRAR, STRAUS & GIROUX NEW YORK

Published in Italian under the title
L'uomo come fine a altri saggi

First American edition 1966

Library of Congress catalog card number 65-26572

The quotation from Ernest Hemingway's
A Clean Well-Lighted Place is reprinted in
this edition by permission of Charles Scribner's Sons;
those from *The Betrothed* by Alessandro Manzoni,
translated by Archibald Colquhoun,
copyright 1951 by E. P. Dutton and Company, Inc.
(Dutton Paperback series), and from
The Decameron by Boccaccio, translated by J. M. Riggs,
reprinted by permission of E. P. Dutton and Company, Inc.,
the publishers.

"When Art Becomes Propaganda" first appeared in the
United States in the *Saturday Review*.

Printed in the United States of America

CONTENTS

Translator's Note 7

Preface 9

Man as an End 13

The Man and the Character 64

Presence and Prose 72

Recalling *Time of Indifference* 76

Extremism and Literature 82

Psychoanalysis 87

Machiavelli 89

Communism in Power and the Problem of Art 108

Boccaccio 134

Roman Walks 156

Notes on the Novel 167

The Short Story and the Novel 178

Answers to Nine Questions on the Novel 183

Alessandro Manzoni, or the Hypothesis of a Catholic Realism 192

Eroticism in Literature 228

Nothing Amen 231

Dialogue on the Painting of Renato Guttuso 237

The 'Vulgarity' of Giuseppe Verdi 248

TRANSLATOR'S NOTE

THE ESSAYS published in this volume are put in the order of their original dates of publication. There is only one exception: the title essay, *Man as an End*, is put first. The dates are important and the reader should note that the earliest essays, which appeared during the Fascist dictatorship in Italy, were considered dangerous at the time.

In quotations from the essays on Boccaccio, Machiavelli and Manzoni, use has been made of translations of these writers already in existence in English. These are: *The Decameron*, translated by J. M. Rigg (J. M. Dent, Everyman Library); *Machiavelli, The Literary Works*, translated by J. R. Hale (Oxford University Press); and *The Betrothed*, translated by Archibald Colquhoun (J. M. Dent). The quotation from *A Clean, Well-Lighted Place*, published by Jonathan Cape Ltd, is by permission of the Executors of the Ernest Hemingway Estate.

The Man and the Character and *Presence and Prose* were first published in the periodical *Prospettive* in 1941. *Recalling 'Time of Indifference'* in *Nuova Europa* 1945. *Extremism in Literature* and *Psychoanalysis* in *La Fiera Letteraria* 1946. *Machiavelli* in *Quaderni dell' Associazione culturale italiana*, vol. III 1950. *Boccaccio* appeared in the volume *Il Trecento*, Florence 1953. *Communism in Power and the Problems of Art* 1953, *Man as the End* 1954, *Answers to Nine Questions on the Novel* 1959 and *Eroticism in Literature* 1961 all appeared in the review *Nuovi Argomenti* (edited by Alberto Moravia and Alberto Carocci). *Notes on the Novel* appeared in *Tempo Presente* 1956. *Nothing, Amen* appeared in *L'Espresso* 1961. The following essays were originally written as prefaces: *Roman Walks* for an edition of Stendhal, Florence 1956; *Alessandro Manzoni, or the Hypothesis of a Catholic Realism*, for an edition of the *Promessi Sposi*, Turin 1960. *Dialogue on the Painting of Renato Guttuso* was published in Palermo in 1962.

The translator also wishes to acknowledge his gratitude to Professor Filippo Donini of the Italian Institute, London, for help with the translation of G. G. Belli and over other points.

BERNARD WALL

PREFACE

The essays collected in this volume are all literary—a statement that may seem surprising when the essay from which the book's title is taken is not literary. But apart from the fact that I am a literary man, and that whatever I write must be concerned with literature up to a point, I believe that *Man as an End* is directly and immediately concerned with literature. For *Man as an End* is a defence of humanism at a time when anti-humanism is the fashion. As literature is by its very nature humanist, it follows that any defence of humanism is a defence of literature.

The reasons why the modern world is anti-humanist are not at all mysterious. At the source of the anti-humanism of the modern world there is unquestionably a death-wish—a longing for death and destruction and dissolution that may well be the last spasm of the great suicidal orgy of two World Wars. But there are other, less extreme reasons which are more customarily associated with certain alienations of feeling: the exhaustion, weariness and decay of traditional humanism; its immobilism and conservatism; its hypocrisy when confronted with the tragic events of the first half of this century.

For all these reasons I would like to point out that *Man as an End* is in no way intended as a defence of traditional humanism, now over and done with; rather, it is an attack on the anti-humanism known as neo-capitalism and a cautious approach to the hypothesis of a new humanism.

Now it would be interesting to ask why, despite the apparent contradiction, today's anti-humanism coincides with the victorious achievements of neo-capitalism. That is, with the predominance of a conception of life which appears to be bound up with humanistic values.

For it might well be supposed that a conception of life that has changed the face of a large part of the world within a matter of twenty years, and achieved the humanist operation of allowing ever-increasing masses to enjoy what was once the privilege of the few by putting at the disposal of these masses an endless quantity of factory-produced consumer goods—it might well be supposed that a conception of life that has made men more prosperous, and hence freer, deserves the name of humanism.

But this is not so. In the modern world it would be hard to find the solid confidence, the full-bloodedness and the richness of temperament that were the hall-marks of humanism at its dawn. The man of the neo-capitalist age, with his refrigerators, his supermarkets, his mass-produced cars, his missiles and his television sets, is so bloodless, insecure, devitalised and neurotic that he provides every justification for those ready and anxious to accept his decline as a positive fact, and reduce him to the position of an object among other objects. But unfortunately neo-capitalist man is unable to forget his own nature which, after all, is human. And so his anti-humanism falls short of real conviction. Beneath the bright, abstract appearance, we find—if we look carefully—boredom, disgust, impotence and unreality.

The arts, as usual, play their part in disclosing the characteristics of the modern world. They mirror, in exasperated form, the negative characteristics of neo-capitalist humanism. And what are these characteristics? I would say they could be summed up in one word: nothingness. For the outstanding characteristic of the arts is the discovery of, the representation of, the description of, and the obsession with—nothingness. This nothingness has no real connection with the old anarchistic nihilism, which was first and foremost denial and revolt.

This nothingness is an autonomous nothingness and an end in itself; it denies nothing and revolts against nothing. It is the nothing to which Hemingway refers in his well-known short story, *A Clean, Well-Lighted Place*:

Our nothing who art in nothing, nothing be thy name, thy kingdom nothing, thy will be nothing, as in nothing . . . Amen.

Probably the origin of what we might call the 'nothingness' of the arts lies in their transformation into consumer goods. In the past it was understood that the arts were humanist, inasmuch as they were the highest, and at the same time the most complete and lasting, expression of man. But now it is the alienation of man that is expressed first and foremost in the arts, in other words something contrary to completeness and lastingness. It may seem strange that an art that has nothingness or alienation at its heart should at the same time be an article of consumer goods or a product for the masses: but the contradiction is only on the surface. For modern art is a substitute, that is, something non-genuine, counterfeit and mechanical. This is because it seeks to place at the disposal of the masses what at one time was only for the few, while leaving the masses in their disinherited inferiority and not bringing them up to the level of the few. In this way art as an article of consumer goods reflects a society divided into classes in which everything is at everyone's disposal in appearance only. In reality real culture remains the privilege of a few: for the masses there are the substitutes provided by the culture industry.

All this, let us say in passing, goes to show the usefulness of the avant-gardes in art in the modern world. They have a precise function in the culture industry in that they manufacture the prototypes from which mass production can proceed.

But is it really true that the masses must inevitably be abandoned to their anti-humanism? My answer is No: there could unquestionably be humanist arts for humanist masses tomorrow. The anti-humanist masses in the modern world are merely the neo-capitalist masses. This is why neo-capitalism is fetishist; and every form of fetishism is bound to be anti-humanist.

What does neo-capitalistic fetishism consist in? Neo-capitalism, in its reaction against Communism, has behaved in somewhat the same way as the Counter-Reformation in its reaction against the

Reformation; by extending the industrial revolution and flooding ever larger groups with consumer goods, it has borrowed the means of its adversary; but it has preserved its aim intact—as how could it not?—which was, and still is, profit, or fetish.

So we must have no illusions. We shall have an ever larger number of cheap, well-made consumer goods; our life will become more and more comfortable; and our arts, even the most demanding and difficult ones, indeed those especially, will become more and more accessible to the masses; at the same time we shall feel more and more despair. And we shall feel more and more that at the heart of this prosperity lies nothingness or a fetishism which, like all fetishisms, is an end in itself and cannot be put to the service of man.

I say all this to explain not only the title of this book, but also its composition, which may seem to lack homogeneity. As I said at the beginning of these introductory notes, it is natural enough—given my conception of literature—that a moral essay such as *Man as an End* should stand side by side with essays on Boccaccio, Machiavelli, Manzoni, and the art of the novel.

Finally it seemed to me that there was a certain unity of inspiration in the essays collected here, the more noteworthy in that this was unconscious, and in that they cover a span of some twenty years.

This unity seems a guarantee that I have expressed myself sincerely and impartially over those twenty years, and without regard to fashion. After all, a book is not a book but a man talking through a book. I hope the theme of this book will not strike the reader as incoherent or useless.

Alberto Moravia
October 1963

MAN AS AN END

1 *Machiavellianism as Sadism*

Polemics about the end and the means have now lasted for more than four centuries—from when, in his exile, Machiavelli wrote *The Prince* to incite Cesare Borgia, Duke Valentino, to achieve the end of uniting all Italy under his sway without regard to the means. Machiavelli wrote in Florence, which was a little republic of Renaissance Italy, and his primary concern was with Italy, which was one little part of the world of the time. Yet his observations and theories have been proved valid outside his own time and in worlds infinitely larger and more complex than his own. Moreover, like all discoverers, Machiavelli did not so much invent as give a permanent name to something that had always existed; or, better, he defined this something so well and deduced such exact and rigorous consequences from his definition that ever since his time this something has spontaneously been called Machiavellianism. Significantly no name had been found for it before Machiavelli's time, that is to say before the spiritual and political supremacy of the Church had been rejected by the European monarchies, and politics had effectively and practically been separated from Christian morality. This amounts to saying that, though Machiavellianism had always existed, it was only in the age of Machiavelli that conditions occurred which made it possible to deduce from it a whole theory of political practice. And I say this precisely because of my conviction that even attitudes apparently constant in the human soul, and hence capable of giving the illusion that laws can be deduced from them, may well either slumber and remain latent or—if not exactly disappear—at least go back to sleep, that is revert to being man's good or bad potentialities, to being his inclinations and temptations.

The truth of this could be shown by comparing Machiavellianism and Sadism. Sadism, too, had to wait many centuries before receiving its name and the theory justifying it, from the Marquis de Sade. This does not mean that before de Sade the mixture of lust and cruelty that today goes under the name of Sadism was unknown. It was certainly known and widely practised. But we needed de Sade or the French civilisation of the eighteenth century with its mixture of eroticism, illuminism and demonism, for the vice to be given a permanent name and, so to speak, be erected into a theory. With its official consecration in the world of the spirit, Sadism has since done nothing but grow, exactly like epidemics once the health authorities have finally decided to write about them in official bulletins. The German concentration camps of the second World War were nothing more than de Sade's novels transferred to reality and lived. But the very excesses of Sadism suggest that it could disappear from one moment to the next or, better, as we have already said, go back to sleep like a volcano that has broken a centuries-old lethargy with a memorable eruption.

I have compared Machiavellianism and Sadism because I want to make clear from the outset that, to my mind, Machiavellianism is a deformation of politics in exactly the same way as Sadism is a deformation of love. On the other hand, just as Sadism, whether in de Sade's books or in current practices, is not confined to the strictly erotic field but seems to invest all human activities, so Machiavellianism is no longer a merely political affair. It is no longer concerned, as in Machiavelli's day, with what to do so as to win and consolidate political power, for it invests all relationships between men, political and non-political. The world of mankind is unitary, and every time one idea becomes pre-eminent over others it tends irresistibly to go beyond its proper field and enter others with which it has nothing in common.

But leaving Sadism aside, with its many affinities with

Machiavellianism (for Sadism is a contamination of eroticism and is in character abstract), I maintain that the deformation Machiavellianism produces in politics lies in the forced marriage of politics with abstract reason, that is to say in the creation of political science and technique. Before Machiavelli, politics consisted in prudence, cunning, intuition, the capacity to temporise, wisdom, and a whole lot of distinct practical expedients often mutually contradictory. When Christian morality reigned supreme, it would not tolerate the existence of any human activity that was independent of that morality or ordered by new laws and principles. With Machiavelli politics became independent from Christian morality; all those practical and reasonable—as distinct from rational—expedients were erected into a single rational principle, and where before there had been no more than changing and discontinuous relationships, there arose laws. Politics, as we have seen, became a technique.

But no human activity can be independent of ethics and become a technique without sooner or later causing the same independence in other activities and transforming them in a similar way. In Machiavelli's time Machiavellianism was an almost private affair for princes and rulers; but since then it has taken giant strides. It has found two ways of general infiltration: on the one hand, not one but all human activities have been transformed into techniques, and on the other, politics have become supreme and this supremacy has turned the whole of man's world into a political world.

2 *The modern world is a Machiavellian world*

The various advances made by Machiavellianism have been not continuous and regular but discontinuous and in leaps. As the Church lost ground to her enemies and became Machiavellian in its turn, that is to say subordinating all moral and religious considerations to the conservation and defence of the institution of the Church, other currents of a universal and humanist tendency attempted from time to time to limit, combat and overthrow Machiavellianism—e.g. liberalism after the French Revolution, nineteenth-century socialism, pacifism, and so on. As everyone knows, Machiavellianism lay behind the policies of the great enlightened monarchies, suffered a partial eclipse at the French Revolution, made a come-back with the Treaty of Vienna, seemed to be put in the shade first by English liberal politics and then by the propagation of socialist ideals, but exploded once more under Bismarck at the very heart of European peace and progress. Since then the strides made by Machiavellianism have been triumphant, like a headlong, irresistible river that swells and increases in power thanks to the very obstacles it overcomes on its way. Machiavellianism now seems inevitable, it is taken for granted and seems to have no alternative. In the field of pure thought it appears invincible, and it is the ineluctable centre towards which all roads in politics seem to lead. Efforts can be made to halt it at the beginning or half-way along thanks to decency, timidity, humanity, or restrictions on the spirit of logic; but no one can hope to find a road that does not lead to it if followed to the bitter end. Some peoples and governments are less given to system and are more empirical, and these can still boast that they have been Machiavellian only in part and in given circumstances; more consistent peoples and governments have been entirely Machiavellian. In the first case we have seen politics moderated by devices of prudence and humanity; in the second we have seen inhuman ferocity. But there is no denying that the prudence of the first and the ferocity of the second were influenced by the Machiavellian spirit.

Yet the immediate practical result of the struggle of these Machiavellianisms does not justify their wide and obstinate employment. Hitler and Mussolini died ignominiously after causing catastrophes in Germany and Italy; the great democracies of the West gained the victory but emerged from the ordeal in a very worsened condition; Stalin's Russia was invaded and devastated by the armies of his German ex-ally. The only result of the universal and indiscriminate practice of Machiavellianism in modern times has been to provoke the two biggest wars in history and to bring infinite suffering and immense destruction on mankind. But despite all this, Machiavellianism shows no signs of being abandoned in the near future, very much the reverse. Even if its vitality is due to the absence of any different kind of politics rather than to positive and convinced loyalty, it is more alive than ever. Everyone agrees when it comes to disapproving of it and condemning it; all deny in words that they practise it; but if we look at the facts we find no one prepared to forgo it.

And this because even if the two greatest world powers, the United States and Soviet Russia (to mention only them), *wanted* to be un-Machiavellian they would not be able to be so. Four centuries ago politics had it within its power to be un-Machiavellian, that is to say, to avoid being a technique. Today politics is inevitably Machiavellian because the premises for a non-Machiavellian system of politics are entirely lacking. These premises have been skilfully suppressed one after the other in the intervening centuries, and we would somehow have to re-create them if we wanted non-Machiavellian politics, that is to say politics subordinated to a higher principle. Or better, once the ancient premises ceased to be valid and were allowed to go by the board, we would have had to create new ones of a fundamentally different kind.

Therefore, if we are to investigate the reasons why Machiavellianism is inevitable and ineluctable in politics we need to leave politics aside and get down to something deep in human relationships, something that seems at first sight to have nothing to do with politics. So it would be inaccurate and cause a certain confusion if we discussed Machiavelli and Machiavellianism in this inquiry. Machiavelli applied the principle of the end justifying the means to politics, yes, but this principle is valid outside politics and as such is to be studied, defined and understood outside Machiavelli's formulations. From this point onwards, therefore, there will be no further mention of Machiavelli's name. It might well have been unnecessary to mention his name earlier on had it, and what goes with it, not seemed a help in clearing the ground for the series of ideas that are to follow.

3 There are two ways of building a road

I am a conquistador from across the oceans, and my government has assigned me the ownership of a vast piece of land as a reward for my services. Even before taking possession of my land I have examined it on the map and decided to build a road. The land is criss-crossed by holdings of various sizes, by a river, numerous streams, large scattered farmsteads and other buildings. Here and there are churches and chapels dedicated to local divinities. There are wells in plenty where people draw their water, oil-presses to press the oil out of olives, mills to grind the grain, little artisans' workshops, a sports ground where the boys play ball on Sundays, and other similar amenities for public use. My land has been inhabited from time immemorial, and numbers of monuments and ancient ruins bear witness to the passing of other civilisations and other conquerors. The land has great beauty owing to the special and unique character of the blending of man's work with nature. Finally the configuration of my land is not uniform: here it is minutely cultivated like a garden, there cultivation is impossible owing to rocks or marshes. The rock is extremely hard and the marshes pestilential.

Why do I want to build a road? Because I am a new landlord and have new ideas. Because I am convinced that the road will be of great service to the inhabitants and also to myself. I have a thousand reasons and none. It is enough to say that I want to build a road.

I have two possible ways of building the road. The first way is to respect the boundaries of the homesteads, skirt round the large farms, span the river at its narrowest point, leave the chapels, oil-presses, mills, wells and sports ground untouched, and avoid the marshlands and rocky areas.

The second way is just the opposite and consists in building the road without bothering about the obstacles. In this case my road will cut across the farm land, span the river at its widest point, flatten the homesteads. I shall hack down mills, oil-presses, chapels and workshops, fill in the wells, eliminate the sports ground. Furthermore I shall dynamite hundreds of thousands of cubic yards of rock and dry up hundreds of thousands of square yards of marshland.

Nothing binds me to build the road in one way or the other. The law is on my side. There is a decree of my government whose execution is guaranteed by force. I can do whatever I want: I can even kill off the inhabitants down to the last man and destroy all the farms and farmland. But I want to make the road.

The first way is certainly the longest and, at least temporarily, the most expensive. It will involve going to live on my land for a few months or even a few years so as to make a serious study of the configuration of the landscape, of all the twists and turns my road must make if it is to respect the existing properties and buildings while not barging off into the rocks and marshlands. I shall have to get to know the inhabitants individually so as to discuss the plan of the road with them. I shall have to form my own idea as to the usefulness or necessity of the various wells, oil-presses, mills, workshops, sports ground. I shall have to study, and get to the heart of, the inhabitants' religion, and familiarise myself with the divinities to whom churches and chapels are dedicated. I shall have to learn about the history of my land so as to make a correct evaluation of all the monuments and ruins. I shall have to get to know and appreciate the various beauties of my land so as to enhance them rather than harm them. Finally I shall have to sound the land to find out where there is rock, where marsh, where clay, and so on. In the course of this long, patient and exhaustive examination a singular thing will happen to me: as I get to know my land better I shall find myself growing to love it more and more, so that by degrees the end I had first set myself, namely building the road, will give place to another end, namely the land itself. True, the road would have benefited the land; but my original end was to build the road at all costs. Now I shall discover that my real end has become the land itself, or rather the particular idea I have formed of it and of its good after thorough examination. This substitution of ends will have become so complete that I shall finally decide either to build the road with innumerable twists and turns, or to put off building it until a more suitable time, that is until, for whatever reason, the obstacles have fallen of their own accord, or, again, to make no road at all supposing I have come to the conclusion that the road would be useless if not downright harmful. But whatever the reason, these three possible decisions bear witness to the fact that henceforward my end is no longer my road but my land, that is my respect for my land or for the idea I have formed of how my land should be; bear witness to the fact that something irrational, namely love for my land, has finally prevailed over my first purely rational idea of building a road.

Now let us consider what I shall do if I pursue my second way. First, instead of visiting my land, I shall draw two parallel straight lines from point A to point Z on a topographical map: this will and must be my road. Then I shall call in a squad of surveyors, accountants, engineers, constructors, planners, and various other technicians, and give them the job of making a completed plan of the road as marked out on the map. Of course I shall lay down certain preferences and requirements in accord with what might be called the ideal aspects of the road as I have imagined it and want it to be carried out: cost, so much; time, so much; length, so much; width, so much; and so on. My technicians will study the matter as technicians, and as technicians they will draw up the plan. It will be a perfectly rational plan, with so much allotted for cost, time, and all the other conditions. Any uneasiness I may feel will be dispelled when I see the plan. It corresponds to the requirements of reason in every aspect; it could be put into effect today, ten centuries ago, or ten centuries hence, on my land, in central Africa or in Siberia. I feel perfectly happy about it and give orders for the construction to start: funds are paid out, workers taken on, material collected, plant installed, and so on. But suppose that after ten days or a fortnight uneasy rumours begin to reach my ears. Some of the farmers protested when the workmen began pulling down their houses, there was a clash, the police had to intervene, casualties occurred; a mine intended to blow up a rock killed four workmen; the bridge over the river was carried away by flood; during the demolition of an ancient miraculous chapel the people again rose up in revolt—ten more casualties; boys greeted technicians on the sports ground with stones; the water in two of the wells was poisoned, etc, etc. When I get news of these, and numbers of other incidents of the same kind, I become very angry; I re-examine the plan of the road, find it rational in every respect, and forthwith accuse both the farmers who opposed the building of the road, and my technicians who failed to foresee and forestall such incidents, of crime. The criminal guilt of both farmers and technicians strikes me as all the more irrefutable and unpardonable in that, when summoned to answer for their failures before my court, all they can produce in defence are irrational and highly personal reasons against the sacred and perfect rationality of the plan. For instance, in attenuation of the revolt following the demolition of the chapel, a farmer mentions the devotion of the faithful to the saint venerated there, and dares to set this devotion against the strict calculations of the plan. A technician on his side offers the tiredness of the workmen as an excuse for the improper functioning of the mine. To this I reply that the plan allowed for the mine going off on a given day at a given hour and a given minute, and there was no earthly reason why this should not have happened. In the end I become convinced that, for some unknown motive, there is manifest ill-will against the construction of the road, and so I give new orders. The road must be built at all costs and in the time and manner prescribed in the plan, and any means must be used to attain that end. Where money can be used for bribery and ruthless buying and selling, let it be used; where physical violence is required, let there be beating-up, imprisonment, torture or hanging; where deceit may help, let any promise be made—people's minds must be seduced with illusory prospects of future wealth, the outcome must be painted in rosy colours, nothing must be spared to stimulate enthusiasm. My hirelings rush off to carry out my orders. A third of the population is corrupted, a third is wiped out, and a third is besotted. After a few months, and in the time prescribed, the road is inaugurated. True enough, on the day of the inauguration I realise that my land has changed in appearance, and where at one time there were cultivated fields, houses, and the works of man, now there is a wilderness; but to make up for that there is my road, straight, shiny, irresistible, as far as the eye can see. My aim has been achieved. Reason has triumphed after all, and I have the knowledge that within a year, or ten years, or a hundred years, other men will take the place of those I have wiped out, other cultivated fields will spread out over the wilderness, and new inhabitants will eventually use and benefit from my road. But such forecasts are unnecessary, superfluous; I do not need them to silence any qualms of conscience—that can be done by the single phrase, Reason has triumphed. I am not a fanatic, remember, but outside reason I can see nothing but unreason—darkness, chaos, fog, confusion. Is it surprising, then, that I cling to reason with my whole strength?

So here we have the two ways of building a road. As I have already said, my land is mine entirely, to do what I like with. Yet it is impossible for me to decide which of the two ways has more advantages or disadvantages. The first way may lead me to giving up building a road at all; the second destroys my land in the interests of my road. But the main difference between the two ways—apart from all considerations of profit—is this: if I pursue the first way my end is the human beings who live on my land; if the second, my end is reason which dictates to me the plan of the road.

So it is plain that the choice will depend not so much on my personal interests as on two things outside myself: the human beings who live on my land and reason. In other words both the ends confronting me transcend me personally and so provide a morally valid justification for the means I adopt in attaining them.

For a while I can be buoyed up by the theory that the two ends are really one, that human beings and reason are the same thing expressed in different words. But men are not made up of reason alone—indeed, when I examine their lives, their customs, their religion, their affections and their passions, I perceive that reason plays a very modest part. Reason, which was my guide in drawing up the plan, does not reckon with men as they really are. For men could be substituted animals, plants, stones, even algebraic cyphers and formulas, and the result reason produced would remain unchanged.

So the choice will depend on me, on what I am. That is, on what I am in relation to the men on my land. If I am capable of viewing them as men, and not as inanimate matter, then I will surely adopt the first way; if the reverse is true, then I shall have to adopt the second way, even though it may go against my temperament. There we have my dilemma.

4 The only truly rational means is violence

Broadly speaking, the means I can adopt to achieve my end—that is, to build my road—can be reduced to two categories: persuasion and violence.

At first sight persuasion might seem to be highly reasonable, but in fact it is bound up with a whole lot of non-rational things: respect for the individual, loyalty to tradition, affection for religion, aesthetic feeling, charity, pity and sympathy.

Whereas violence, which at first sight seems totally irrational, is in fact strictly bound up with reason. For if my end be to build that particular road, then the means most in accord with reason are those that allow it to be built exactly as I planned it, in the most efficient, most direct and quickest way possible without regard to anything but the road. Now this method is bound to be violent. All other methods come under the heading of persuasion and, as we have seen, with persuasion I can even reach the paradoxical conclusion of not building my road at all.

Moreover violence is implicit in the very plan of the road. As I have said, I drew two parallel lines on the map from point A to point Z. If, while drawing those two straight lines, I really believed I was drawing a road made up of stone, asphalt and chalk, then I had already made my choice, I had already opted for violence. For those two straight lines of mine can have no existence in reality without recourse to violence, that is to destroying, flattening-out and eliminating everything that prevents my plan from being exactly carried out.

The proof: violence is the only really rational means because, if I employ this means, I can only be stopped by reason, that is—in the concrete case of the road—by the rational calculations made in my plan. These do not lay down that I will kill *all* the inhabitants of my land, and raze *all* their houses to the ground; I will kill only those inhabitants and eliminate only those houses that need to be killed or eliminated in accord with the dictates of the plan. But no inhabitant will owe his life, and no house will owe its preservation, to any consideration other than what is contained in the plan. In a word, I will establish a relationship of reason with my land. This relationship will inevitably be one of violence either inflicted or not inflicted in accord with reason, in other words with the dictates of the plan.

But in the case of persuasion I shall be stopped on the path of violence by entirely irrational considerations which have nothing to do with my plan. It may happen that I shall adopt violence in this case too, but it will be the least possible amount of violence, or violence derived not from what is in my plan but in accord with what is tolerable to the inhabitants. In other words there will be no violence once an agreement has been reached between me and the inhabitants to the effect that I shall inflict no violence other than what seems to me compatible with the idea I have formed of them, and they shall undergo no violence other than what they seem able to tolerate without undue harm.

Now what, in last analysis, will the use of violence involve? We have already seen the consequence of the way of persuasion, that is the substitution for the road, as the end, of the human beings whom the road should serve. In other words the road becomes the means, the human beings the end. In the second case, however, the road remains the end, the road is reason and the most rational means of satisfying reason is violence. And what of the human beings? They are still there; they still live, work, pray, eat, drink and sleep. But all of them are included in the one word: violence. They have become means. For violence is only violence if exercised on human beings; it is only violence if it arouses pain and revolt in their spirit.

But, as we have seen, violence is exercised on human beings so as to attain the end of reason; and the minute violence is exercised on human beings, human beings cease to be the end and become the material used to attain the end, that is, the means. So suffering and revolt, which are signs that violence is being used, are born in human beings whenever they feel they are being used as means for an end that does not directly concern them. Or, once again, precisely when violence is used on them.

It follows that the most rational way of attaining an end is to use men as means or, rather, that the use of violence implies substantially the use of men.

So, logically, the most rational means for attaining an end other than man is man himself. That is, the use of violence as a means implies the use of man as the means. It follows that employing man as the means comes from not considering man as the end, from a lack of respect for man, a lack of knowledge as to what man is, and a lack of a clear and adequate idea of man.

5 *Only madmen make use of reason*

When we say that a clear idea of man is required in order to see him as the end, and that this idea is lacking when he is used as means, we mean in effect that no end exists outside man and that the setting-up of any end other than man is tantamount to the setting-up of no end, or setting-up an end that ceases to be an end the moment it fails to justify the means. But what is an end that does not justify the means? It is precisely an absurd end, an end that bears no relation to man.

Let us take an example. I am suffering from a violent headache and rightly want my suffering to cease. My end, then, is not to suffer any more from my headache. But is it really true that my end is not to suffer any more from my headache? Is it not rather to be in a position to do the things that my headache prevents me from doing? And by doing these things to be the thing that I am—myself? So the end that at first seemed final and definitive, on closer examination gives way to a vaster and more distant end, which finally reveals itself as me being myself. So: I have a headache, and instead of having a headache I rightly want to be myself.

Now let us look at the means. I have various means at my disposal for getting rid of a headache, but really they can be reduced to two: I can take an aspirin and go to bed with a hot water bottle and plenty of blankets, or I can call in a friend, offer him a well-sharpened knife and ask him to cut off my head.

In the first case I am adopting a suitable and inoffensive means, but not a rational one—for it is not certain that my headache will go; I may have an allergy to aspirin, my headache may come from a mounting bruise, the aspirin may have lost its strength, and so on and so on. Whereas in the second case I am adopting an unsuitable and offensive means but one that is rational because there is no doubt that if I have my head cut off the pain, whatever its cause, will cease because I will cease to be myself.

In the first case my end will be to be myself; in the second, to stop my headache. If I am irrational, that is if I love myself more than reason, I shall have a pretty good idea of myself from the physical point of view and know that by having my head cut off I shall not only stop suffering from my headache but also die. If on the other hand I am rational, that is if I love reason more than myself, I shall see no cause why I should not have my head cut off so as to stop suffering from my headache since the only really certain means of no longer suffering is to have it cut off.

But the man who has himself beheaded so as to stop suffering from a headache can only be a madman. And that of course is what he is.

Only madmen, that is to say only men who are so out of their minds that they have lost all sense of man and his physical integrity and are hence unable to see any difference between a knife and an aspirin save on a rational or abstract level—only madmen, we repeat, are capable of such abstraction. They do not hesitate to have their heads cut off if only they can get rid of their headache. How do their minds work? The end—the termination of the headache—is posited outside themselves, on an entirely rational and abstract plane, and there is no logical dividing-line (consisting in knowing their own body and its laws) between this end and the use of the means, any means. Hence the use of the knife as more certain and more rational; in other words the use of themselves, or their own death, as a means to attain the end of ceasing to suffer from headache. The triumph of reason at man's expense.

And the truth that it is only madmen who make use of reason, and let reason dominate their thoughts, and see nothing but reason, can be shown more plainly still from an example in recent history. The famous Himmler-Stadt, or city of extermination, or city of death, not life, where a perfect organisation exterminated millions of men every year, gives an excellent picture of a rational end carried through with rational means, in other words of an inhuman end carried through with man as the means. We take it that there is no need to point out here that the Himmler-Stadt was the product of a sick mind, the distorted invention of a madman.

6 Reason is sometimes reasonable

At this point someone will surely say that if we tried to drive reason out of every situation we would end up with a world more absurd than one controlled by reason alone. To which we reply that it is a question of measure, that (if the play on words be permitted) reason should be reasonable. Reason should serve us for reasoning, that is for distinguishing, recognising and appreciating means and ends according to their proper value. Reason is an instrument indispensable in human activity, or better, a condition without which no activity happens; but it is not, and cannot be, the substance from which our life and destiny are fashioned. We are men, not automata; we eat meat, not ideas; we drink wine, not syllogisms; we make love to people of the opposite sex, not to dialectics. If reason is reasonable it can tell us, as it sometimes does, that the only right and possible end is man; hence the means for attaining this end cannot be man, for man is the end. But reason, in consternation, will also tell us that to set man and not reason as the end is to set as the end something irrational, ineffable, incommensurable, unknowable. By this we mean something irrational, ineffable, incommensurable and unknowable to reason—which, as being only part of man, cannot know the whole. Such are the very humble limits of reason's province. If we let reason escape from its ancillary sphere into fields that are not its province, then it will quickly and easily become tyrannical and paradoxical; it will actually dare to show us that the end is not man at all, but the well-being of a given society or the output of a given factory or the glory of a given nation, and man is no more than the means. In other words, it will try to show us that those ends justify the death, suffering and oppression of millions of men. Naturally reason will point out to us that it is aiming at the happiness and freedom of man through the well-being of the given society or the output of the given factory or the glory of the given nation. But this we cannot believe. Reason cannot substitute one end for another at the last moment as in a conjuring trick and having chased man out through the door, bring him back through the window. There is a contradiction in terms here, and we can justifiably reply to reason that while it is entirely rational to achieve the well-being of a society or the output of a factory or the glory of a nation through the death, suffering and oppression of millions of men, we cannot make those men free and happy through that sort of well-being, output and glory.

Reason cannot set up man as the end because man cannot be known or defined in terms of reason. Reason can tell us about man's chemical make-up, it can explain man's similarities with the other animals and with the vegetable and mineral kingdoms, but it is totally and absolutely incapable of telling us what man is, which is why all its definitions of man presuppose man as a means and as subordinated to reason. In fact, if man is not man but now an animal, now a vegetable, now a mineral, reason will find it easy to deduce that man is not an end but a means—in other words, a slave, a beast of burden, raw material for soap or for fertilisers. Reason finds no difficulty in accepting these paradoxical and macabre consequences. For reason to stop on this slope it would have to deny itself and fall short of its own nature.

Reason delights in ends that have nothing to do with man precisely because it can ransack them and analyse them, explain them and get to know them inside out because they are made of nothing but reason. There is nothing ineffable, incommensurable and unknowable, for instance, about the State. Reason can take the State to pieces and put it together again before our eyes, like a meccano set. The State is a creature of reason and of reason alone, and that is why reason delights in it.

But there is another explanation of why reason prefers any end to that of man, and that is because reason is quantitative. It does not know what man is, but knows very well what ten, a hundred, a million men are. Man is not an end for reason because reason does not know what he is, but it knows full well what a million men are. Here we are talking of a million men as we would of a million shoes or a million dollars or a million bayonets. If a robber attacks a car and kills the occupants to appease his hunger, reason will condemn him. There will be talk of ethics, but really it will be a matter of numerical relationship, one man's hunger is not worth four men's lives. But absolute abstract reason will have no objection to a political minority being exterminated by a majority, because the safety of a million men is worth the life of ten thousand. But, in fact, in both cases we are dealing with the same thing, and the violence, or the down-grading of man from the end to the means, is identical. In last analysis all our laws have a quantitive justification. This is so true that when there are a million robbers instead of one the laws are changed.

7 *We are all Christians; even Hitler was a Christian*

Respect for man has disappeared. Man is no longer taboo and he has a much lower place than in the pre-Christian era when, at least within the city walls or within the tribal environment, the religions of cities and tribes guaranteed that sacred character to man which was later to be extended to all men without exception by Christianity. Christianity has evaporated, but so has the ancient anthropocentric and humanist idea that Christianity had salvaged from the ruins of the pre-Christian world. For this reason it is inaccurate to speak of the neo-paganism of the modern world. If anything we should say that in the modern world we can perceive the outline of a new cave-man civilisation, a new pre-history.

So Christianity has failed, then? No, it has not failed, just the reverse. Its success has been complete; but on the historical plane, in other words on the concrete plane, its activity is exhausted. Christianity is a religious movement bound up with a development in history, that is to say a movement limited in time and space. It answered certain needs and carried out certain tasks. Today the needs have changed and the tasks have been performed. Christianity has made all men Christians without exception, and as it cannot make them more than Christians it no longer has any practical part to play. The men who in our own time, by aberrant experiments and destinies, are used as means to attain certain human ends, are in fact neither pagans nor Neanderthal men—they are Christians. And their executioners are Christians too. And with the fat of Christians exterminated by other Christians during the last war, soap was made; and with their ashes the fields of other Christians were fertilised. Hitler was every bit as much a Christian as the Pope and Roosevelt. A proof of this was that, though his reason or reasons of state allowed him to commit nothing but crimes, he never managed to delude himself entirely into thinking that these crimes were not crimes—which is why he took such care to conceal them and destroy their traces up to the last minute.

The truth of all this is manifest both in the impotence of Christianity to save man a second time from slavery, and in the uneasiness that slavery arouses in us. In other words we are Christians psychologically, but on the ethical plane—that is, on the operative plane—we are no longer Christians, precisely because we are Christians psychologically. Every system of ethics is created to bend and order and shape a rebellious and hostile psychology. For long the early Christians were psychologically pagan, which was the reason and explanation of their acceptance of the Christian ethic. It took twenty centuries to make man psychologically Christian, hence depriving Christianity's ethical function of authority.

We now find that we are faced not by one end only but by innumerable ones which, though perfectly rational, are all materialist and inhuman, and on all sides man is turned into a means to attain these ends. Whereas Christianity had nothing rational about it, St Paul's statement that 'there are no more Jews or Gentiles' is in some way opposed to reason. The universality of Christianity in contrast with its great variety of climates, social conditions and historical situations, was irrational too. And Christianity had the quality of setting man as an end and not making use of him to attain that end.

Today Pascal's saying: *Verité au deça des Pyrénées, mensonge au delà* is universally true. We have horizontal truths according to class, vertical truths according to nations, State truths, race truths, party truths, sex truths and group truths. Providing he finds associates, anyone can in practice create an independent system of truths. The world has been broken to pieces, and the brothel-keeper who sells the prostitutes' bodies for profit is every bit as justified in doing so as the head of State who declares war on another State. In the brothel, as in the State, reason reigns supreme inasmuch as the end, that is the preservation and prosperity of the brothel and the State, is attained with adequate means, that is with the means of man—with prostitution in one case, and social and military discipline in the other. But in both the brothel and the State there reigns contempt for man, and the air is unbreathable. This is the fundamental characteristic of the modern world. Since Christianity has evaporated and man is no longer the end but the means, the modern world is like a perfectly organised nightmare. This characteristic of the modern world is exemplified in all recent literature, whether explicitly and consciously in the pessimism of a man like Kafka, or implicitly and perhaps unconsciously in the optimism of socialist realism. But both the pessimism and the optimism are, in last analysis, alike for both inspire a feeling of suffocation and claustrophobia. It is well known that when there is not enough air everything around seems to conspire to give us less—even the sky seems too low. In varying ways all modern poetry expresses this feeling of suffocation. Whether by affirmation or denial it warns men: the modern world is absurd.

8 In a nightmare everything, even the sun and the stars, becomes nightmare

The modern world is very like one of those Chinese boxes inside which you find a smaller one which in its turn contains a smaller one and so on. In other words the general nightmare of the modern world contains lesser, always more limited, nightmares, until the final one which is every man's sense of being himself a nightmare. The modern State, whose end is the State and whose means is man, is a nightmare of such gigantic proportions that the man who lives inside the nightmare is probably as unaware of it as an ant crawling on a tree is unaware that it is a tree. But in the modern world, as in any other world, each macrocosm is reflected in the microcosm, and every microcosm repeats the properties of the macrocosm. The man who lives in the wide bosom of the State realises that the State is a nightmare because the factory in which he works is run in the same way as the State, and his section in the same way as the factory, and his sub-section in the same way as the section, and so on and so on till we come down to him, the solitary isolated individual. If we take society instead of the factory, and from society descend to the class, and from the class to the group, and from the group to the family, and from the family to the couple, and from the couple to the same lonely and isolated man, we get the same pattern. One could go on indefinitely with examples.

To put it in other words, modern man—whether in the womb of the masses, or with his workmates, or with his family, or alone—can never for one moment forget that he is living in a world in which he is a means and whose end is not his business. Yet we should not suppose that the modern world is so pitiless and lacking in cunning as not to try to make man forget this reality (at least in the majority of cases). On the contrary: the modern world does all it can to convince man that, far from being used as a means, he is still the supreme end. That is to say —to use the words of the governments—everything is done in the modern world to protect and strengthen human dignity and exalt man. Endless laws protect property, life and the rights of man in every variety of way. While he is working he is constantly assured that he is working for the well-being, freedom and happiness of all, and hence of himself. Honours, rewards and incentives, in the form of badges, medals, bonuses, promotions, public praise and publicity of every kind, continually confirm in his mind the usefulness and dignity of his work, and the social importance of his person. When he leaves his work, culture comes to meet him—in the form of books, cinema, theatre, radio, newspapers—to occupy his leisure hours and give him the feeling of being more, much more, than a mere cog in an anonymous machine. Finally religion throws wide the doors of its temples and assures him that he is not only a worker and a mind, but also a soul.

All this exists in theory and in the words of governments, as we have said. But it only needs some kind of decisive crisis to break the close rhythm of his distractions, and man is forced to serious reflection. Then it is not long before he sees that work is slavery, that honours, rewards and incentives are deceits, delusions and bromides, that culture is flattery to seduce him, a noise to prevent him thinking, and that religion is a further nail to hold him tight on his cross. So it is above all in times of crisis that man discovers he is a means, not an end. It is precisely during crises, wars, revolutions, economic disasters that he sees, with perfect lucidity, that he is but a means among other means, and that the work, honours, culture and religion of the modern world show themselves in their true light, revealing the ruthless contempt for man of which they are woven. In other words, man finds himself suddenly dispossessed of his royal crown and thrown upon the scrap-heap, a castaway among castaways; and all those things that should confirm him in his feeling as a man are unmasked and stripped of the sacred character with which they had been invested and shown up as no more than trappings and deceits.

It can scarcely seem surprising, then, that in the course of this 'tale told by an idiot, full of sound and fury' which is man's life, nature and the mystery of nature display the same nightmare characteristics as the world around him. Everything, from love to the sense of the infinite, from procreation to sunlight, seems perverted and reduced to the status of a commodity, a tool, a mechanism. For him love is not 'the love that moves the sun and the other stars' but a mere friction that combines lust and delusion. He experiences nature as an absurd background to an absurd activity. In a nightmare a flowering tree can oppress us and terrify us as much as a knife pointed at our heart; we would prefer it that neither should exist.

9 *The cave-man guessed he was a man*

So man is nothing but a means in the modern world, and a means that is always used rationally, or with the maximum of violence. Not for nothing has modern science attained its high degree of complexity and technical perfection, and have statistics become an important branch of science. Man in the modern world may say that the way in which he is used is ruthless, absurd, cruel and ridiculous, but he cannot say that it is not rational. Neither the worker in the factory, nor the peasant in the field, nor the servant in the household, nor the bureaucrat at his desk, can ever maintain that his condition is not rational. Should he say it, reason is there to point out the statistics and give him the lie. Man's desperate appeals, therefore, derive and can only derive from something other than reason, from the very thing that makes him feel how cruel, absurd, ruthless, undignified, and—in a word—inhuman is the treatment inflicted on him. This something is not very clear or defined; if it were, man would cease to be a means and become an end again. It is man's dim, uncertain, mysterious, contradictory suspicion of his own sacred character.

This suspicion resembles the emotion felt by an explorer at the sight of some fantastic, worn-away idol found in the depths of an African forest and taken home. The explorer will of course place the idol on some surface where the light will best display its strange and exotic beauty. But he will feel all the time that the idol is more than this would suggest, that its destination should be different, in a word that over and above the beauty of the carving the idol contains a powerful charge of magic. This charge does not lie, as the superstitious think, in the object itself which is no more than a piece of wood but in its form, or the intention that the particular form of the idol reveals. In other words the explorer is committing a sacrilege, and it is irrelevant whether he himself is non-religious or has a religion with other idols. The sacrilege will seem all the more flagrant if the explorer happens to be lacking in aesthetic feeling, if he picks the idol up and throws it on the fire so as to warm his hands on a winter evening. But even in that case a suspicion will remain. In what will it consist? Precisely in the difference, shining in the flames, between the carved and painted idol and the other logs blazing in the hearth.

The cave-man, too, dressed in skins, hairy and armed with a club, had this same suspicion when he sat on the lifeless body of his enemy, opened the base of the skull, and sucked out the brain by way of ritual. It did not occur to him to do this to the bears or the deer that constituted his more normal food. The cave-man really felt more than a suspicion: he already had a good idea that man should be the end and not the means.

And if the example of the cave-man seems too barbarous, and seems to suggest too irrational an idea of man, it should be noted that even at that time reason stood for the use of man as a means; reason would have liked the cave-man to devour his kind in all tranquillity, as he devoured the deer or the bear; reason was not lacking to the cave-man, far from it. If the proper environmental adjustments are allowed for, the cave-man was no less rational than the New York scientist. Hence it was against reason and in spite of reason that the idea of man's sacred character was born.

When the cave-man cut into the base of his enemy's skull and devoured his brain by way of ritual, he suspected there was a difference between that corpse and the others from which he normally took his food. It was a difference that had nothing to do with any taste or smell peculiar to human flesh—there is nothing so like a beef-steak as another beef-steak. No, the real difference lay in the cave-man's awareness that he, too, was a man and not a deer or a bear. But all the cave-man knew was that he was a man; he did not know *what* a man was. A dark awareness which, as we have said, is much the same as a suspicion.

But has there ever been more than a suspicion that man is a man? I doubt it. There was no more than a suspicion at the origin of the Greek myths, no more than a suspicion at the origin of the Christian idea of man made in the image of God. It is precisely this uncertainty that confers ineffability, incommensurability and mystery on man. It is precisely because one can only suspect the sacred character of man that every human civilisation is so fragile and so miraculous, and that the notion of that character is lost so easily and with it the notion of civilisation itself.

10 In the beginning there was a state of mind

What is there to distinguish a state of mind from the definitive formulation of that state of mind? What, for instance, distinguished the state of mind before Christianity from Christianity itself? What distinguished the state of mind before Christianity from Christianity itself was the rejection of the moral, religious and social work of paganism, the breathless striving for something not so much better as absolutely new. In other words, the state of mind preceding the great revolutions of mankind is usually largely negative as regards an existing order that convention agrees to be positive. The state of mind presents itself as an awareness of a defect to be remedied rather than of an acquisition to be made—as an awareness, that is to say, of need. The day the transition from the state of mind to the expression of the state of mind (in a clear and recognisable formulation) is effected, then the long (or short) period of the satisfaction of the need will begin. Or better, the need will gradually lose its character of need—that is to say of dark, painful, mysterious, ineffable and urgent impulse—and will become a visible and identifiable process. Thus the obscure and irresistible craving that urges the animal to mate brings into existence first, the act of mating and then the animal itself. But neither the animal, nor indeed man, knows at the outset that he wants to mate and give life to another animal or another man. The impulse to love is rather expressed in terms of a painful and incomparable uneasiness. All the animal knows is that it does not want to sleep or drink or eat but it does not know that it wants to love. So, from the very beginning, life in its most definite forms, in its freest and most autonomous forms, bursts forth from a dark and urgent state of mind.

When, today, we speak of the modern world and its tragic shortcomings, we immediately demand the infallible remedy, the perfect system of ideas, the complete religion, the miraculous panacea, and when this demand goes unsatisfied, we are left frustrated, incredulous and sceptical. But it is as if we asked a boy, timidly courting for the first time, what he will call his child, what job it will have, and what will ultimately become of it. The boy, who has no desire for children and hardly even knows why he is wooing the girl so ardently, will be shocked and horrified. Our indiscreet impatience about the destiny of the modern world derives primarily and to a large extent from our much-vaunted consciousness of history. We would like to know, on the basis of analogies with the past, whether we are moving towards a new Christianity, towards a new paganism, towards Plato's republic, or towards Marx's world without history. Men have always given life to children, but this gives us no authority for thinking that they will always go on doing so, and certainly none for asking our boy in question what his child will be called and what it will do.

In the modern world there is a state of mind marked by an ever-increasing rejection of the modern world and an ever more pressing need for a better and different world. That is all. It would be quite arbitrary and misleading to deduce the character of the future world from it. Moreover we are not dealing with deductions and prophecies here, but with difficult and concrete action—in other words, with the gradual enrichment, the gradual clarification, the gradual organisation, and the gradual expression of this initial state of mind. Hence a big step will have been taken once the specific character of that state of mind has been defined. But this definition, applied as it must be to such vast and intractable material, will take centuries to formulate. Or rather, an infinite number of definitions will be formulated before the right one is found.

People who want infallible remedies and perfect systems must realise that such remedies and systems are proposed every day without making the slightest impression on the evils that afflict the world. On the contrary, the very existence of such a plethora of remedies and systems is an additional indication of the mortal crisis besetting the world. Nor is it any use adopting one of these remedies, or one of these systems, blindly—telling ourselves that it is better than nothing. History is full of blind alleys and wrong turnings.

The world was not made in a day nor in seven days and as time is a conventional measurement, the seven days of Creation may perfectly well be the billions of light years of which astronomers speak. Yet precisely because the astronomers' billions of light years are equivalent to the seven days of Creation, the world might well be saved in a minute, a second, in that split second in which a state of mind found definitive expression and was converted into creation.

11 A brick and a skull are of equal value provided one builds the wall

When we say that man has a sacred character, we do not mean that in the future this character will necessarily resemble the one attributed to man by Christianity twenty centuries ago. We should not be misled by the term 'sacred'. Christianity attributed a sacred character of a religious and ritual kind to man because the epoch in which Christianity flourished was religious and ritual. The ancient world was an eminently religious world in which nothing was absolute that had not received the chrism of religion. But today the world is no longer religious, or at least no longer religious in the same way. All over the world the religions are languishing and seem quite incapable of self-renewal. But today all the Churches see as their end their own preservation; in other words their end is no longer man but themselves and so for them too man has dwindled to half his size. In a word, they in no way escape the general perversion and absurdity of the modern world.

Thus today the sacred character of man cannot find support in any of the existing religions and it is very doubtful whether it could find it in a new religion, at least for the time being. Rather, we would expect it to spring from a new definition of man made in accord with the experience and the needs of the modern world. Here we seem to be in a vicious circle, for we have also said that a new definition of man will only occur when man's sacred character has been defined in a new way. But if we look closer we shall see that all reality is made up of these vicious circles so long as it is static and apparently incapable of development. That does not prejudice the solution of the problem, for the solution must be sought outside the vicious circle in which the problem seems irremediably to turn. This is only one further confirmation of the feeling of anguish peculiar to the modern world—that of being in a maze with no exit.

Yet the sacred character of man must not be sought in what man today is, for as we have seen man today is only a means, that is to say, nothing. On the contrary, it is in all that man does not want to be, and refuses to be, that we should look for his sacred character.

In the modern world, as we have said, man is used as a means, neither more nor less than an animal, a vegetable or a mineral. And indeed it would be hard to deny the animal's extraordinary resemblance to man, or, rather, man's ever-increasing tendency to resemble the animals, so much so that at times there are grounds for thinking that man is no more than an animal among animals and not the most gifted at that. For what at one time distinguished man from the animals was that man, alone among the animals, set himself up as the end, whereas the other animals, being incapable of setting themselves up as ends, became means for man. For instance, the subordination and inferiority of the horse with regard to man lay in the fact that the horse did not set up the horse as an end, whereas man set up man as the end, hence the horse, as it did not set up the horse as an end, had to be a means for man. But since man no longer sets man as the end, but sets various inhuman things as ends instead—such as the State, the nation, money, society, mankind and so on—it is both moving and disconcerting to see how much closer to the animal man has grown, and how he is subject to the same destiny and partakes of the same properties. What difference is there between the beehive, the ant heap and the modern State? In the beehive, the ant heap and the modern State, bees, ants and men are means for the beehive, the ant heap and the State, whereas the ends are the beehive, the ant heap and the State, No one can deny that Christianity could show that the beehive and the ant heap were closed, automatic, absurd worlds, ends in themselves, and for that reason fundamentally different from the human world of man that was not an end in itself but had man as the end. But modern reason is totally unable to show this—on the contrary, it is obliged to admit that no such difference exists. It is needless to dwell on this point, for in our everyday speech we talk of cities as beehives and ant heaps and the feeling is widespread even among the uneducated that the modern State is not very different from the social organisations of certain insects. In other aspects, too, the resemblance is increasing rather than diminishing. For instance, what is the difference between a young man, painstakingly educated by his family and the State and then sent off to fight and die in war, and the soldier ant, the soldier bee, the fighting-cock or the bull in the arena? What is the difference between a man destined from birth to a given kind of work that he will go on doing till he dies and the ox the farmer buys in the market and puts to drawing the plough until it dies? So long as man considered himself as the end, he could die in war or do the same job all his life without thereby becoming an animal among the other animals. But as soon as he accepted the decline in his status from that as end to that as means, then he became a soldier or a labourer and no more than a soldier or a labourer, just as the fighting-cock is no more than a fighting-cock and the ox no more than an ox. Whence it becomes a mere matter of convenience as to whether man shall take the place of the cock or the ox and be used in the same way and for the same ends; in other words, is it more entertaining to watch two cocks pulling themselves to pieces, or two men, and is it cheaper to have an ox drawing the plough, or a man?

Not only negatively, but even positively, does the resemblance of man to the other animals increase when he is degraded from being an end to being a means among other means. Nowadays we say that man is gentle as a lamb, brave as a lion, swift as a horse, strong as an elephant, faithful as a dog, and so on, precisely because gentleness, courage, speed, strength and loyalty are useful traits for describing various uses of man as the means and because in certain circumstances we can turn the comparison inside out and say that the lamb, lion, horse, elephant or dog have human qualities. Furthermore, in the modern world we have man making love with the lust of a goat, procreating in the arbitrary and prolific way of rabbits, bringing up children with the care of cats, defending and nourishing them with the passion of wolves. From the moment that man is no longer an end but a means, his amorous, procreative and productive qualities are put first: they are shown to be exactly like those of the other animals and, like those of the other animals, they are studied, examined, and organised so as to serve the various ends of society, money, the State, the nation, and so on. Luckily for man, this study of his qualities and properties has led to the discovery that there is no species so profitable, so cheap, and so adaptable as the human species—otherwise man would have become extinct long ago as bisons have become extinct in North America and tigers in Europe. But we are already on our way along this road and after the German racists, who established scientifically that

Slavs, Jews and Gypsies are useless and consequently exterminated them, we shall surely see racists in other countries proving with equal rationality that, for the ends of their given society, other races of men are unnecessary, and acting accordingly. And this is the way stock-breeders proceed; according to whether given kinds of horses or fowls or dogs are in demand and correspond to utilitarian needs, they modify breeds or suppress them outright. For instance, certain dogs in fashion fifty years ago are now virtually extinct because fashion has changed. Transfer the fashion from the context of ladies' whims to political obsessions, replace the breeder of fox-terriers by the white-overalled scientist who fecundates women by injecting male semen taken from a selected human stallion, and you have one of the most possible of all possible worlds of the future.

But the resemblance of the means that is man to other means does not stop at the animals. The day may come (though it has not come yet) when we shall say that man is not only gentle as a lamb, strong as an elephant, brave as a lion, and so on, but that he is tough as rope, detergent as soda, fertilising as manure, malleable as leather, and so on. These similes have not yet come into everyday use, but the facts that could justify their use have already happened—in the last war human hair was made into rope, human fat into soap, human ashes into fertiliser, and human skin into parchment lampshades. It is just a matter of waiting for a few more wars, for every war, that is to say every state of necessity, confirms the usefulness of man as a means and brings him nearer to the simplest, even the most inorganic, forms of life. What more can we say? As things are now, stones, bricks and cement are obtainable even in wartime. But should the day come when these materials are lacking (owing to war or for any other reason) walls will be built with human skulls as in the time of Tamerlane. But notice: Tamerlane was an atrocious man and his walls of skulls were atrocious not only for those who provided the skulls but also for him who ordered them to be built. Whereas should skulls be used for building in time to come, the operation will be a rational one; in other words, owing to the lack of other materials the end in view, i.e. the construction of the wall, will provide complete and rational justification for the means, i.e. the use of skulls. Which amounts to saying that human material will take its place and not too low a one we hope, among the other materials used by the building industry.

So man is a means, and from now onwards he will owe his survival on the face of the earth uniquely to the fact of being a means. But the use of man as a means may lead either to the extermination of entire families of the human race or to the total extinction of man. The earth is littered with the ruins of civilisations that perished because they degraded man from the status of end to that of means.

12 Even if you burn man, he will always leave a residue

In a famous phrase, Pascal defined man as a *roseau pensant.* In so doing he laid down that the whole difference between a man and a reed, the difference in which man's dignity consists, is that man thinks whereas the reed does not think. If both man and reed were swept away in the same avalanche, the man would know that he was being swept away and the reed would not. In Pascal's definition there is an element of illuminism and rationalism. The presupposition on which the phrase is based—namely that man is endowed with thought—is anything but convincing. In fact we have no proof that the reed would not know that it was being swept away in the avalanche, or that man would. And even if we admitted that man is endowed with thought, we should not therefore take man's superiority over the reed as proved, for the reed in its turn might be endowed with other qualities compensating for the lack of thought. In other words, the effects of thought in man—or at least in millions and millions of men—are so confused and tenuous and contradictory that thought may seem a mere instinct peculiar to man, rather as an extremly acute sense of smell is peculiar to dogs, or extremely sharp sight is peculiar to certain birds of prey. So thought proves nothing, and if we look closely we shall see that with the majority of men it does not appear to extend beyond very simple mental processes such as the other animals would surely be capable of if nature had not endowed them in other ways. Let us suppose that the sacred character of man does not derive from the fact that he thinks, but from something quite different.

Certainly man has never fallen so low as today, and yet we can be sure that the fall is not decisive. Despite the many proofs to the contrary, the modern world is not becoming a beehive or an ant heap. In other words the inevitable automatism that the use of man as the means in the pursuit of material and inhuman ends has brought to the modern world, is not and never will be as complete as it plainly is in some insect communities, or as it is described in certain utopian or satirical books.

What prevents, and will always prevent, the triumph of automatism and absurdity is that the use of man as the means (unlike the use of animals, vegetables and minerals as the means) always leaves a residue, and this residue cannot itself be used as the means. Animal, vegetable and mineral, used properly as the means, leave no residue. A pig fattened for slaughter leaves no residue. In other words it never occurs to us to make anything of a pig but sausages, nor to do nothing with a pig, but just let it live. Even if the whole world became vegetarian and the pig were no longer fattened and slaughtered, it would still be a means and nothing but a means, without anything left over and this because, unlike man, the pig neither sets itself up nor is capable of setting itself up as an end.

Hence it follows that the residue left over by man when used as the means lies precisely in his sempiternal capacity for being an end and for setting himself up as the end. We shall now examine in what this residue consists, in other words what becomes of man's capacity to be an end when he is reduced to a mere residue by being used as the means. For it is in this residue and in nothing else that man's sacred character, or rather the potentiality of his sacred character, consists.

In the modern world we note on the one hand that the use of

man as the means lies at the origin of the feeling of absurdity and nightmare that the world itself inspires, and on the other that this feeling of absurdity remains unchanged whether man is used as the means in a totally paradoxical and unsuitable way, such as for making fertilisers, or in an apparently right and suitable way, such as for managing a bank or commanding a ship. On close inspection we will get the feeling of a similar waste in both cases, of a similar margin of residue or a similar degradation giving rise to a similar sense of absurdity. In other words, precisely because of its ruthless utilitarianism, the modern world sees all the more acutely the waste that lies in using man as a means. And it also sees that this waste has nothing to do with fitness and suitability, that there is no end that can *completely* justify the use of man as a means and that however man is used there will always be a residue of waste. In other words, the use of man as means—whatever be the end—is bound to be irrational because man will never be exclusively and completely a means. This irrationality puts a brake on rational automatism and prevents the modern world from becoming a beehive or an ant heap.

This is proved by the fact that if the use of man as a means did not leave any residue, then such use would be a perfectly rational operation, and the modern world would truly be nothing more than an ant heap, or a rational world from which the sense of the absurd has been banished, and in which no ant would get feelings of absurdity about its own destiny or even about the ant heap itself. And this is the way things really are. We only see the ant heap as absurd when we compare it with the human society to which we belong or to which we would like to belong. In itself, inside itself, it is not absurd, it is merely what it is.

For this reason, when we say in horror and bitterness that the modern world is on its way to becoming an ant heap, we are speaking not as ants but as men degraded to the level of ants. For ants the ant heap is the best of all possible worlds and it may well even not be an ant heap. It is, and is bound to be, the end which the ants serve, and are bound to serve, as the means. Theirs is a really rational world without any flaws and without any waste, a world in which everything is useful and from which everything useless is banished.

The modern world will not become an ant heap though it is unquestionably trying very hard to do so. This tendency is one of the most outstanding aspects of the modern world. As it is a rational world, setting itself rational ends and wanting to attain them by using man as the means, it makes a fierce attempt to ignore, reduce and destroy the absurdity and the irrationality that undermine it. The residue left by the use of man as the means is either never mentioned or persecuted. The political police, money, propaganda and a thousand other methods of coercion are employed unscrupulously against the residue left over when man is used as a means—to destroy it, minimise it, stifle it, and annihilate it. The whole of modern society, everywhere under the sun, is engaged in this struggle against the human residue, that is, against the sacred character of man. Every method is used to prove to men that in given political, economic, and social situations they are bound to be happy, and those who are unhappy are mad or criminals or monsters. In other words, no method is spared in the effort to change human society into a perfected ant heap.

But, by natural consequence, the more the modern world furiously tries to become an ant heap the less it does so; the more it tries to reduce the human residue the more the residue grows; the more it tries to be rational the more absurd it becomes.

What happens to nightmares when they reach their climax and can no longer be borne? The nightmare disintegrates and the sleeper wakes up. The modern world is a nightmare from which men will wake up.

13 Man is man because he suffers

When Pascal formulated the difference between a man and a reed by saying that man is a thinking reed, his real meaning—in the terminology of this essay—was that the residue of man, or what forms man's sacred character or at least man's dignity, is thought. But consider the case of a scientist specialising in some very narrow and purely practical branch of science, for instance a man of thought who puts his thought at the service of efficient radio sets, and we have a reed whose mental activity makes him in no way superior to the non-thinking reed. For thought is by no means a non-combustible residue, and if man were made of thought alone he would go up in flames once thrown into the furnace of the useful. The man of thought manages to avoid being mere means, even when used as a means for an end that is not thought. Thought is a servant and in a rational world, composed of rational ends and means, it can be the most grovelling and abject of servants. For instance (to return to Pascal's metaphor) how many people suspect there is servitude if their thought is identical with the State's thought? And how many people know when they are being swept away by an avalanche? The majority prefer to let themselves roll along with the avalanche and delude themselves that they themselves are the avalanche.

The fact is that when we have given various names to the residue left by man used as a means—such as absurdity, irrationality, sacred character, and so on—the time must come for pronouncing the real name of this residue: suffering. The non-combustible, unchangeable, uncontrollable residue that survives every use of man as a means is not thought, as Pascal and all the illuminists following him suppose it to be, but suffering.

This suffering has nothing in common with the suffering of animals, either when they lose their freedom by being put at man's service or when they are cruelly and ruthlessly treated by man. For the suffering of animals, whether of the untamed horse when first broken-in, or the patient mule flogged by the carter, does not derive from a sense of profanation, as man's suffering does. The horse and the mule do not set themselves up as ends, hence do not feel degraded at being used as means. For them their condition has merely been changed for the worse. The untamed horse is a means that is as yet unaware of being a means, or of being potentially a means. It is not an end that knows very well that it is, or is potentially, an end, and does not wish to be used as a means. The flogged mule is a means which would like to change its end but not to cease being a means.

Whereas man's suffering—that unchangeable, non-combustible residue that renders absurd both the use of man as a means and the world in which this use is practised—man's suffering, we repeat, derives precisely from a sense of profanation, sacrilege and degradation that only man, among all the creatures, seems in a position to experience. This suffering is the proof that man can only be an end, indeed the only possible end, and that—whatever the efforts made—he will never become a means.

The whole texture of the modern world is formed of this suffering. It finds expression in the ugliness of cities, the stupidity of amusements, the brutality of love, the slavery of work, the ferocity of wars, the decay of the various arts to the level of palliatives, propaganda and flattery. It is manifest in all man's activities. Indeed it is the frame on which the whole fabric of modern civilisation is spun.

The modern world is, to a supreme degree, a profane and profaning world. Wherever we turn our eyes in the modern world we see things bent to unworthy uses; great inventions such as journalism and the radio only serving to diffuse lies, stupidity and corruption (when they are not playing their part in increasing the already enormous total of violence); wonderful scientific discoveries, from aeroplanes to atomic energy, being used for war; boundless wealth being squandered in a thousand ways to increase, not remove, our ills. Beauty, goodness, intelligence, enthusiasm, will, and the impulse to self-sacrifice—in a word, all the finest human qualities—are subjected to a continual and flagrant rape. 'The right thing in the wrong place' is the motto adorning the black escutcheon of the modern world.

The modern world is like those trees the Japanese shut up in boxes so as to weaken and dwarf them. In the contortion of their branches that cannot grow freely, you read their dumb and eloquent suffering. The modern world is like those trees: all the branches of its activity are twisted and evoke a sense of suffering.

14 But man is not man because he is content to suffer

So the residue left by man, whenever he is employed as the means, is suffering. But one of the great discoveries of mankind, from Christ onwards, is the cathartic, transforming, liberating and uplifting function of suffering. Indeed, Christianity made suffering the corner-stone of its whole moral and religious system. By accepting on behalf of all men to expiate man's sins on the cross—that is, by accepting to suffer for the whole of mankind—Christ purified, unloaded and freed men from sin. Hence every Christian could suffer for the whole of mankind, and suffering was a means of purifying himself and others. Throughout the centuries, from Christ to Dostoievsky, the energising and propulsive function of suffering has been explained, confirmed and preached to us in a thousand ways. How comes it, then, that though suffering has increased beyond measure in the modern world, it has lost its ancient function and no longer seems endowed with the liberating, purifying and cathartic effect it once had?

It is beyond question that there has never been so much suffering in history as there is today, and never has suffering been so supremely useless. The death, oppression, want, and slavery of millions upon millions of men have not only failed—through volume of suffering—to bring about any betterment in the conditions of mankind, but have produced even greater quantities of death, oppression, want and slavery. Today the cathartic machinery of suffering seems to have become clogged, and suffering seems to produce bestiality, barbarism, stupidity, corruption and slavery. This, be it said in passing, is one of the principal aspects of Christianity's setback in modern times.

One of the ways in which the truth of this is shown is by the modern world's fear of suffering. Though there is more suffering now than in any previous time, the modern world rejects suffering as something useless and harmful, and spends its time searching for a cheerful way of life. Suffering is banished by modern life as a tedious intrusion and bore. The United States and Russia—both representative countries of the modern world in their different ways—claim that they do not suffer and that they do not want to suffer. As a natural result (for the contradiction is only apparent) they both produce an ever-mounting volume of suffering. For the fetish of material happiness is the most inhuman of all inhuman ends, and more ruthlessly than any other end, it compels the employment of man as the means.

But man has not really changed, nor can he change. Today suffering is just as powerful a source of energy for purification as it was twenty or thirty centuries ago. Instead of rejecting suffering as something useless and harmful, the modern world should look within itself and examine whether it itself has not rendered suffering useless and harmful. In other words, the machinery of suffering still holds fast, but something has clogged it.

One of the many ways in which Christianity has degenerated is in its attitude to repentance, to the sense of suffering following on sin and purifying from sin. The vicious monk, Rasputin, fabricated sins precisely so as to be able to repent. Rasputin's reasoning was as follows: the good Christian is the man who repents that he has sinned, and the more he repents the more Christian he is. Hence, the good Christian is the man who sins. It follows that the more one sins the more Christian one is. Such perverted reasoning was not only Rasputin's—it is that of many Christians today.

Analogously: we have said that everywhere in the modern world man is used as a means. On the other hand, that which permits a man to consider himself a man and not a means is the suffering he experiences when he is used as a means—the residue of suffering that his use as a means leaves over. Now what has happened is this: man in the modern world is man and not a means precisely because he suffers; yet he does not suffer—that is, feel himself to be man—except by accepting to be a means and even trying to be a means. To put it in another way: if he were not a means he would not be a man, and if he were not a man he would not be a means. Here we have a sort of Rasputinism applied to suffering—suffering provoked in order to be experienced. Obviously in a vicious circle of this kind, the possibility of suffering having a cathartic function disappears, and suffering becomes the solidest of bases for human slavery.

Although man in the modern world recognises that his dignity as man lies in suffering, far from making use of suffering to remove its causes, he cultivates it precisely so as to experience it. These causes can be summed up in one: the use of man as means for ends which do not concern him. Whether we are dealing with State bureaucrats or factory workers or soldiers, we will see, if we look carefully, that they all place their dignity as men in suffering at being bureaucrats or workers or soldiers, though they only manage to attain this dignity by being bureaucrats or workers or soldiers more than ever. In the modern world this automatic procedure is called civic sense, sense of duty, patriotism, enthusiasm for production, and so on. But the fact remains that the sickness and unhealthiness of the procedure is manifest in man's state of immobility, in his iron persistence in using man as a means and the disastrous nature of the outcome: intellectual stultification, vulgarity, moral baseness, latent despair and pessimism, oppression, violence and war. And what else could be the outcome? It is not by restricting ourselves to suffering from an evil that we get rid of the evil, but by seeking for the good.

The vicious circle in which the modern world turns is very like the one in which the sadist turns. He would like to be loved, but he has to cause suffering so as to be able to love, so the more he loves the less he is loved. He fails to realise that to be loved he ought to love. That is, he ought to get out of the vicious relationship of 'suffering equals love' which constitutes his way of loving.

It looks as though the cause of the modern world's descent into the vicious circle of Rasputinism where suffering is concerned is a lack of vitality—one of those accidental and a-historical causes which nonetheless play their part in history so as to modify it. Lack of vitality seems to leave the modern world incapable of breaking out of the vicious circle in which it rotates, for only some explosion of vital energy could interrupt the non-stop circular movement. In other ages this vital energy was known as the barbarian invasions; in our day it is represented by peoples of more recent history and more integral strength who are taking on—as though they were new—the problems of the older and tireder peoples at the point at which they left them. For resolving a problem means nothing but inventing and creating and the distance between a problem and its solution can only be crossed by life, that is by creation and invention. Even a tree has a problem, that of thrusting forth its leaves and branches in springtime. But this will not happen if the sap running through the tree's fibre is thin and tired. Rather, an excess of sap is needed.

15 Man should not suffer from being a means; he should suffer from not being an end

The most exact, consistent image of the modern world is provided by the concentration and extermination camps. In the concentration camp all the data of the modern world are pushed to their logical conclusion and thus are shown up in all their significance and eloquence. For in the concentration camp the supremely inhuman end of extermination is carried out with the maximum of violence and with man as the only means. In the concentration camp both the butchers and their victims are the means, and in theory—like the parts of a perfect machine—they should be means and nothing else. The concentration camp, within the concentration camp's limits, is perfectly rational, more so than any factory, any State, or any nation. The famous answer given to an application for provisions: 'Buchenwald should be self-sufficient', throws light on this rationality and confirms it. That, surely, is the motto of every nation, factory and State in the modern world. Everything in the modern world, from the State down to the individual, should be self-sufficient and it is of little moment if this involves death.

Yet, despite its rationality, the concentration camp is absurd; and it is absurd both for the butchers and the victims precisely because it encloses within its barbed-wire fence an enormous residue of suffering. But how is it that the concentration camp does not explode, or disintegrate, or vanish? The concentration camp does not explode, or disintegrate, or vanish, because, alike for the butchers as for their victims, suffering is not a motive for rebellion, rather, despite the horrible torments inflicted and received, it confirms that both are men. In other words, both butchers and victims suffer from being employed as the means and yet they need to suffer (or to cause suffering, which is the same thing) so as to preserve their feeling that, in spite of everything, they are not means but men. So the circle is completely closed and the concentration camp goes on devouring men.

For the concentration camp to explode and vanish, both butchers and victims would need to make a superhuman effort to get out of the vicious circle in which they rotate. But to get out of it they would need to transfer their suffering onto another plane, in other words, *cease to suffer from being a means, and suffer from not being an end*.

That is to say, man in the modern world should no longer suffer from being a bureaucrat or a worker or a soldier, but from not being a man. This may seem the same thing, but it is not. To suffer from being a bureaucrat or a worker or a soldier is a passive moral position; to suffer from not being a man is an active moral position.

But in order to transpose this enormous mass of suffering from the vicious circle in which its energy is exhausted into some direction without limits, man would have to posit as his end an image of himself against which he could measure his strength and suffer from falling short of it.

It is the creation of that image that would finally free man from being a means, and free his life from the slavery of suffering. That image, the image of man as the end instead of the means, would deliver man back to joy, would hand him over to the joyful feeling that he was approximating to the best in himself by his own effort, approximating to the self he has set himself as the end.

The modern world has made up its mind that suffering equals existence, that suffering is the first and last proof of existence; whereas suffering should be felt as impotence, as non-existence, as incapacity. But suffering will only be felt in this way when man has been wrested from his present use as a means and restored to his nature as the end.

So a new concept of man is needed, one organised round a negation of the equation, suffering = existence. Christianity got round the difficulty by unloading mankind's suffering onto Christ who suffered for all men on the cross. The modern world needs to get round it by a new awareness of the cathartic character of joy. This joy will lie in man's discovery that he can be an end, in his effort to be an end, in his full and absolute awareness of being an end. Man needs to rediscover his pride in being a man, in other words in being the centre and the final end of the universe.

But the first step out of the vicious circle in which man is struggling will be his awareness of not being a means but an end. And for this awareness he must rely on himself, that is, on his own will, his own inventiveness and his own creativeness. In other words, if man himself does not realise that he is man, who else will ever be able to make him realise it?

16 To despair means to act

In ancient times man had recourse to asceticism and contemplation so as to attain awareness that he was an end and not a means, that is, to mortification and the near-suppression of the vitality that was being dissipated—or so he felt—in the employment of himself as the means. As living seemed to involve being a means, he refused outright to live, or at least he pushed his refusal as far as was compatible with physical survival. In other words, ancient man committed sucide as regards the political, social, and moral life of his time. And indeed, to the pagans, the early Christians appeared as suicides, especially those who, in order to be more fully Christian, elected to pass their lives in deserts or in the depths of caves. So ancient man expressed the dilemma clearly: he must either be an end, or not be at all.

The employment of man as a means, and the setting-up of material and inhuman ends, are both signs of an extraordinary dispersion and dissipation in mankind. It is only when such dispersion and dissipation have taken place within mankind that man can set himself on a level with animal, vegetable and mineral and, through his incapacity to set himself as the end, propose conventional and provisional ends for himself. For man, after all, needs an end for living, and when this end ceases to be himself he selects as an end something that does not seem too ignoble: the State, welfare, the nation, efficiency of production, and so on.

So recourse to reason alone, the adoption of a material, limited and inhuman end and the will to attain this end by all possible means including the means of man, these things in every civilisation are a sign of despair. It is only when men have lost all idea of man, and despair of ever finding it again, that they accept the principle that the end justifies the means.

A common characteristic of these states of despair is that they force mankind to resort ever more frequently and obstinately to those ways of life, and of understanding life, that can only lead to more despair. And those ways of life, and of understanding life, can be summed up thus: the predominance of action over contemplation.

There is a very close link between the worship of action and the use of man as a means to attain ends that are not man, just as there is a very close link between despair and recourse to reason alone. And there is a very close link between despair and action, and between reason and action.

The dominance of the values of action over those of contemplation is, first and foremost, an indication that man has abandoned both the search for a satisfactory idea of man and the desire to set up man as man's end. It also indicates that he finds it impossible to act in accordance with man as the end, that is to act as a man, and hence agrees to act anyhow granting only that he acts.

The principle of 'the end justifying the means' is a principle of action, indeed it is the principle of action *par excellence*. But of action detached from any real justification, of action—in brief—justified by nothing but ratiocination. And as we have seen, reason taken alone in the attainment of a non-human end involves violence, that is, action for action's sake.

The man of action is a man of despair who tries to fill the void of his despair with acts connected mechanically and encompassed by arbitrary and conventional starting and finishing-points—as, for instance, the starting-point of the manufacture of a car and the finishing-point of the same manufacture. The man of action suspends his despair as long as the manufacture of the car lasts, and he suspends it because in his mind he suspends any really human sense of aim; he feels himself a means among other men who are means like himself. True enough, once the car is finished he will find himself more lifeless and inert than the car itself, but he will quickly dissimulate the crisis of despair with promotion in rank, a medal, a pay rise, or simply by turning his hand to yet another car. In a word he will immediately plunge back into the flux of action and oblivion it brings.

It follows from this that the concentration camp is the most suitable image for representing the static, though apparently frenzied, mechanism of the modern world with its suffering equals life and life equals suffering; and the modern army is the most suitable image for providing the sense of this same world in movement. The soldier is action and nothing but action. His action is continuous, uninterrupted, lacking even those moments of pause possible for a worker between one car and the next. The soldier is an automaton, in other words a means upon whom the state of being a means is imposed by the rhythm of mechanically interconnected action. His end is the most inhuman of all inhuman ends—death. It little matters whether it is his own or the enemy's. This is how the special character of action is manifest in the modern world: it is born of despair; it is developed by the mechanical interconnection, on the plane of pure violence, of one act after another; and it reaches its fulfilment in destruction and death.

The predominance of action over contemplation came into being slowly; it arose with the gradual darkening of the idea of man within man himself. At the beginning it was a kind of substitute for expression, or action springing from the idea of man as the end. Then little by little the darkness grew and the man of action took the place of the man of expression. In other words little by little, as the idea of man became more and more obscured, action became void of content, it lost any justification, and became an end in itself.

Action as an end in itself affects the human spirit in a deeply disintegrating way. It substitutes mechanism for nature and breaks any real link between the man who works and the material on which he works. In the realm of love, action as an end in itself leads to vice, in work it leads to technique, in politics to Machiavellianism, in ethics to a system of mere precepts, in literature to propaganda, in art to decoration, and so on, and in all these activities it leads pure reason to prevail over life. Action for action's sake is the triumph of the technician, of the specialist, of the man-as-means. The man of action knows his own field of action precisely because, if it is to be effective, action needs to be restricted and concentrated. The man of action is a human machine, and as such he can be employed, and employ himself, for any end whatsoever.

But action as the end in itself has this characteristic: it consumes more than it produces. It is a wearing-down process for which no production can compensate. As it forces men to be pure means, it consumes them ruthlessly like logs in a stove. Hence once again war is the most persuasive image of pure action. On an absolute plane war is action that only stops with the disappearance of the last soldier, that is, with the lack of all serviceable means to attain the end which, precisely because the last soldier has disappeared, is in its turn null and void. That is to say, pure action ends in void.

17 The modern world will not become a Thebaid

It is the predominance of action over contemplation that constitutes the secret drain on the modern world. The modern world is rather like a man who goes on a diet of eggs and red meat, yet fails to notice the steady flow of blood from an open wound. He grows weaker and weaker and one day he will die.

Ever greater recourse to action, as to the only mode of conduct, increasingly obscures any possible idea of man in the modern world, and compels man more and more to set himself material ends and make use of man as the means. The Nazis were men of action, that is soldiers; their end was the race, their means were men, and the most original and whole-hearted outcome of it all was the concentration camp where men were cremated and turned into fertiliser at full steam.

If man wants to rediscover an idea of man and break out of the slavery into which he has fallen, he must be aware of his being as man and, to attain this awareness, he must abandon action for contemplation once and for all.

I know that this statement calls up echoes of the past. The hermits were the supreme contemplatives. But the hermits belong to the past and there is no question or possibility of putting the clock back.

Contemplation in the modern world does not necessarily imply asceticism and mysticism. No, in the modern world it implies, purely and simply, transferring human energy from one plane to another. The first thing is to effect this transfer, then we shall see. Possibly asceticism and mysticism may be reborn; possibly other things will come to light of which we know nothing as yet and hence cannot name them.

The millions of men who are lost in admiration at the mechanism of a car or a vacuum cleaner remain totally indifferent to the sublimest moral proposition. They notice the irregular beat of an engine missing out on a cylinder, but are completely unaware of the injustice, corruption and cruelty of the modern world. Millions of men suffer from being mere means, but they prefer to rationalise their life of suffering rather than withdraw into themselves and discover a new idea of man, or an end.

This moral, mental and spiritual poverty in the modern world might seem at first sight to indicate extreme weakness and fatigue. But the modern world is neither weak nor wanting in energy. On the contrary, it is very strong and very energetic; the only trouble is that its strength and energy have been channelled from contemplation into action.

We can compare man's inner power to a river blocked by a dam so as to form an artificial lake to be a source of energy. But the dam has had a fault for centuries, the lake is nearly dry, the energy almost nonexistent, and all the surrounding villages in darkness. The need is to rebuild the dam so that the level of the water may rise again. In other words, in order to rediscover an idea of man that is a source of true energy, men must rediscover a taste for contemplation. Contemplation is the dam that makes the water rise to form the lake. With it men can accumulate a new energy of which action has deprived them.

It is not possible to define at this stage the kind of contemplation that can be practised in the modern world. Contemplation presupposes an object to be contemplated and today this object is not there. But it is a mistake to imagine that the modern world must necessarily turn itself into a Thebaid so as to rediscover the idea of man. The ancient world, the pre-Christian world, was adequately contemplative but contemplation was present in, and so to speak mixed up with, the daily life, which was infinitely simpler and more human than ours. That is all that can be said.

If it be true that some day machines will allow man to devote the greater part of his day to himself instead of to the problems of production, if that paradise is possible, we shall certainly see people abandoning the stupid pastimes that occupy the modern worker's margin of leisure today and returning on a large scale to contemplation—that is, to the search for wisdom. Yet no one can predict when and how the machine-system will restore to man the freedom of which it seems at the moment to have deprived him, nor what use man will make of that freedom, nor to what idea of man contemplation will give rise.

The modern world is so different from the ancient world that, although we can and should rediscover the needs of the modern world from those of the ancient world, we cannot say quite how such needs will be interpreted and fulfilled. At a given moment in the ancient world men withdrew into caves to pray and live in communion with God. And ancient civilisation preserved its equilibrium precisely because, while soldiers and politicians were being active, other men were not being active at all, indeed action for them was sin. But it is difficult to say what the modern equivalent of the ancient contemplatives would be. It might even be that contemplation would not be confined to a few, so to speak, specialists, but would find its place in the daily life of every man, rather as happened in the best periods of the pre-Christian world. Or that in the modern world the absolute function of the Christian contemplatives would be fulfilled by philosophers and scientists. These are all hypotheses and none have so far been confirmed by factual proof. All we can say with any certainty is that every epoch responds to unchanging needs in its own distinctive way.

18 The first condition is a world to the measure of man

But what is certain is that no contemplation or wisdom, and hence no new idea of man, will emerge until the world has been cut down to the measure of man. For what strikes us most today is the obvious disproportion between modern man and the world in which he finds he has to live. This world is inhuman precisely because it is gigantic, and modern man is not man precisely because he lives in a world not made to his measure. In the modern world there is no direct relationship between man and the nation, or the State, or the industrial organisation, or the city, and so on. Man in the modern world has a direct relationship with infinitely more restricted organisms and societies than those with which ancient man and Christian man had a direct relationship. Ancient man could have a direct relationship with his city, his country, or his workshop; but modern man can scarcely have a direct relationship with a district or a street of his city, with a city or a region of his country, or with even a department of his factory. And this contradiction follows: that modern man is smaller than ancient man in proportion as the organism to which he belongs is greater. The first consequence of the smallness of modern man is his incapacity to have a satisfactory knowledge of the world to which he belongs and, in last analysis, satisfactory knowledge of himself. On the other hand the immensity of the organisms to which he belongs strengthens modern man's sense of his own nature as a means, and his sense of the impossibility of setting himself up as an end.

But the social and political organisms of the modern world, though sufficiently huge to frighten the man who belongs to them, are not sufficiently huge to lose their hold on him and leave him to think of himself. The modern State is not universal enough to allow man to stop experiencing it as oppression and limitation. Though it is made to the measure of monsters and idols and not to the measure of man, it persecutes man even in his own home and even within his own conscience. And there follows this disconcerting consequence: man is compelled to belong to organisms too vast to be human but too narrow to be universal. These are the Nations, the States, the Modern Societies, all at grips with one another and as ruthless with those they claim to defend as with those they wish to destroy.

For all these reasons, the world urgently needs to be brought back to man's measure. Only in a world made to his measure can man rediscover, through contemplation, an adequate idea of himself, cease to be a means, and propose himself to himself as an end. A world of this kind naturally presupposes the destruction and disappearance of States and Nations, and hence of the enormous cities in which States and Nations centralise their directive organisations. A modern world made to the measure of man needs to be made on the one hand to his physical measure, that is according to his physical capacity to move, see, embrace and understand, and on the other to his intellectual and moral measure, that is according to his capacity to enter into a relationship with ideas and moral values. A world, in brief, in which there will be no great metropolises such as Moscow, New York, London and Paris, nor any States and Nations such as Russia, Britain and the United States. The big cities should make way for groups of houses or much smaller centres of habitation; the States and Nations for a civilisation as vast as the earth. Man will live in the first, and produce and work in the second.

Thus the measure of man is the universal and the particular, not the gigantic and the minimal.

[This essay was written around 1946, shortly after the end of the war and reflects the state of mind of that time. It makes no claim to any systematic analysis of philosophical value; it is merely a reaffirmation of confidence in the destiny of man.]

THE MAN AND THE CHARACTER

LITERARY *genres*, however much they are attacked by criticism, have an obstinate vitality. It is not easy, nor perhaps very instructive, to explain why epic poems are composed at certain periods of history, and plays at other periods; yet such ups and downs in literary *genres* exist, and at the moment when the question might well have seemed buried, it has raised its head as more alive than ever. Obviously literary *genres* are something more than empty forms determined by historical and practical conditions in which poetry—which never perishes—is sometimes incarnated and sometimes not as the case may be. Doubtless preferences of sensibility and rhythm, which are neither fortuitous nor inactive, contribute to creating these *genres* and keeping them alive. But to decide why in the world a *genre* is born, has a varied and eventful career, and then dies, would involve inquiring into the mystery of the relationship that links art with the age that surrounds it. Above all, why does a *genre* die? Especially because one cannot see why, once a means perfectly adapted to expressing poetic sensibility has been found, this means should be slowly emptied of all vitality and be finally rejected. If the *genre* is of no importance, why is it that no heroic poems are written today? Here it can be seen that, quite apart from any question of language, structures, too, are essential for understanding artistic achievement.

When I think of the number of literary *genres* which seemed likely to live for ever and yet have died out, I cannot help wondering whether the novel, the last in the series, is also doomed to the same fate. The novel is a literary *genre* like another, and its life has not been very long—it is hardly two centuries old. Other means of expression, which we now consign to the ark (and rightly), flourished for much longer, while interest in the novel seems to get a new lease of life at every season, which testifies to its inexhaustible vitality. And the novel will assuredly carry on its good span of life until a more actual form evolves, one better corresponding to the demands of the age. But meanwhile we can already detect certain symptoms in the novel that seem like portents—if not of death, at least of serious illness. In its very vitality and ceaseless development, in the continual modifications and transformations that it undergoes, we seem to recognise signs of the imbalance undermining it.

For if we consider what the European novel was and is, how it came into being and how it has developed onwards and upwards from the eighteenth century, through the nineteenth, and as far as our own day, we can see how steady that development has been. Few literary *genres* have had such a logical and clear-cut development as this. Its early origins lie in the memoir-writers and moralists of the seventeenth and eighteenth centuries. Those wooden characters, those portraits of contemporaries, were already characters in novels yet to come, but still bound in the chains of apologias and chronicles. For we need to emphasise the fact that before the novel there were characters, and before there were characters there was the inclination to moralise on vice and virtue, and to portray and pass judgement on contemporaries. When La Bruyère re-wrote Theophrastus with his eye on the court, and Saint-Simon drew an occasional full-length portrait of a contemporary in the midst of his huge mass of information and trivia, they were establishing the antecedents for the novel as we know it in France, both the eighteenth-century novel and the most recent novel of today. The novel was born of them, and of others like them who were concerned with men, the world, and values. Many innocent people wonder how in the world it happened that, though Italy had such an excellent portrayer of his age as Boccaccio, and such a good poet of adventure and action as Ariosto, she never afterwards produced a novel worthy of such forerunners. But this was because Boccaccio and Ariosto were not forerunners; each in his different way was an apex—Boccaccio of a kind of Mediterranean and Eastern tale, and Ariosto of a tradition of chivalry. The novel's antecedents cannot possibly be found either in Boccaccio's richness and fluency, or in the aery architecture of the *Orlando Furioso*; they lie, rather, in an unpoetical and bitter inclination to re-evoke and to judge. In other words the novel's birth lies outside poetry and derives from man's warfare of words against men and the world; its origins, that is to say, tend to be metaphysical and moralistic; for behind the moralists and writers of memoirs we can perceive a general Christian tendency—a religious feeling which, while earthly and immanent, nevertheless retained its ancient breadth and comprehensiveness.

It will be said that I am seeing things in a distant perspective, and attributing qualities, characteristics and functions to the novel that do not rightly belong to it. But when one realises that the novel today is the only *genre* in literature that deals explanatorily and explicitly with man, one has to acknowledge that such a solemn reference to it is not excessive. I repeat: the origins of the novel are religious and metaphysical, and to prove it we could go much further back than our own age, as far indeed as *The Golden Ass* of Apuleius. In a word, the beauty and grandeur of the novel derive almost invariably from the strength, depth, sincerity and breadth of feeling of the author. Of course it has to be understood as a primary condition that there should be poetry in it—but this is not enough to define the novel and give it its distinctive character. The novel's character derives not only from its particular structure and organisation, but also and principally from the ethical commitment, from the determination not to present human beings fortuitously, nor outside human conventions and values.

So we begin with moralists and memoir-writers, then. And whether the man they present us with is shown against the generic background of classical character-drawing, or against the shifting and picturesque background of gossip-writing, he is, we feel, not a mere splash of colour, a voice, a decorative feature—that is to say, something passive, dependent and partial—but someone in possession of the most human of all properties, freedom. Freedom from his creator, freedom from the other characters surrounding him. We are not discussing here the novel that vies with the civil register such as is advocated by the naturalists. We are not interested in the sort of objectivity that turns out machine-made collections of types and characters, but in the purely poetic capacity to represent one's own hopes, one's own fears, one's own resentments, one's own loves, in human form; to tell one's own story through characters instead of through the warm flow of lyric poetry; to define oneself by subdividing oneself and multiplying oneself in one or a hundred creatures. In other words, the character is not the fruit of a more or less minute and precise observation, but the form taken by moral judgement. Let us note in passing that it is for this very reason that the characters in a novel are often smaller than the author, often the author himself, but only in rare cases bigger than the author—even when judgement seems to take the form of an affectionate intuition that cannot be put into words.

If we accept this definition of the novel as character, all we need do now is follow its developments, mentioning the usual names—Stendhal, Balzac, Flaubert and Zola, or Austen, Brontë, Thackeray and Dickens, or Gogol, Tolstoy and Dostoievsky. But this is always done, and always has been done, and usually ends up with the surprising statement that the novel of the past should serve as premiss for a hypothetical modern novel that has not yet made its appearance. But more interesting to us is to show how the character, as indispensable condition of the novel, has undergone a process of modification with time, and how the very existence of this character has been more and more reduced and is now threatened with complete elimination.

The character in the nineteenth-century novel, as is well known, drew his main reason for living from some sort of faith on the part of the writer in the existence of objective reality. The characters in the nineteenth-century novel are almost all seen objectively, and the delicate operation whereby the writer expresses himself through the character takes place in a mysterious way that remains obscure to everyone and most of all to the writer himself. There is no question but that Stendhal, Balzac, and even Flaubert (in spite of his famous statement, *Madame Bovary, c'est moi*) believed they were portraying the truth. Really they were trying to compete with the civil register; and the result of this rivalry was that at a certain moment the novel extended its ambitions in an incredible way. The aspiration of the nineteenth century was for the novel to represent a world. It became a substitute for life, and was as multiform and organic as life itself. The greatest novels of the last century, whether *Vanity Fair*, *Le Père Goriot*, *War and Peace*, *L'Education Sentimentale* or *Le Rouge et le Noir*, are all stamped with this ambition. Then little by little, as less gifted artists followed, the original moralism and spirit of judgement declined to give place to an arrangement or mechanical process. They started by giving the character a name, surroundings, a job, a physical appearance. Then they made him talk and act, more or less in keeping with these attributes, for three or four or five hundred pages. But art has no truth apart from poetic truth. Soon the naturalists' view of the true was shown to be false, even extremely false, as false as the cardboard tragedies of the last of the neo-classical plays, or the epic spirit in the last epic poems. But at the same time a revolution was taking place in the way the writer conceived and moulded his characters. The mystery of the writer's self-expression through his characters, to which I alluded just now, came out into the open. Suddenly the '*tranche de vie*' lost interest and seemed futile and useless; and the character no longer appeared as a copy of the real but as the result of an alchemy taking place within the writer. For the first time people grasped that what mattered was not the character's approximation to truth so much as the nature of his relationship with the author, the way in which his ghostlike figure took on substance and shape under the pen, the love or hate in which his secret bond with his creator consisted. This discovery led to the complete abandonment of the naturalists' methods in favour of a kind of character who was avowedly lyrical and autobiographical. With this the novel seemed once again to have found the path of poetry.

Why do we feel, for instance, that Dostoievsky's novels are more modern than Tolstoy's? Because Tolstoy's characters are hardly ever Tolstoy, whereas Dostoievsky's are nearly always Dostoievsky. In other words we are more interested in the writer than in the characters he creates. It would be useless to look to Dostoievsky for the description of a whole society such as we find in *War and Peace*. For him the great question is to give substantiality to his own mysterious and contradictory instincts. Recently, in connexion with Dostoievsky, we have had a lot of talk about the subconscious. We are not of the opinion that psychoanalysis has anything to do with art, nevertheless the attempt to make a psychoanalytical exegesis goes to show the prevalence of purely subjective elements and undermines any talk about verisimilitude.

With Proust, the change that has taken place since the age of the naturalists is still more apparent. Proust's concern is not to introduce characters in some clear-cut and definitive way, and then set them free to act in accordance with external cause and effect, but to fix and describe their relationship with the character called 'Je' and relate, in enormous wealth of detail, the changes slowly wrought on these relationships by time. In other words the character in the traditional sense of the word does not exist with Proust, because time so transforms it in the eyes of the protagonist that it ceases to be an independent entity but is rather a changing and unstable aspect integral with the character of the protagonist himself. Swann, Charlus, Saint-Loup and all the rest are not characters but moments in the sensibility of 'Je', that is, of Proust himself. And he is the only character who really exists. The prevailing tendency here is significant. Not content with disintegrating the traditional character into so many contradictory moments of memory, Proust puts him on the same plane as a piece of music, a cathedral or a landscape. In his impressionistic way, he does not establish any difference in value, for his driving motive is above all to resurrect time past or to re-create reality through the modifications of sensibility. It is only a step from this to abolishing the character and turning the novel into something between an essay and a book of lyrical memories.

Running parallel with Proust, Joyce too wears out the formula of naturalism by showing that once the heterogeneous elements that go to make it up have been analysed, the character loses all existence. His Bloom is not a man but a crossroad at which utterly different kinds of traffic meet. He is richer than any other character because he can think, feel and be the most diverse things, and at the same time he is as poor as can be owing to his lack of any core round which this tumultuous material can be arranged. So, from their common starting-point of impressionism, Proust and Joyce inevitably dissolve the personality, Proust in the changing flow of time, Joyce in the mass of objects set before him by consciousness. With them the character swells, spreads out beyond human limits, becomes the time that passes or the mass of objects, and in the end explodes and dissolves. Unquestionably these two writers can be viewed both as the grave-diggers of the nineteenth-century novel and the founders of the new novel. Perhaps rather than founders they are restorers, having restored to narrative the lost sense of poetry.

So today the character is in danger of being eliminated in favour of exclusive interest in the writer. Tree-like forms of memory, shadows of fantasy, monologues and soliloquies, seem all that is left to the only kind of character henceforth possible—the character who calls himself 'I'. This reduction coincides in a significant way with the careful search for a narrative language that satisfies the increased aestheic demands of the age. In other words the novel, for so long a matter of content, now seems to have been resolved in form. So, after the pure lyric, are we going to have the pure novel? We have obviously travelled a very long way from the nineteenth century.

This crisis in the character obviously corresponds to a similar crisis in the concept of man. Modern man can be seen as a mere numerical entity within the most terrifying collectivities that the human race has ever known. He can be seen as existing not for himself alone but as a part of something else, of a collective feeling, idea and organism. It is very difficult to create a character out of such a man, at least in the traditional sense of the word.

But at this stage we need to point out that what matters more than character is the metaphysical and moral experience from which the character itself was born. In this sense the novel is not dead. But to be reborn in a way worthy of the name it will have to await a new conception of man.

1941

PRESENCE AND PROSE

WHEN STENDHAL spoke of the *Code Civil* it was probably not because of a need for simplicity (the prose of the *Code Civil* is not necessarily simple; on occasion, when the laws demand it, it tends to be fairly complicated), but rather because of a need to attain complete domination over his material—in other words, because of a need for freedom. Many writers of the naturalist epoch were simple enough, but not therefore free. This absence of freedom can be seen in various ways: in satisfied enjoyment of detail, in forced faithfulness to the data of space and time, or in the context of the syntax which emerges as a composition of impressionistic phrases set variously one beside another. When for instance Verga wrote in *Jeli the Shepherd*—

> . . . meanwhile the sun had begun to set behind the Croce hill and the robins set out after it towards the mountains as darkness grew, and followed it through the wastelands of cactus. The crickets could no longer be heard, and in that hour there spread through the air a sort of huge melancholy . . .

his short phrases, each of which illuminates and supports the others, are certainly simple, but he is not being free. His accepted task is to tell the story of Jeli the Shepherd: but in this piece Verga has forgotten Jeli and is concerned with the sunset. In other words, this description, like all descriptions, is unnecessary except insofar as it adds something to the *atmosphere* surrounding the figure of Jeli in an indirect way: by indulging in it Verga effaces himself, so to speak, and at most his presence is a question of sensibility or of choice of detail. This amounts to saying that, like all the naturalists—Flaubert included—Verga is not free, because his presence is often too approximative and doubtful. When he spoke of the *Code Civil* Stendhal was referring to the freedom that comes from a sort of mathematical development in which all the material is inexorably swept along, systematised, subjugated, and dominated to such an extent that it kills stone dead the element of autonomy that allows for the spirit of playfulness, decoration and arabesque.

Of course any real artist is free up to a point. The impurity of art as compared with what are called the exact sciences would appear to consist in this preoccupation with origins, and in this limited freedom. But everything is relative. The extreme slavery to detail in our more recent prose-writing is epitomised in Gabriele D'Annunzio, whose lack of freedom is revealed on every page, word by word, and the rounded-off perfection of the writing seems over and over again to affix maximum attention and immobility to every detail as if it stood by itself and had no connection with what comes before and follows after. Sometimes D'Annunzio's phrases are put together coldly, externally, like lists in a catalogue, without even the unity conferred by Verga's breath of physical and full-blooded poetry. Page follows page composed not structurally but according to purely extrinsic demands. This is the very antithesis of the freedom that owes everything to a rigorously thinking mind; we are in an occasional, ornamental, fragmentary world. For what is fragmentary writing if not the expression of a physicalness open to every kind of suggestion but incapable of rising to the order and contemplative lucidity of systematic thought? Modern Italian prose, which nearly all derives from D'Annunzio—above all our so-called 'art prose'—has tried various ways of remedying this original vice; either by hiding its native impressionism under the cloak of essays, or by looking for the freedom and mastery we were talking about just now in the broad flow of traditional eloquence which submerges everything in its abundant waters.

Yet the fact remains that the freedom the writer gets from a complete and absolute mastery over his material is something quite else. It has often seemed to me that this kind of freedom must be something more than a mere literary matter. For example, mannerism, to which many writers have recourse nowadays so as to escape from the naturalist fashion, is a cure worse than the illness. Mannered writers fail to realise that they cannot free themselves from slavery to time and space by a mere tone of voice. The manner is no more than imitation presence. The truth that the writer is absent from his prose is made all the more obvious by his attempt to disguise his absence.

But, to return to Stendhal, it seems to me that his longing for a prose like that of the *Code Civil* amounts to a rejection of the author's presence in terms of mere feeling. The confirmation of this lies in his *esprit*, his capacity for a playfulness, a lightness and counterpoint unshackled by any sort of realistic impediment. The *Code Civil* prose is by and large the outcome of a judgement that precedes representation, and is so absolute and final that it serves as an immovable and reliable background for the characters and their behaviour. Moral doubt, uncertainty of values, and the lack of any convention lie behind all forms of 'realism'. The concentration is on details because of the knowledge that nothing exists outside details. Once the ground has been cleared of the necessity to construct reality with nothing more than the data of time and space, then reality—previously rendered misshapen and top-heavy by lack of judgement—recovers its lightness. Then the prose becomes simple, it darts forward where previously it was sluggish, and is married to an ideal space and time. And the writer's presence is no longer a matter of the content he prefers; it is a voice and a song.

Prose of this kind, of course, demands an over-riding intelligence. Its lyricism is the offspring of a counterpoint of an intelligence that provides in advance the solution it aims to reach, so as to leave for the reader's delight only the foreseen and needful ins-and-outs of the demonstration. The result is just the opposite of those books in which we are warned not to read the end until we reach it, otherwise we shall lose interest. It is clear that along this road we really can reach the *Code Civil*, or perfect, completely rational aridity. But this is at least better than the boneless, swollen, ultimately analogical prose that many people seem to prefer.

Tension and clarity in prose have a direct relationship with the cruelty used by the intelligence in marshalling the material. One only needs to think of Machiavelli's cruelty, above all in *The Prince*—on which the accusation of immorality made in all ages against the Florentine writer largely rests. Such cruelty has its origin in the resistance of the intelligence to the promptings of feelings of an inferior order. Deep down in certain decorative, literary, humanist, traditional, educational and pleasing kinds of prose lies a compromise. A compromise over form which none the less mirrors a human compromise.

In other words prose is inevitably in direct correspondence with the writer's most rigid and essential faculties of logic. It is inevitably the expression of a sincerity that is not only complete but supremely coherent and hence pushed to the furthest boundaries of imagination. The logical links that abound in ancient prose show this function clearly. They constitute so many necessary steps taken by the intelligence on its way to its distant targets. For all his fascination with sixteenth-century fashions, this function is obvious in Leopardi. But in some modern writers, whose timidity is only rivalled by their arrogance, logical links of this kind turn into mere decoration, more or less completely useless, like the columns and arches found only too frequently on the façades of our public buildings. These links precisely exclude the possibility of dwelling on detail. And detail, when reduced to its real level of importance and, so to speak, treated with contempt, attains far greater prominence and vividness than in the pages of modern writers. All the varieties of adjective and all the close analysis in the moderns are inadequate for defining it; whereas with the old writers a single noun set down in the context of the prose attains an incomparable highlight of meaning and suggestive power.

1942

RECALLING *TIME OF INDIFFERENCE*

I HAVE been asked by the review *La Nuova Europa* to tell the story of how I came to write *Time of Indifference*. I find it difficult to comply with requests of this kind, because the real reasons for a book can only be found within the book itself. In other words a book, like a flower or an animal or any living organism, is its own sufficient explanation and justification. An inquiry into the whys and the wherefores of a book may have some interest—especially if carried out by a critic and not the author—but at best such an inquiry can only touch a small part of the book. The failure of so much of our psychoanalytical, moral and social criticism only goes to show that it is as unconvincing to reduce the achievement of art to a mere matter of content as it is to reduce it to a mere matter of form. The fact is that artistic creation involves extreme effort on the artist's side, effort without reserve, effort in which the whole of his interests and means are at stake. Thus inquiry into a book which goes beyond the confines of the book itself inevitably leads to delving into the life and character of the writer, so that in practice talking about one's own book amounts to a sort of confession. But I am not in favour of confessions, and an artist can only confess in black and white. Which brings us back to our point of departure, namely that the explanations of a book reside within the book itself.

Nevertheless authors can say something about their own books and, let's face it, they are often very ready to do so. It just happens that this does not apply in my case—I get bored talking about my books, and especially about *Time of Indifference* which I have seen so often bracketed with my name that I have developed a kind of antipathy for it. However, I shall do my best. I shall talk about it as I would talk about any other experience of mine of which I was asked to give an account.

I began writing *Time of Indifference* in October 1925, and I finished it in March 1928. I had written a good deal before *Time of Indifference*, but was never sure if I could really see myself in what I wrote. I had written a good many poems and short stories, and even two novels, most of which were imitations of this or that author with whom I had become infatuated as I went along. With *Time of Indifference* I felt for the first time in my life that I had put my feet on solid ground. I suddenly felt that I had crossed over from the stage of good intention to that of spontaneity. I hope all whose ambition it is to write will experience this crucial transition once in their lives. It is the transition from the desperate career of literature to literary expression as a means of knowledge. I do not say that this transition necessarily leads to works of poetry, but it at least gets away from the limbo of empty will and spiritless words.

When I began *Time of Indifference* I had no exact plan in mind—either as to the meaning and purpose of the work I wanted to write, or as to the theme of events, characters, and general set-up. I began, and then carried on because for the first time I was enjoying writing. Up till then I had just struggled along. Suddenly I felt I had found the beginning of a thick skein; I pulled, and to my astonishment saw that the skein was unrolling. In other words, from the beginning of the work I felt the urge to carry on, not from practical will-power but from a sense of rhythm which for the first time entered into the words and regulated their disposal. I wrote very little each day, content if I set down just a detail or a phrase.

I began without any ideas as to content, though I had no lack of literary outlines. Over a long period of years I had read innumerable plays and novels. I had become convinced that the summit of art lay in tragedy, while on the other hand I felt more drawn to writing novels than writing for the theatre. So I got the idea of writing a novel that combined the qualities of story and drama, a novel with few characters, very few scenes, and the action confined within a short space of time; a novel in which all that existed were dialogue and background, and in which all the comments and analyses and author's interventions were meticulously eliminated in perfect objectivity.

The truth is that my preference for tragedy was not the fruit of cold critical reflection but of a deep inclination towards freedom. Today I find it difficult to recall the state of mind I was in then. All I can say is that before writing tragedy I wanted to live it. Crime, bloody and insoluble conflict, passion, violence—all had an infinite attraction for me. Normal life did not appeal to me—it bored me and seemed to lack flavour. Very probably at that period I found in writing a substitute for experiences I had not had and could not manage to have.

On the other hand I became convinced that writing was pointless unless the writer entered into competition with the Creator and invented independent characters with independent life; it never entered my head that art could be anything but the creation of characters. So from the start, and largely due to these unshakable convictions, I found myself up against a whole array of very serious difficulties.

Unquestionably I had plenty to say. But I was absolutely determined not to say anything extraneous to the inevitable channels of the characters. But the trouble was that I had only a very limited knowledge of people, and still less of human experience.

The biggest difficulty I had to face lay in establishing a relationship between myself and my characters. I felt that making characters who were mere spokesmen of my feelings and my ideas would come relatively easily, but that was not the aim I had set myself. The element of moralism and the lack of poetical freedom that the critics—some more, some less—detected in the book must surely be ascribed to my determination to underline the distance between myself and my characters. I could never be certain that I had done enough to make the characters separate and distinct.

Much of the 'realism' in the book comes, not from any inclination of mine towards realism, but from this insecurity. The truth is that I am less of a 'realist' than any writer imaginable. Even today I have great difficulty in forcing my attention so as to achieve a 'realist' representation of reality.

However the particular structure of *Time of Indifference* was neither willed nor pre-established. My original idea was to make the novel cover two isolated days—like a two-act play. Almost inevitably and against my will I made the two days consecutive which helped to give the theatrical shape to my novel that had been one of my original ambitions.

Once the action had been confined to two days it followed that I had to describe not only the emotional development of my characters, but everything they did. Hence all those dinners and suppers and similar events with which the novel is full. In this way, though without intending it or setting it as my goal, I came to give a complete and lifelike picture of the daily life of a middle-class Roman family at that time. The picture has been called bitter and cruel. In fact it reflects very faithfully those feelings of boredom and impatience that, as I mentioned earlier on, normal life aroused in me.

I would find it almost impossible to say in any detail how I came upon the idea of indifference, which is the key of the book. All I can roughly say is this: as I have already explained, I set out to write a tragedy in the form of a novel, but, as I wrote, I realised that the traditional tragic motif, or indeed any really tragic event, slipped through my fingers as soon as I tried to formulate it. By this I mean that tragedy was impossible given the sort of background and sort of characters I was dealing with, but if I had changed the background and characters then I would have turned my back on reality and created something artificial. In other words I began to see the impossibility of tragedy in a world in which non-materialist values seemingly lacked any right to exist, and where moral conscience had become so hardened that people acted from appetite only and were more and more like automata. So the spirit of tragedy became transferred from outward events (such as the seduction of the daughter by the mother's lover) to the inner experiences of Michele, an impotent character in revolt, who, while participating in the general lack of feeling, had retained enough insight to suffer from his participation. Today all this may seem naïve and simple, not to say clumsy, but at the time of writing it was anything but clear, and the few motifs that finally emerged seemed indissolubly tangled up with all the others that I eventually dropped. In any case the issue was never one of ideas, but of feelings more or less ordered and enlightened by reason.

To this I can add—should anyone want to probe further—that what had priority in the composition of *Time of Indifference* was a quite special state of mind caused by my experiences in those and the preceding years. Without going into the value or otherwise of these experiences, I can say that the state of mind was strongly romantic, and though it was the outcome of experiences extrinsic to art, it was in keeping with all the decadent and realist literature of the preceding quarter of a century. In other words, for a long period there was no critical line of demarcation between literature and life. Perhaps this is still the case today.

At this point someone will surely ask why I make no mention of the concealed social and political intentions lying behind the criticism of the middle class so often attributed to my novel. My answer is that if I do not mention these intentions it is because they did not exist. If being antimiddle-class implies a clear conception of class, then nothing was further from my mind at the time. I was born in, and belong to, a middle-class society, and I was middle class myself (at least as to my way of life). At most *Time of Indifference* was a means of making myself aware of my condition. Moreover if I had had any clear class-consciousness I would not have written *Time of Indifference.* As I see it, it is impossible to write a novel against something. Art lies in inner, not external, feelings. I wrote *Time of Indifference* because I was inside the middle classes, not *outside* them. Had I been outside, as those who endow me with socially critical aims seem to think, I would have written a different book from inside whatever society or class I belonged to. It is quite another matter to say that *Time of Indifference* ended up as an antimiddle-class book. The fault or merit of this belongs to the middle classes, especially in Italy where they have hardly any qualities capable of inspiring (let us not mention admiration) even the remotest sympathy.

All this is so true that only long after the publication of *Time of Indifference* did I realise the real bearing of the book and begin to feel revulsion for the middle-class way of life as a whole. But I should point out that I began seeing that way of life as a moral, rather than a material, phenomenon. Comfort is always preferable to poverty, and I know many violently antimiddle-class people who would hardly be able to go on being what they are in any deep or sincere way if the material restrictions in which they are struggling were removed. They are antimiddle-class because they are poor, just as many middle-class people are anti-proletarian because they are rich. However useful they may be in the political struggle, their conclusions remove all interest from the attributes themselves. I think one can only be genuinely antimiddle-class on a wider plane, one that annihilates all social distinctions and aims at building a world for all men.

But to return. It was noticed that the punctuation left much to be desired in *Time of Indifference*. This was because at the time of writing I made no use of punctuation and only separated one sentence from another by a dash or a space. Though I wrote in prose, every sentence sprang out with rhythmical independence, like a line of verse. Then, when the whole composition was finished, I distributed punctuation more or less at random. But in many places sentences were so constructed that no reasonable punctuation seemed possible. Now, too late, I realise that I should perhaps have omitted the punctuation and left the book as I originally wrote it.

1945

EXTREMISM AND LITERATURE

THE BEST-KNOWN and most spectacular case of compromise in literature is the one known as the Victorian compromise. In what does compromise in literature consist? It consists in the presence of a quantity of restrictions in form and content imposed on art by any given society. In the nineteenth century it was the middle class and industrial society of the Victorian era that imposed these restrictions—but plainly any society or collective organism, even not middle class, can fall into the same error. Yet the most typical compromise is the Victorian one because it took place within a régime of complete freedom, without State or other intervention. An English critic whose name now escapes me, writing on morality and literature, observed how the cynical and libertine outspokenness of the eighteenth-century theatre would have been unthinkable twenty or thirty years later in the devout England of Queen Victoria. Another critic, writing of Dickens's *David Copperfield*, notes the incongruousness of its conclusion: Mr Micawber, loaded with debts and incurably unemployed, ends up by leaving for Australia where, so far as we can see, he becomes a quite different man, prosperous, active, well organised and important. This is a typical case of compromise: the appealing characters had to end up well to satisfy the wide readership, and Dickens could think of nothing better than sending Micawber off to Australia as if a new continent could change an old and jaded man. Australia was providential in Dickens and, *mutatis mutandis*, is exactly like joining the Fascists or the Nazis, as many characters in books of the last twenty years have done, or building factory chimneys in Siberia, like the heroes of Soviet

Russian realism. It seems obvious that, following the great literature of the last century, Russia is going to have a Victorian-type literature imposed by the new society of bureaucrats that has emerged from the Revolution. It is similar to the conversion to Catholicism in Catholic novels: it is, in a word, the brutal intrusion of social conformity into the logical, detached and pure climate of art. We could go on with a list of the best-known names of the English nineteenth century. The Victorian compromise has as inevitable outcome a writer like Kipling with his hypocritical explanation of the white man's burden, or the right of the British white man to govern the coloured peoples.

But it would be better to define compromise in literature in depth rather than to give examples. By and large, in cases where definite material interests are not involved, it amounts to a sort of self-censorship of an almost Freudian kind that the writer, whether aware of it or not, imposes on himself before setting pen to paper. Freud's conception of censorship is well known. He explains why the things which inhibit the writer's work are nearly always the most important, the things that concern him most. Or, inversely and equally characteristically, the writer works himself up into an artificial glow about matters that do not concern him and that he does not care about, but knows to be acceptable to the majority of readers or the society to which he belongs. So a double process of falsification takes place: the writer seeks a refuge from himself as otherwise he knows he would be carried on too far in dangerous directions, and at the same time he accepts the ready-made framework society proposes to him. All this can be done sincerely enough in literatures in an ancient and illustrious tradition, with a high standard of formal decorum.

In other words the writer who practises compromise lacks the courage to get to the bottom of things while knowing full well in his heart that this bottom exists, that is, he does not dare to be *extreme*. He preserves a conventional golden mean, like someone who avoids saying what he thinks at a polite reception for fear of not being asked again. When the moment comes for saying the truth, the whole truth, and nothing but the truth (it is the writers themselves, remember, who bear witness to this) the compromising writer feels his elbow jogged by the guardian angel of conformity, no matter whether the society be Victorian, or Soviet Russian, or simply literary society as in the case of Tasso. The main suggestion the guardian angel makes to the writer is *not to be logical*. The fight against logic is nearly always carried on in the name of the golden mean. But that measure is not the measure that belongs to works of art. We are up against another quite arbitrary measure, one that society—mistaking its own prejudices and proprieties for aesthetic and moral laws—attempts at times to impose on the artist. If and when he is imposed upon he is no longer free and his work, which has come to terms with society, is in danger of perishing outright whenever society gives way to another less narrow one, or simply to one fortified by other prejudices.

As I have already said, it is the writer's duty to be *extreme*. I will add that there is not a single instance of a great writer who was not extreme, in other words consistent and unshakably and wholly sincere. The word 'extreme' will make some people turn up their noses; it will make them think of a revolutionary and bohemian type of literature. I would like to dismiss these fears by taking Giacomo Leopardi's work as an example. For it would be hard to find any of these compromises with contingent and historical reality in Leopardi's work, although, oddly enough, many people tried to justify such compromises later by appeals to his authority. The lesson to be learnt from Leopardi is not just a formal and literary one, as some people would have us think. It lies in the heroic consistency with which he developed his themes to such an elevated and dangerous point, without regard for the sleepy academic world in which he had to live, and above all without regard for himself. He paid for his consistency in suffering and blood. They tell us that poems such as *La sera del dì di festa* or some of the dialogues in which Leopardi's despair, following its thread of passionate logic, reaches the point of paradox, are inferior, poetically speaking, to other more peaceful poems or more balanced dialogues. That may be so. But Leopardi's poetry, the purity and loftiness of his song, are inseparable from the extremism of his position. True, other poets as great and as extreme as Leopardi were not so deperate. But here you must turn back to what I said about the bottom that the writer has to attain even at the cost of his own life. Obviously this bottom changes in depth and place according to times and circumstances. The tiresome vitriol of truth scarcely scratches the surface of some periods and these are the ones in which we would all have liked to have lived. But there are other, weaker, more lying, more corrupt periods in which the appearance of truth, by corrosion and sudden combustion, produces a downright void. So we have the despair of Lucretius and Leopardi, the cynicism of Machiavelli, the *Angst* of the Existentialists, and so on. I am choosing examples at random, and my only aim is to clarify my own thoughts.

In the second half of the nineteenth century, after Leopardi and to a certain extent Manzoni (but not, to be sure, Manzoni the Catholic novelist), compromise was widely practised in Italy. It explains the mediocrity and provinciality of a large part of Italian culture after 1870.

We need only recall the musty smell of the polite drawing-rooms and scented garçonnières, whichever it was (without prejudice to the rhetorical and harmless smell of gunpowder about so much so-called civic poetry) that spread through our literature with the works of Carducci, Pascoli and D'Annunzio. These things are well known, and it is boring to repeat them. There are those who mourn to see so much ability wasted on so slight a result. Seventy years of literacy and intellectual compromise have done nothing visible to increase the extremely slender cultural equipment of our good and prudent middle classes. It would have been just as well if no one had done anything but put their feet up on their desks, or, better, never gone near a desk at all. Carducci, remember, with his silliness, was a contemporary of Baudelaire, Rimbaud and Lautréamont; of Dostoievsky and Tolstoy; of Nietzsche and Ibsen.

Of course the writer should respect measure, but as I have

already pointed out this measure is a question of rhythm, proportion and balance rather than of charm and social conformity. It is a very consoling fact that a positive moral world can always be rediscovered wherever the artist has done no more than remain faithful to himself. What matter if this world is discovered by posterity rather than by short-sighted contemporaries? Books are not written for today or for tomorrow. An ideal library that contained all the literary masterpieces of mankind would be a catalogue of extreme positions beyond which there is only nothingness. Whereas compromise relegates literary works to the geological depths of writing, with old documents, *curiosa* and other fossils of the kind, which may deserve our study, but not our admiration.

1946

PSYCHOANALYSIS

I HAVE no deep knowledge of psychoanalytical theories; the truth being that I have not even read much Freud. Psychoanalysis is a science, and only concerns the artist insofar as it helps him clear his mind as to the significance of certain experiences that he *ought* to have been through earlier himself. In other words I think all Freud did was to give scientific formulation to something which was, so to speak, in the air. After all, culture is not just contained in books. It runs through men's actions like blood through their veins. The artist, insofar as he is practising, can neither ignore it nor do without it. Without realising it, I knew Freud (or at least I was a Freudian, even before I had read him), through experiences that had convinced me of the major importance of the sexual factor in art. But of course as regards the aims of art, it is not so much the sexual factor in itself—a thing that has always existed—that counts, but awareness of its importance.

Freud's case is very similar to that of Marx. Both of them posited a material definition of the origin of seemingly autonomous and 'ideal' activities: with Freud this is the sexual instinct, with Marx the economic drive. At first it might appear that this sort of determinism would enslave and destroy those activities. In reality, however, it serves the liberating function proper to all rigorous and lasting criticism—that of purifying them by cleansing them of the fog of our more self-interested illusions and hypocrisies. Before the advent of Freud and Marx, families and societies were 'innocent'; now we know what lay hidden beneath that innocence.

It has often been observed that Marxism, though open to debate when putting forward positive solutions, is impregnable when diagnosing the negative evils of the bourgeois world. The same can be said of Freud in all that concerns sex. Thanks to the ethical requirement animating their works, both contribute to a renewal of the concept of man and the importance of man.

I am not aware of any novels or other literary works directly inspired by Freud. But Freud's influence on art is to be found wherever there is frankness and objectivity about the sexual act. I do not believe in the possibility of poetry when conformism—whether conscious or unconscious—is present. Great classical art knew nothing of conformism, even though it often remained silent about certain matters. Conformism as regards sex is a survival from the nineteenth century. Freud sets us free from this spirit of conformism, and enables us to tackle the subject without embarrassment, without sentimentality, and without cynicism. In other words, by unveiling the mystery, he has enabled us to handle it in a poetic way.

1946

MACHIAVELLI

IN THESE notes I shall be dealing only with *The Prince*, *Mandragola*, and a few of the lesser works; I shall exclude the *Histories*, the *Discourses* and *The Art of War*. My reason is that I do not intend to write an essay on Machiavelli's political works but on some of the traits of his character, and it seems to me that these are much clearer in the first works mentioned above. Moreover I am particularly anxious to get at a definition of Machiavellianism and the degree to which Machiavellianism is inseparable from Machiavelli. But by Machiavellianism I understand not a political theory but a moral passion that found a perfect and unselfconscious portrayer in Machiavelli. Hence these notes go to make up a psychological portrait rather than a critical essay.

It may be objected that Machiavellianism is a libellous legend created at a later date by critics who could hardly be called disinterested, and that in his works Machiavelli in fact did no more than develop a rigorous and consistent line of thought. To this we answer, yes, in much of his work and often even in *The Prince* Machiavelli is no more Machiavellian than any other political thinker. Nevertheless certain facts remain that are totally inexplicable if we view Machiavelli as no more than an essayist on the same level as, say, Montaigne or Guicciardini (Machiavelli's contemporary). These facts consist in a complicity (not confined to words alone), an extravagance, and, in last analysis, an incoherence that we either have to ignore, as do most of Machiavelli's admirers, or else make a fiery and moralising denunciation of them, in the manner of Machiavelli's enemies. In fact neither of these attitudes stands up to examination; both appear evasive and lacking in commitment.

Successive generations have revolted against certain statements and developments in Machiavelli's teaching, just as they would revolt against any attitude or teaching or theory in which they instinctively felt personal interest to be at work rather than free thought. In other words, no system of thought can offend—however unfamiliar or even erroneous it may appear at first sight—if it is thought, thought pure and simple, and sooner or later what appeared so strange and even erroneous may well come to be accepted as normal and obvious. For instance many of the ancients viewed Christian thought as a diseased paradox, but before two centuries had elapsed it had come to be the thought, and to form the life, of all mankind. Machiavelli's thought, on the other hand, after the lapse of four centuries, still seems to the most broad-minded reader as having embarrassing, strange and extravagant elements, and far from becoming the norm, and forming the life, of men, it has remained attached to the figure of its creator like a vice or some other purely personal attitude. In fact Machiavelli's thought seems in many ways to differ from thought, to be something that looks like, but is not, thought. Posterity's primary irritation when considering Machiavelli's work lies in the fact that what was really a personal attitude was so very well disguised as thought and so very well developed with the methods proper to thought. To sum up, any estimate of Machiavellianism is made difficult by the presence of real thought intermingled with what is not thought—Machiavelli's political science being at the service of emotions and passions that have little or nothing to do with the science itself.

The huge mass of detailed and exact observation in Machiavelli's work, coupled with his rigorous logic and excellence of construction and method, all impose themselves on the attention and admiration of even the most ordinary reader and form the basis and foundation of Machiavelli's glory. But there is something else besides these qualities, something that Machiavelli neither could, nor wished to, hide. Few writers have been as sincere as Machiavelli, and it has to be admitted that it is this quality of candour that reveals the greatness of the man. For it is a constant characteristic of great men to give themselves openly and unarmed, trusting only in their strength and their complexity.

Now it is this candour which allows us to draw the line between Machiavellianism and Machiavelli's political science. A writer other than Machiavelli, someone with more foresight and discretion, could have blurred certain corners, disguised certain parts of his thought—in other words not have written *The Prince* at all. Machiavelli's fame as the initiator of political science would have been just as assured by the *Discourses* alone. We would have had a Machiavelli no less deep, penetrating, exact, methodical, and new. A Machiavelli without Machiavellianism—or so little of it as to pass unnoticed. We owe *The Prince* to Machiavelli's sincerity. *The Prince* is a poetical work which not so much concludes and crowns Machiavelli's work as adds to it by providing the note of, and the evidence for, Machiavellianism. It is in the light of *The Prince* that Machiavelli's other writings reveal whatever measure of Machiavellianism they contain.

We know, of course, that there always has been Machiavellianism, and always will be. Nevertheless, Machiavelli's calling as an initiator remains intact: it was he and he alone who uncovered its various parts scattered throughout history and assembled them within one vigorous and terrifying body. In a similar way, Sadism existed before de Sade: but it was de Sade who first described it and gave it its name. It seems to me that if sympathy had been lacking—the sort of sympathy that makes a fire seize hold of very dry things—Machiavelli would never have uncovered, built into a system, and given a name to, the sort of moral disease known as Machiavellianism.

Many critics have seen in *Mandragola* the fount and origin of a supposed Italian theatre that somehow—no one quite knows why—never developed. (Goldoni is something quite different and cannot be called Italian theatre.) But in my view, far from being a beginning, *Mandragola* is the most tired and anaemic of ends. I am referring here to its harshness, corruption and cynicism. Now if this harshness, corruption and cynicism were real, and really felt by the author, then *Mandragola* would be a vital play such as could well have been a genuine starting-point for an Italian theatre. But the only reason why cynicism, corruption and harshness exist in *Mandragola* is not because Machiavelli intended to put them there but because we modern readers, who live in quite another world and have quite other conventions, see them there. In other words, Machiavelli thought he was writing a kind of farce; and if the farce turned out to be cruel and bitter this was without his intending it and, up to a point, without his knowing it. There is an almost complete lack of that irony and detachment which, in writings of this kind, normally establish a distance and a difference between the author and his creatures and reveal a moral anguish, strictly controlled, so as better to achieve the effects originally intended. There is no irony or sarcasm in *Mandragola*, only the kind of gloomy delight, arid complacency and exhausted sincerity of someone who had no intention of, and (had he intended) was incapable of, seeing much beyond Lucrezia's fatuity, Nicia's silliness, or Timoteo's corruption. The seriousness in *Mandragola*, which verges on the morose even in the comic parts, is the outcome of an effete and bloodless ethical background, not of real indignation.

> God knows that I have never thought of bringing harm to anyone; that I have kept in my cell, said my office, looked after my parishioners. Then comes this devil Ligurio, who made me dip first my finger into mischief, then my arm, and then the whole of me—and I still don't know where it's all going to end. But my consolation is this: that when a thing concerns many, the responsibility can't be left to anyone in particular . . .

says Friar Timoteo when he has let himself be persuaded by the pimp, Ligurio, to promise him first an abortion and then the trick of the mandragola or mandrake. Now all this could have been satirical, or even downright anguishing, if it had cut its way, like a diamond on glass, into some sort of disapproval or moral feeling or faith in Machiavelli; if, that is to say, Timoteo's pettiness and abjection had been played out against a background of some important fact that Machiavelli really believed in. But here, all is void. To describe the appalling trap into which the Friar has let himself be drawn, Machiavelli can think of no comment other than two phrases of political prudence: '[he] made me dip first my finger into mischief, then my arm, and then the whole of me' and, 'When a thing concerns many, the responsibility can't be left to anyone in particular'. Owing to his lack of personal relationship with Timoteo, Machiavelli merely copies him from life, that is, composes him out of the raw materials of reality. In other words, Machiavelli doesn't shudder as he writes Timoteo's monologue because he is writing it on paper and not on his own flesh.

For all these reasons Timoteo emerges as arid and sketchy and lacking in depth. Rather than described he is, as it were, scratched scrappily on stone. And the other characters fare no better. Take Lucrezia, for instance. Lucrezia's innocence ought to be offset by Timoteo's 'religion'. Though Machiavelli's irreligion may have historical explanations, we have really no idea what reasons can be produced for his total indifference to Lucrezia's outraged innocence. She is described by Callimaco as 'virtuous, and won't let herself think of love'. But on closer scrutiny we see that she is merely silly. Silliness, ignorance, fatuity—these are the characteristics that betray Machiavelli's worn-out ethical sense. Often Boccaccio's women, too, are introduced to us as 'virtuous', and then turn out to be merely stupid, if not worse. But this transition from stupidity to corruption is so subtly described, with such joy and wit, detachment and taste. Boccaccio, besides being a greater artist, has a fresher and more integral moral sense. Lucrezia is silly for no other reason than that Machiavelli attempted to make her virtuous; she is silly through no fault of her own, but through Machiavelli's fault; she is silly because she is inadequately felt and portrayed. She has no moral conscience nor moral feeling; she hangs mechanically on the lips of her confessor; she accepts improbable terms like a frightened animal led to slaughter, and once she has got into bed with

Callimaco she suddenly loses all her famous 'virtue' and proves every bit as coarse as her lover and the other characters.

Quite apart from the Friar and Lucrezia, none of the other characters in *Mandragola* escape this silliness and stupidity. Nicia is stupid, not only because he is stupid by nature but also because his very stupidity is stupid, that is to say it is mechanical, verbal and exaggerated; Ligurio is stupid—he is a kind of Iago without tragedy or warmth or any motive save gain; and finally even Callimaco's love is tinged with stupidity. Boccaccio is full of loves of this kind, but they are clothed with such grace and freshness—just as, with him, moral blindness is clothed in the brilliant colours of youth. Whereas here, just as Lucrezia's innocence is merely physiological and material, so Callimaco's love is merely lust.

> The longing comes over me to be with the girl I love; it shakes me and changes my whole being—even my legs are trembling, my stomach fluttering, my heart is pounding as though it would burst, and my arms feel useless, my tongue wordless, my eyes dazzled, my brain awhirl.

Here is a long catalogue more suitable for anatomical science than for expressing the feelings of love. De Sanctis sees this description as 'natural love, with its own special colouring' and thus differing both from Petrarchian love and 'cynical vulgarity'. But in Ariosto, a contemporary of Machiavelli and, like him, a child of the Renaissance, love is quite a different thing. The truth is that it is Machiavelli's moral exhaustion that reduces love to a merely physical manifestation. In a word, Machiavelli is a materialist through lack of vitality rather than through conviction, and unknowingly rather than consciously. He probably thought, in good faith, that he was representing the world as it is rather than 'as it ought to be'; that he was representing innocence in Lucrezia, love in Callimaco and religion in Timoteo. But in fact he has given us physiological innocence made up of ignorance and passivity, lecherous love made up of physical paralysis and frenzy, and mechanical religion confined to conventional devotion. In matters of innocence, love and religion, the knowledgeable and brilliantly intelligent Machiavelli saw things no differently from the common people of his own century or, indeed, of ours. For that mentality has endured, and will endure yet awhile.

So *Mandragola* reflects a deeply tired spirit as regards private values, religion and moral conscience. *The Prince*, and the other political works, are a magnificently successful attempt to whip this spirit into life by means of the only passion that still stirred in it: political passion.

It would seem natural to accept Machiavelli's political passion as an obvious fact. Machiavelli was involved in political activity, nursed political ambitions, and was interested only in politics. How could he not have a passion for politics? And yet, as I see it, things are not so simple as this would imply. Guicciardini, like Machiavelli, was a political man by profession, yet we do not find political passion in him, or, if we do, it is subordinated to his serene and sad clarity of vision. The problem of Machiavelli's political passion is, in last analysis, the same as the problem of his political science: at what point is it legitimate to subordinate every other value and affection to politics; why does this happen; and when it happens, to what extent can politics compensate for the deficiencies its supremacy involves? Once again, comparison with Guicciardini will help us clarify the matter. Guicciardini had a very different cast of mind from Machiavelli. His ability was less vehement, less imaginative, less artistic—and yet, perhaps for this very reason, he had a more integrated moral personality, a sharper conscience, and a more balanced intelligence. His adoration of the 'private person' bears witness to a respect for human freedom that it would be impossible to find in Machiavelli. True, the 'private person' seems to be nothing more than the sum of the material interests of the individual; but there is no reason for thinking that favourable circumstances might not bring about developments in the moral personality of the 'private person'. When Guicciardini falls back on individual happiness, he is in fact being an optimist; the 'private person' may at first sight seem no more than an egoist, but on closer examination we see that he is at least a man, whereas the subjects of Machiavelli's Prince are not men but inert material. Consequently while nothing can be expected from the subject, we can expect from the 'private person' (when the times are propitious and his withdrawn cultivation of his private interests has yielded fruit) a deep, rebounding renewal that will give fresh life to the whole nation. Guicciardini's idea seems to be, 'Give unto Caesar the things that are Caesar's', but surely this is also Christianity's answer to all those who want to solve public affairs before private affairs. The 'private person' has no passions, least of all political passions; he has first and foremost to save himself. Machiavelli's man has nothing left to save, and, owing precisely to his lack of private interests, political passion is his only anchor of salvation. Owing to his corruption and impoverishment, he is not free in himself, hence has to see freedom in terms of the illusion that he is taking part in politics. To sum up: both Guicciardini's man and Machiavelli's man are far from the ideal of a balanced welding of private life with public life. Guicciardini's man sacrifices every other value to the 'private person', Machiavelli's man sacrifices every other value to politics. But the former, as Voltaire says at the end of *Candide*, at least 'cultivates his garden'.

Machiavelli was so desiccated and exhausted, so worn out and infirm, that for him politics was much more than a mere occupation and duty, much more than an intellectual diversion. It was a mainstay of life and a reason for living, an artifice for making him feel morally alive. His desperate clinging to political life, when moral and religious life had died, is the main explanation for Machiavellian abstraction, unnourished by any deep ethical feeling, and it also explains the particular form to which Machiavelli had to have recourse to express it.

Just consider: Machiavelli was a republican and, more than that, he had an absolutely clear, sound and unshakable concept of what freedom was, of its advantages, and of the fatal consequences of its suppression. All this is shown at every stage of the *Discourses* and *The Prince*. As if this were not enough, he had himself been submitted to torture at the time of the Boscoli and Capponi conspiracy, so his convinced and reasoned appreciation of freedom was backed up by physical experience. And yet it was this self-same Machiavelli—who held freedom in such esteem and defended the Republican régime—who offered his services to the Medici family as soon as they returned to Florence and wrote the most perfect treatise in favour of autocracy ever known. All this seems supremely contradictory, but the contradiction is no more than an apparent one.

In the most famous of his private letters, the one written to Francesco Vettori on December 10, 1513, Machiavelli gives a very lively description of his life in the country. We are shown Machiavelli out hunting, in litigation with the villagers about a few piles of wood, stopping in the road to talk to passers-by, and playing cards by the hour with a miller, a butcher, and two bakers. When evening falls, Machiavelli doffs his day clothes plastered with mud and clay, puts on the robes of court and palace, and enters the ancient courts of men gone by, and speaks with them—or, as he tells Vettori further on in the letter, he writes *The Prince*. It is a very fine letter, above all in the vigour with which he expresses the contrast between his own thoughts and dignity, and the coarse, uncivilised world around him. But in this contrast there are signs of a kind of cruel and bitter satisfaction, as of a man whose sense of his own value is enhanced if he is scorned and misunderstood.

> So, trapped among this vermin I rub the mould from my wits and work off the sense of being so cruelly treated by Fate—content to be driven on along this road if only to watch for her to show some sign of shame.

This is not the tone of a man who knows his own value and, when he sees he is misunderstood, withdraws proudly to his country house and lives the life of a humanist. Here we can almost feel a sensual pleasure in abasement which, of course, acts as a stimulus—like a spring that only acquires its total strength when pressed down. 'Content to be driven . . .', the phrase clearly reveals a turgid and twisted unhappiness. Reverses to Machiavelli are a kind of tonic. His moral exhaustion will not allow him the serene independence of a free and victorious spirit; it makes him need these desperate stimulants. But they are dangerous remedies, for once the sensibility has grown used to them it can no longer do without them. His appeal to the Medici that they should at least set him to 'roll a rock' stems from the same mentality as the one that dictated the phrase about being driven by Fate. In the first there is a kind of pleasure in abasement in order not to adapt himself to it, not to experience it as such; in the second there is a desire for any kind of function, even a humiliating one, so that he may feel that he exists. In both Machiavelli is trying to spur on a sensibility otherwise lazy and inert. On a higher plane even *The Prince* is only a lever for lifting the mortal weight of his apathy.

The truth is that Machiavelli needed to live, needed to feel himself to be living—a need that does not arise with really vital men whose activities are all balanced and equally alive. In misfortune, these men can take refuge in their 'private lives' which may consist, as we have already pointed out, not only in their private interests but in a serene and upright conscience, a taste for independence, and a sense of mystery. Whereas the exhausted, inadequate man feels the need to hit at his sensibility until he draws blood and twist his emotions to make them stronger, as with rope. And this gives rise to various contradictions. We get the Marquis de Sade who needed to go through the action of the bloodiest hatred in order to love. This is Machiavelli's case at a different level of ideas. Had he been a normal, organised and balanced man, he would not have written *The Prince* but the *Ricordi Civili*; he would not have tried to serve the Medici but would have retired in contentment to the country. His need to avoid drowning in the apathy, indifference and boredom of a life devoid of emotion or occupation spurred him on to wound himself to death so as to feel alive; to serve so as to have a function. So *The Prince*, that panegyric of autocracy in the mouth of a republican, was born of a compulsive desire for life expressed in terms of conscious cruelty.

And so what he had failed to do for religion in Timoteo, for innocence in Lucrezia, and for love in Callimaco, Machiavelli managed to do for freedom in his final character, the Prince. For while Timoteo's corruption, Lucrezia's ruin and Callimaco's lust neither cut deeply into any of his ideals nor contradicted any of his aspirations, but were rather in entire conformity with what he took to be daily reality, the Prince—in every action and saying—wounds and draws blood from what little living flesh Machiavelli still retained in the paralysis of all his faculties. In *The Prince* all the tension, the rigour, the cruelty, the strict consistency and reasoning, are underlined by suffering. But this situation does not really go hand in hand with the balance, true clarity, and coherence of a free intellect. All self-indulgence, even when it is sad, even when it hurts, extends beyond reasonable and sane limits. And that element of lop-sidedness, of disproportion, of monstrosity even, that exists in the so-called political science of the Prince, we owe to Machiavelli's passion twisting itself on itself so as to feel more alive. To call the maxims of *The Prince* political science is like calling the not disinterested advice of the Marquis de Sade an *ars amandi*. In both cases a detail of the operation is made into a law—and this because of the writers' incapacity to feel alive when combining their favourite activity with other activities pertaining to the spirit, because of their incapacity to love, or be in politics, while at the same time respecting the independent existence of all the other values.

There is no intention here of denying that when Machiavelli wrote *The Prince* he meant to compose a purely political work, that is, to depict—following the models provided by the great monarchies beyond the Alps and by the Italian princedoms themselves—the ideal figure of a statesman capable of driving out the barbarians and unifying Italy. We are not questioning Machiavelli's patriotism, nor indeed any of the other qualities and merits attributed to him by critics over the last ten years. We are concerned to prove, not that these qualities and merits are not present, but that they hardly counterbalance those pre-existent psychological characteristics that lie at the root of the contradictions and excesses that go to make up what is called Machiavellianism. In other words the grandiose machinery of Machiavelli's doctrine is set in motion by an engine that has nothing to do with politics. Hence the explosive, lyrical and peremptory character of *The Prince*. It is rather as if an engine, carefully assembled and prepared, suddenly started turning violently and unpredictably on its own, thus threatening the whole machine.

In *The Prince* Machiavelli expiates at some length on the ways of acquiring and holding princely power, and on the hazards that accompany such exploits. In enumerating the different kinds of princedoms he mentions, among others, the ecclesiastical ones, and this is where we have the ironical fragment about the Papal States:

> Those people have States and do not defend them; subjects, and do not govern them; and their States, though not defended, are not taken from them; and their subjects, though not governed, are not concerned. So these princedoms alone are safe and happy. However, as they are subject to higher causes to which the human mind cannot attain, I shall not speak of them; for as they are exalted and upheld by God he would be bold and presumptuous indeed who spoke of them.

Now in this quotation we find—apart from Machiavelli's antipathy to, and rancour about, the Church and its policy in Italy and the world—a final and definitive condemnation of those medieval politics which are inseparable from the 'higher causes to which the human mind cannot attain'. I mean that in a negative form it reflects the distinction between politics and morals, between politics and the ideal, which lies at the foundation of Machiavelli's glory and of his political science. We should note in passing that Machiavelli's judgement on the Papal States, though brilliant and justified by the long medieval constriction, is unfounded historically because he is considering the States at the very moment when their historical, psychological, moral, political and cultural justification had collapsed, and papal policy—both in practice and in aims—differed very little from that of all the other Italian princedoms. Machiavelli would not have been able to make the same judgements on the Church and its policy at, say, the time of Hildebrand or even of Boniface. But to continue.

My point is that the violent separation of politics from morals, politics from ideology, and politics from religion, does not really lead to the creation of a political science so much as to that of a political technique. For while it is very doubtful whether science can be detached from, or take no account of, ethical values, technique, being concerned only with implementation and not with what precedes it or follows it, is by its nature neutral and abstract. Technique, in fact, is only one moment of the scientific process, and not the most important one at that. When we were examining *Mandragola* and the minor works just now, we described Machiavelli not as immoral, but as morally worn out, and thence follows his ability to achieve that separation and give so much importance to political technique. Technique, which is certainly valid in the construction of an engine or the harnessing of a river, has in our view the merely negative value of a restriction or a falsification if applied to what we are obliged to call the things of the spirit. But who most readily apply technique to activities that have nothing to do with technique? Precisely those men in whom moral conscience is either on the way to extinction or not yet born, men whose spiritual atrophy goes hand in hand with an acute and captious intelligence, men in whom the forces of the intellect are unbalanced, and hence arbitrary and purposeless, owing to the lack of other deeper forces. Technique, the key to all doors except those of the spirit, is idolised primarily by men and nations that are either worn out or barbarous, by men and nations, that is, whose moral life is either in a decline or still to come owing respectively to fatigue or primitiveness. Men and nations of an integrated civilisation make use of technique, but do not put it on an altar. Furthermore technique, in worn-out or primitive men and nations, panders to the pride of those who think that by its means the spirit will be ousted, and that the same results will be achieved in some mechanical way as are achieved by others along the slow and hidden paths of culture and virtue of spirit. In a broad sense such men and such nations are deeply irreligious—if we take irreligion to mean complete scepticism or complete ignorance.

Guicciardini, to whom we have to refer when discussing Machiavelli, has a harsh comment to make about those who repeatedly invoke the example of ancient Rome.

> How they deceive themselves, those who are always quoting the Romans. For a city would have to be conditioned just as Rome was, and then govern itself according to that example; which example, to those with disproportionate qualities, is so disproportionate that it would be like wanting an ass to run like a horse.

Now in my view Machiavelli's defect was not so much his constant quoting of the Romans as the extrinsic, rhetorical manner in which he did so, harking back to the supposed political technique of that great people precisely because he was unable to perceive the other forces—far stronger and deeper than the political and military ones—that had gone to make up its greatness. These forces were not merely technical, but religious. They were the very forces that had made the greatness of the Papacy that Machiavelli derided, the forces that come from considering not how one lives, but how one ought to live; not what happens, but what ought to happen.

And now we come to the most famous and most debated chapter of *The Prince*, the last, in which Machiavelli seemingly unexpectedly leaves the 'Prince' and 'the lion and the fox' in the air and embarks on his exhortation to drive the barbarians out of Italy. There are two broad theses about this chapter (if we discount the one that holds it to be of no significance): one, that it is in total contradiction with all that goes before it, and two, that the whole of *The Prince* was written with this chapter—in which Machiavelli finally prophesies the liberation and unity of Italy—in view. As I see it both these theses are mistaken. The last chapter is not in contradiction with what precedes it, nor is the whole book written with this chapter in view.

The last chapter is a vehement exhortation to drive the barbarians out of Italy and re-establish the motherland. But the whole of *The Prince* is a work of destruction of the very elements that go to make up the motherland. A motherland is neither an abstract idea nor a mere geographical entity, it is soil and men, it is culture, traditions, religion, customs, arts, affections and freedom. When all these elements are either non-existent or corrupted, repressed or destroyed, then little remains of the motherland and it is indeed an abstraction behind which forces with varying aims and natures are hidden, for instance the interests of a class or a family. So Machiavelli's 'Prince' has of necessity to destroy all the elements we have listed, first so as to achieve power, then to preserve it. But had Machiavelli really conceived *The Prince* in this way, he would have done very much the same as the Jesuits and the other casuists of the Counter Reformation who built up their systems of prudent and calculating sophistry, destructive of all true religious feeling, with a view to the greater glory of God. With this difference that would have made it worse, that whereas the men of the Counter Reformation sought to restore an ageing and defeated order, hence had the excuse of being at the end and not the beginning of a long and irrecoverable historical process, Machiavelli, as all admit, was a herald and precursor of absolute monarchy as well as a patriot working for a united Italy. And it would indeed be curious if Machiavelli, who saw the Italy of his time as the most corrupt country in the world and had given in *The Prince* and other works a memorable picture of this corruption, could find nothing better for Italy's redemption than the Borgia-like figure of his Prince who used means directly begotten of this corruption. For all these reasons we refuse to believe that Machiavelli, elsewhere such an acute evaluer of the good and the bad in policies, explicitly set out to write *The Prince* for the sake of the last chapter. Or that the patriotism and the indignation against the barbarians that undeniably animate the last chapter also governed the structure of the twenty-five others. My real belief is that the last chapter is in fact what it sets out to be, an exhortation to liberate and unify Italy, whereas all the rest of the book is a kind of extremely logical, coherent and cruel outlet for Machiavelli's moral passion. And my belief also is that there is no contradiction between these two parts which, though so different in inspiration and substance, are bound together by a link that is primarily psychological.

As I see things, this link has to be sought in Machiavelli's spirit. That is, as we have said, in the intrinsic weakness of a man worn out as regards ethical values yet unable to recognise his exhaustion—for any such recognition would have been a strength, and in characters like Valentino would have had to be immediately translated into action. Despite all his realistic feeling, Machiavelli in some way lacked pride in his own abnormality. Probably he had a residue of Christian conscience that prevented him, once he had formulated certain theories, from taking them to their logical conclusion. A Machiavelli who really deserved the reproach of Machiavellianism would have finished *The Prince* at chapter twenty-five, thus giving us a fine book rather than a scholarly one, perfect rather than useful, lived and acted rather than thought, a real Medusa's head that would have fascinated and puzzled uncomprehending readers throughout the ages. A Machiavelli who was a poet and not a practical thinker would have contented himself with treating the fantastic figure of the Prince in indestructible prose. But Machiavelli wrote *The Prince* neither out of conscious Machiavellianism, nor out of a conscious desire to cram into one book all the observations and experience of his political career; nor did he write it as a poet who woos and caresses a terrible figure in a rarefied æsthetic atmosphere. No, he wrote it, as we have already said, in order to drag himself out of the stagnation of indifference, to prove to himself that he was alive, to hurt himself and feel himself hurt. Such a Machiavelli, beset by such an 'autobiographism', once he had wallowed with almost sensual delight in his own sincerity, needed a catharsis—any kind of catharsis that would release him from the frightful anarchic individualism in which his own coherence had hurled him, and re-admit him into the warmth of mankind. A catharsis, in other words, that would silence the feeling of excess and immoderacy that work on *The Prince* could not fail to have aroused in him. Given the premises we already know, this catharsis could not be religious. If Machiavelli, at the end of *The Prince*, had looked forward like Savonarola to the advent of a new Christianity that would cleanse the Italians in some radical way, he would have been totally inconsistent. The idea is inconceivable. So he found his catharsis in patriotism. With a characteristic metamorphosis into rhetoric of his decadent tendencies, Machiavelli sought to achieve the impossible transmutation of a huge sum of negative values into a single positive one: the motherland.

For all these reasons we should see neither a long premeditated climax nor a political gesture in the lyrical exhortation of the last chapter, but only the craving for liberation and redemption of a man who throughout the whole book had been holding himself strictly within the confines of an iron and intolerable coherence. If this is so, then the accusations of immorality levelled against Machiavelli in all epochs inevitably fall to the ground. To sum up, the last chapter is nothing but the exhaustion of a worn-out runner at the end of a race, a kind of entreaty for pity and repose.

Above all, repose. For, as we have said, Machiavelli did not realise that in *The Prince* he had created a character as fine as, say, Iago, from the literary point of view, and when it came to translating his blood-drenched thoughts into action he must have felt it impossible to end the book in the way he had begun it. In a word it was Machiavelli himself who, with understandable scruple, first accused himself of immorality—an accusation that posterity was to reproach him with ever afterwards. All this may not have been conscious, but this does not alter the fact that we can legitimately think, when faced with the last chapter, that this was the way things really happened. But the operation was necessarily psychological rather than political, or rather, if carried into politics it could only fail. Imagine it: Machiavelli's Prince, with his scepticism, his brutalities, his ambitions, and his methods, suddenly decides—as though weary and sick of his whole being—to sublimate his complex of negative qualities in the positive quality of patriotism. Surely it is permissible to suppose that this urge to sublimation will remain an intention only, and will find an outlet not in action but in rhetoric.

Here we are touching on one of the most secret and delicate points in Machiavelli's personality: the contradiction between the energetic, realistic and exact observer of political affairs, and the rhetorical and literary humanist of certain parts of the *Discourses* and *The Prince*. We know that Machiavelli, unlike so many of his contemporaries, was neither a rhetorician nor an empty and formal literary man; yet rhetoric swells and empties more than one of his pages without his being aware of it. Now the rhetoric, or, as Guicciardini puts it, the harking back in every sentence to the Romans, comes from an inadequate and incomplete sublimation of Machiavelli's decadent spirit, from his vain aspiration for a catharsis to renew and purify him. If Machiavelli had been a mediocre man like Guicciardini, if he had been perfectly aware of his own limits yet organised and balanced within them, then he would not have referred to the Romans nor (if I may be allowed the play on words) would he have referred to them if he himself had been Roman enough not to feel the need to refer to them. But Machiavelli lacked both this sort of mediocrity and this sort of grandeur. He does not accept his own exhaustion, yet lacks the strength (how could he not?) to translate the exhaustion into a positive state of energy. Hence the broad humanistic and literary element of his highly exalted tone, as if—to adopt his own words—about something that he would like to be and is not.

In any case it is something he would like to be. The seriousness of Machiavelli's humanist rhetoric lies in the strenuous aspiration to the service of which he tries desperately to put all that is most living and best in him. So it is a tragic humanism with a psychological background of anxiety and revolt. This distinguishes Machiavelli both from the cold Jesuitical political thinkers and the really rhetorical men of letters who followed him. But it also explains his contradiction; and provides a proof of the lack of disinterestedness of his thought, as well as justifying the persistent distrust of all those who, while bearing these motives in mind, question both the well-foundedness of the theories of *The Prince* and the validity of the chapter that ends the book.

1950

COMMUNISM IN POWER AND THE PROBLEM OF ART

It is one thing to believe and to demonstrate that art is a superstructure but quite another thing to claim that the artist should know this, and base his art on the knowledge. The Marxists always failed to grasp that the artist is unaware of any definition of art lying outside art itself, and that if art accepted any extrinsic definition it would be like a woman describing herself as up for sale. It is surely no accident that explicitly social art is a negligible episode when seen in terms of the history of art throughout the ages? And that poetry springs from a sense of its own autonomy? And that determinism of any kind, and not only the economic kind, withers art like an icy blast on a budding flower?

The Marxists aim at a completely social art, with no loop-holes and nothing left over. A good example of their aim is the girl who loves the worker because he has surpassed the 'norm' of work. They may achieve their aim, but the day they do so they will discover that the 'norm' has taken on an erotic character. In art it is nature, not society, that reigns.

When all is said and done, the last word about art rests with the artist. Chicken broth cannot be made without chicken. It can happen that the chicken escapes to the top of the tower and then the pot boils in vain.

When we look at works of art in the Communist countries, we find that the artist's preoccupation is mainly of a practical kind: that of making propaganda for the State ideology, of operating within the law of this ideology, of avoiding anything that could seem discordant with, or even indifferent to, this ideology. Why does their preoccupation strike us as differing from, say, the preoccupation of the Italian primitives, who after all produced Christian art and nothing else? Because the Italian primitives were of necessity Christians *and nothing else*. Whereas the Communists, even today, are capable of not being Communists. In other words, even now choice is still possible, and hence, alas, coercion is possible, and even the shadow of coercion is enough to bring about the disappearance of poetry. The Communists will have to conquer the whole world before they have an art worthy of the name.

The theory of art as superstructure we owe to the moment in which Marx wrote his books. A bad moment for art, if a passing one. Two centuries earlier Marx would have found no pretext for his theory. The theory of art as superstructure is bound up with the problem of the industrial production of art, and leads to a new social and economic definition of failed art, bad art. Successful art, good art, has no place in it.

Art as superstructure calls to mind all those other definitions that restrict art to some minority status: prisoners' art, mentally handicapped art, the art of the blind, children's art, and so on. But great art is not a superstructure, it is akin to the structure, it does not depend on it.

The educational value of art is enormous, but diminishes insofar as art departs from nature. Banish nature from art—nature with its contradictions, its variety, its imagination, its freedom—and you get an art deprived of educational value, whatever the ideology that inspires it. A stay by the seaside gives strength but a stay in a room with a painting of the seaside has no health-giving effects whatsoever.

The present universal collapse of mankind is no more than the outcome of two frightful wars. One need not be a great prophet to foresee that within a century or two mankind will have rediscovered a decent image of itself. But meanwhile mankind is like a filthy bloodstained drunkard who looks at himself in the mirror and is surprised to find he looks so horrible. According to some, mankind should go on looking at itself in the mirror; according to others, mankind should replace the mirror with an oleograph of a clean, sober man. Few think it would be better if mankind had a brush-up and a rest. And even those who think this, are not prepared to give up either the mirror or the oleograph.

The artists of the Western countries are shocked and saddened by the art of the Eastern countries. But if instead of being shocked and saddened they reflected for a moment and realised that art only exists inasmuch as Western art exists, they would beat their breasts and say *mea culpa*. The same applies to Capitalism in regard to Communism, and in general to every aspect of civilised life in one camp and the other.

There are two alternatives: either, as Marxism wants it, art is a superstructure and in that case—as it is normal to proceed from the superstructure to the structure, from the fruit to the tree—we are bound to conclude that the structure in certain Eastern countries today is not as they would have us believe, or else Marxism, at least as far as art is concerned, is in error, and in that case we are forced to the conclusion that the artists in those countries are not much good. Marxism comes out of it badly in either case, but as I see things that is bound to happen when it trespasses outside the social and economic field to which it properly belongs.

Political freedom is not a *sine qua non* of great art; great art has flourished in ages when there was no freedom. But in order to flourish art has an absolute need of something else: that the social body should be made of the same stuff as the art. If, owing to religious or political fanaticisms, the social body has reduced or suppressed in itself the variety of nature, then art can be as free as you like, but it will not flourish.

Any systematisation of art on the basis of a theory extrinsic to art itself is, at the least, risky and fraught with delusions. Imagine the opposite for a moment: politics conceived in terms of the dictates of æsthetics. In reality such systematisations are dictatorial acts on the part of the predominant activity towards the activities that for the moment seem less important. In this century politics is predominant, hence it would seem logical to infer that all other human activities should be its handmaid. But suppose the political tide were to recede—it would be seen that its ebb had only changed political affairs and left other fields unchanged.

The case of Dostoievsky, whose work is not allowed to be reprinted in his own country, raises the question of ultimate reconciliation with history. Dostoievsky is banned because the game being played by Communism with history has not yet reached its limit. But when will it reach its limit? The day when Dostoievsky is recognised in his own country, as in others, as a very great writer? Or the day when Dostoievsky is no longer mentioned, and even his name has been obliterated from human memory?

The electronics front, the industrial front, the creative-writing front, the cinema front . . . how often have we seen works of poetry put on the same plane and in some way identified with those of engineering and mechanics! Yet it remains that after thirty years or more of Communism, the Soviet State can present the world with gigantic public works but not with a *War and Peace* or a *Boris Godounov* which, on the scale of greatness, are poetic equivalents of the public works. Why? Is it because, unlike the workers and the engineers, the artists have been sabotaging production? Or could we be dealing with two different fronts, in the first of which planning and directives are valid whereas in the second validity comes from the absence of planning and directives?

The hidden vice of so-called socialist realism is, briefly, that it is realist about everything except socialism. And, as in some countries socialism is everything, socialist realism is often not realist at all. Now realism has to be total with no restrictions imposed by consideration, respect, compromise, convention or anything else. Societies in the past, whether feudal, bourgeois, slave-trading or patriarchal, were capable at their best of expressing this sort of realism. But a society that cannot, will not, and does not know how to see itself as it really is, is incapable of doing so.

Class art or official art corresponds pretty accurately to the baser concept of art proposed by the Marxists—art as superstructure. The Communists are only too ready to declare that class art or official art or art as superstructure will cease to exist once the classless society has been achieved. Why is it then that art in Eastern countries, perhaps more than anywhere else, reveals such notorious aspects of class art or official art or art as superstructure? There seems no doubt as to the answer: it is because art does not need a revolution to be real art. All that is needed is that the artist himself, and by himself, should attain the sphere where there are no classes, nor ever were, nor ever will be—the sphere of poetry. This is what true artists have always done, at all times and everywhere and without waiting for the Communist revolution. Art in the Eastern countries has such marked characteristics of class art because the proletariat in those countries still sees itself as proletariat or a class, and has not yet rediscovered mankind in itself—mankind old or new but anyway classless.

The relationship between art and society is not of a moral or moralising order, as all those who attach a negative meaning to the word 'decadence' would like to suppose; it is of a biological order. Art bears a relationship not to the morality of a society but to its vitality.

Art is memory, propaganda is prophecy. But in the past prophets always prophesied disaster. The great novelty is having optimistic prophets.

If art is a superstructure, how in the world can it outlive the structure? Why do we still read *The Iliad* which is a superstructure, so they say, on archaic Greek feudalism? What guarantees eternal life to the superstructure? And why is the transitory structure accorded more importance than the enduring superstructure?

Who is going to deny that Communist ideas on art are on the mark? The very term, socialist realism, contains an irrefutable critical reflection: art has always been realist or it has not been art and it has always been bound up directly or indirectly with the dominant ideology. So realism is inseparable from art, or at least from European art, and so is ideology. What then is odd about the socialist State asking the artists to produce socialist realism? In our view the oddity consists in the fact that, unlike the Church and other totalitarian organisms of the past, the socialist State knows these things, having a very developed critical and historical awareness. In this sense the socialist State, with its intellectual and pragmatist tendencies, participates in the dialectic of decadence from which it would like to think it is exempt.

Having said all this we must now point out that art does not really interest Communism. This is proved by the simplicity of Marxist ideology in matters of art. This is all the more apparent if compared with the complexity of Marxist theories on social and economic problems. Marxism is uninterested in art as, let us say, it is uninterested in religion. The difference between the Marxist attitude to art and the Marxist attitude to religion is that whereas Marxism wants to take the place of religion, it merely wants to make use of art. And in fact all Marxist theories on art concern not so much art in its inner being as art in its relationship to society and the State; in other words they concern the uses of art.

A novel describes a battle. The description of the battle does not please the rulers of a certain Eastern country. The novel is thus recast according to the rulers' specifications. What strikes one most about such a recasting in accord with authority is not the docility of the writer, nor yet the tyranny of the rulers. What strikes one most is the domination of an idea of artifice, rationality, techniques and manufacture over one of poetry, inspiration, originality and creativity. That is, the domination of a classical idea (or at least an idea in tendency classical) over a romantic one. It is as if an æsthetic system that to all appearances had seen its day had started developing again. To take a single example: Boileau would have found nothing to complain about in this sort of imposition by authority on the artist. For what difference is there between socialist realism and the *artifice agréable* of the court poets of Louis XIV?

It is astonishing to see writers and critics in the West, those with the Marxist faith, rising up to defend art from the Eastern countries on which their views could be expected to be severe. When this happens there is talk of party discipline. But in my view we are dealing with a substitution which these people have made in the depths of their souls—the substitution of ideology for reality. For Communists ideology is reality and what ordinary people call reality is nothing at all. If reality fails to confirm the ideology, so much the worse for reality. Nor can we say that such Communist writers and critics are wrong, at least from a psychological point of view. With them the substitution probably happened in dramatic circumstances, as with all conversions. At such moments the ideology genuinely is reality; were it not, the conversion could not take place. Later, when confronted with art or any other human activity or manifestation, they reproduce easily and almost automatically what happened with pain and anguish at the time of conversion.

The Communists always present their ideas on art in strict correlation with their economic and social theories, and merge the two. So anyone who approves of the economic and social theories of Communism, whether partially or wholly, is led to approve of the æsthetic ideas also, or at least to view them with favour. And this inevitably leads to the acceptance of a crude and simplicist conception of art. For though art may perfectly well have a proletarian content, its formal and technical pattern is bound up with maturity in taste, culture and capacity for expression. This amounts to saying that in this very important aspect it depends not on distributive justice but on the level of culture and taste attained by a given society. This fact has never been disproved in history and, whatever its content, art has always been a late and aristocratic product. For the truth is that art always appears at the apex of a civilisation, it is the final flower of the human plant. Whereas whenever culturally immature masses form the prevailing element as, for instance, during the barbarian invasions, an equivalent darkening, if not interruption, of art takes place. The ultimate significance of the Renaissance lies precisely in the rediscovery of the fact of art, of its laws and its autonomy, after the barbarian flood. The barbarians who flocked into Italy in the Dark Ages had no doubt plenty to say, but they said it when, precisely, they were no longer barbarians. In the same way the proletariat (above all in countries where social slumber was accompanied by biological slumber) has no doubt plenty to say, but it will only say it when it has the capacity to do so, that is when it has ceased to be a proletariat. Meanwhile works of art presented to us as works of the proletariat should, at best, be viewed as signs of impatience.

It is a mistake to suppose that socialist realism in the Eastern countries has prevented the appearance of a new Michelangelo or, at least, of a new Picasso. If the socialist régime in those countries were suddenly supplanted by a liberal one, the artists might well imitate the Western artists (though this is not certain), but they would certainly not surpass the rather low artistic level of their present production. For in those countries the revolution has resulted in decapitating the cultivated class, and now rulers and people form one single bloc with the same tastes, the same outlook and the same degree of culture. The leaders in those countries view art no differently from the workers and the peasants. The works of art they select for the admiration of the people are the ones that in all sincerity they themselves prefer. Something similar happens in all revolutions. Even the French revolution, which brought such a long-prepared and cultivated class as the bourgeoisie to power at the beginning of the nineteenth century, produced a crude and transient form of art—early romanticism. In this perspective we should judge the decadent tendencies that followed as a systemisation in a classical sense of that early romanticism.

The Communists can never be brought to admit that the works of art of the Eastern countries are of little artistic value, and how could they? They do not believe in the true but in the credible, not in nature but in reason, not in reality but in ideology, not in poetry but in artifice, not in creative spontaneity but in constructive will. To be sure, they will produce art in the end, but this will be in spite of themselves and unconsciously.

The Communists seem to advocate classical art. We say 'seem' because nothing is certain in a régime as certain as a dictatorship, even a dictatorship of the proletariat. Hence when the Communists set out from the Marxist presupposition that every society, in the moment of its highest functionality and historical necessity, expresses an art which is perfectly objective and realist without reserve or compromise, evasion or incompleteness—in a word, a classical art—they are really contrasting their moment of high noon with the sunset or decadence of every other country, a decadence whose expression lies in an unhealthily subjective, incomplete, abstract, evasive and reticent art. A decadent art. It is obvious that in this case the distinction between poetry and non-poetry falls to the ground and is replaced by the distinction between classicism and decadence, or between completeness and incompleteness, or, in other words, between the society's greater or lesser courage, capacity and will to represent itself as it is in all its aspects, even negative ones, and to recognise itself in this representation, make use of it and turn it into an instrument of improvement and progress. Hence, once again, there is no question of poetry and non-poetry but, on one and the same level, of total or partial poetry, of classical or decadent representation. But inasmuch as Communist society claims to be the heir to all the societies of history, and their crowning glory, it should give rise to the most classical and complete art that could ever be imagined, and this indefinitely and without any interruption. In this way we see how, in the Communist ideology, there is no place for even the smallest negation of reality. Everything is spun out on the thread of logic, everything is rational. Communism cannot fail to produce the perfect society, and the perfect society cannot fail to produce the highest form of art. In such circumstances the artist who wants to argue with Communism seems like an advocate of the irrational or of nothingness, not to say of evil.

It is not easy to see why, once he has accepted and confirmed the autonomy of the fact of language, a given Eastern statesman should not do the same for the autonomy of the fact of art. It is not easy to see why, but we can make a guess. Language, as our statesman has to admit, is neither bourgeois nor socialist; like a locomotive, it is a means. Whereas art can be, and is, an end. But there can be no end save that of the socialist revolution.

Why socialist realism and not, for instance, neo-classicism? Because the last objective form of art in Europe was naturalist. States, whatever people may say, are never in the *avant garde.* The Church stopped at Raphael, who was the great mediator between the world of the Old Testament and Hellenism. States know about history, not about æsthetics.

There is no relationship between the alienation of the worker and the alienation of the artist. The worker is alienated because, in the economy of the market, he is a piece of goods like any other and as such he is defrauded of his surplus value, or of what represents his value as a man. Whereas the artist creates an object that has no market (or if it has, it is not that of necessities which always have a market) and no real price in money or kind. The artist receives the price of his work of art in creating it. In other words, when he hands his book over to the publisher, his music to the conductor, or his painting to the art dealer, the artist has already been paid, and whatever he receives after that is a bonus, or at least a payment with no relationship to the goods delivered. Hence the alienation of the artist consists in the total or partial prevention of his expression, or of his true relationship with society. Whereas the worker, whose relationship with society is determined by his purchasing power and whose expression begins as soon as the whole of his surplus value is paid over to him—the worker, I repeat, is alienated when he is deprived of his surplus value and treated as a piece of goods on a par with the goods he produces. So to sum up: the alienation of the worker is of an economic nature, the alienation of the artist is of an expressive nature. In consequence a worker is prevented from being a man when he is reduced to the status of goods and paid as such; an artist is prevented from being a man when he is reduced to the status of a worker and paid as such. Or again: the worker who is badly hit in his pay cannot be a man and cannot be an artist either; but the artist who is badly hit in his expression cannot be a man and cannot even be a worker—for he was a man to begin with, that is to say endowed with the faculties of expression which are liberated in the worker only when he starts being a man. Finally, when the artist is hit the worker is hit indirectly too, for the worker sees in the artist his supreme human ideal of free and complete expression.

Communism is attempting to take over Western culture and art through its best men and products, so as to leave the bourgeoisie with inferior men and products. This attempt might even be successful. But it remains doubtful whether the result would be what the Communists expect.

It is strange that in the Eastern countries, where a historicist ideology prevails, art should be thought of in terms of moral precepts. But these are the surprises of historicism which ends up by biting its own tail and brings, as logical conclusion, the advent of a society without history. Consequently it is an art without development, fixed to an immobile ideal.

The force of the Communist polemic about art lies less in its own tenets than in the funereal and suicidal character of most Western art. For the Communists nothing is easier than to show how Western art is the expression of an overall *cupio dissolvi* whose origins inevitably lie outside art itself. But all they can do to counter Western art is to propound theories. As regards their artistic production, the best we can say about it is that it is the fruit of goodwill. But goodwill can build factories; it cannot write poetry.

The Communists, though they may well be unaware of it, propose not so much a new art as a suspension of art. Just as in the country, when a field has been sown too often, you let it lie fallow for two or three seasons so that it can rest and regain its strength. In similar circumstances Christianity decided that pagan art, the only possible art at that time, was the work of the devil. The Communists do not believe in the devil, but they believe in the decadence, immorality, corruption and downfall of Capitalism. In reality Communism now, like Christianity in its time, is an instrument of an exhausted nature that clamours for rest. But men do not like admitting that they are determined by simple biological laws, so in the field of art tiredness is called, let us say, abstract art, and rest is called socialist realism.

Of course these notes are concerned with art's relationship with Communism in power. As regards art's relationship with Communism in opposition, things proceed normally, as between the arts and any movement that inspires them. Indeed when Communism is in opposition it is strengthened by many generous and universal impulses and, directly or indirectly, provides inspiration for an exceedingly lively and polemical art that knows no compromise, an art of protest and revolt. But as soon as Communism has come to power the polemical motive notoriously disappears, to be replaced by a eulogistic one. Then art enters into crisis, precisely the sort of crisis on which these notes have attempted to throw light. In matters of art it is obvious that there are only two paths open to the Communist State. On the one hand propaganda and hagiographical art, that is to say art nourished on polemics against the external enemies of Communism, or the re-evocation and exaltation of Communist personalities and events; and on the other hand classical art, or any art from which all trace of social polemics has been expunged (no longer useful in a Communist State), an art which treats of man not as a product of given social and economic conditions, but as something immutable and eternal, which is exactly what classical art does. Moreover classical art is the art *par excellence* of societies which have not yet raised, or have no reason to raise, the social question. Communist society is precisely such a society, as it has resolved the social question once and for all and to everyone's satisfaction.

With Communism in opposition, relations between art and reality can and should be determined—for artists of the Communist faith—by the Marxist ideology. But it is hard to see how, once Communism is in power, such relations can go on being determined by this ideology. For Communism is, after all, an ideology of criticism and the renewal of society. With Communism in power, therefore, and remaining faithful to itself, the Marxist ideology ceases to have inspirational value. So the problem of art when Communism is in power is a problem of the modification of Marxist ideology, a modification all the more difficult in that every victorious ideology tends to turn into an affair of dogma and moral precepts.

Consider what happened with the French revolution. At an early stage, before the revolution, art was steeped in illuministic principles; the bourgeoisie, not yet in power, exercised corrosive criticism of the *ancien régime* by means of art. After the revolution the bourgeoisie abandoned illuminism, which was henceforward useless, and maintained it represented universal mankind and reality. At the early stage we had Voltaire, at the second stage Balzac. But to achieve this the bourgeoisie had to abandon the dictatorial standpoint of illuminism, and get rid of the Terror, of Robespierre, and, indeed, of Napoleon. Of course the Russian revolution was a very different matter and the development described above was modified in the case of the Russian revolution by a new factor: the persistently religious character adopted by the Marxist ideology in Russia and throughout the whole world.

Every time art comes into contact with an orthodoxy it abandons its basic criticisms of society and confines itself to nature, that is, to the immutable and unmodifiable in man. But in the case of Communism we have the curious contradiction of an orthodoxy postulating the mutability and modifiability of man by means of social and economic changes. For this reason, on the one hand orthodoxy constrains art to abandon criticism of society, while on the other it accuses it of not being sufficiently 'committed', or, as they say, party-minded.

Every orthodoxy allows art the autonomy it needs in the measure in which it, so to speak, merges itself and dissolves itself in all mankind, or, if you prefer, expands so as to embrace all mankind. But that is a long and difficult historical process; Christianity did not allow art autonomy for several centuries. Yet it is beyond doubt that, whether it be a matter of centuries or years, of bloody struggles or rapid and easy transformation, without such autonomy art cannot properly flourish. For as I have already pointed out, art looks towards nature, not towards society, and when it looks towards society this means that society has become nature.

The relation between art and Communism may at first sight appear the same as the relation between art and any of the numerous dictatorships that have occurred in history. And in this connection we could be led to make the usual reflections applicable to all dictatorships. Yet on second glance it can be seen that the problem does not alter even when the dictatorship ceases to exist. We see that the relation between art and Communism is, in reality, a relation between art and a given society which is or is not capable of granting art the autonomy it needs. There have been non-dictatorial societies that have not granted autonomy to art, and dictatorial societies granting a wide measure of autonomy. In any case, the autonomy of art has never really been granted so much as won, and sometimes at a high price—for it is a characteristic of all societies to deny autonomy to separate human activities, so as to lead everything back directly and immediately to themselves. This happens most of all when societies are in their first stages, and rules are strict, and interests near and pressing. A society that is permissive of tangential and remote interests is already a cultivated, mature and reflective society.

In matters of art, Communism behaves like the type of mother who will not face the fact that her daughters have grown up, but goes on calling them 'my babies' even when they are twenty, and resents the babies asking for a latchkey. But art will not admit to being Communism's daughter until Communism ceases to regard itself as a mother. Constraint cancels obligation.

A picture depicts a poor little barefoot shepherd-boy grazing his sheep on a mountain side. The boy is smiling and looks happy. On seeing a picture of this kind even someone ignorant of Marxism cannot help thinking, here we have the bourgeois conception of art, one that seeks to project the happiness of a shepherd in spite of his rags and bare feet. But what are we to think of the no less happy workers in paintings by Communist artists? The Communist State tells us, 'My workers do not go barefoot and ragged. They're truly happy in pictures as they are in fact.' To this we could object that, were it true, Communist pictures would be better painted. But being painted as they are, Marxist criticism with regard to these pictures is as justified as it is regarding bourgeois pictures.

Marx said that it was time philosophy set itself not to explain the world, but to change it. But he never said that art should do the same thing. If he had been questioned about it he would probably have said that the task of art, as always, was to represent the world once it had changed. But Communism demands that art should contribute to such a change in a direct and active way. This means, to begin with, a change in art itself, both as regards its means and its ends. And perhaps, what's more, the absolute end of art, at least as it has been conceived for centuries and up to today.

What is the artist's duty in a time of struggle, supposing he wants to take part in the struggle? In my view the artist's duty is notably different from that of other participants who contribute to the struggle with arms and political action. The artist's first duty is to create art, for he knows that an art which is non-art can make no efficient contribution to the cause in which he believes. If he succeeds in creating genuine art, the question resolves itself, indeed it does not even arise. But if he fails to create genuine art, then we need to find out where the fault lies, whether with the artist who was unable to create art because he did not really believe in the cause for which he thought he was fighting, or with the society that required him to create a particular kind of art that was non-art, or in some way prevented him from creating art. Obviously society, through the mouthpiece of its official representatives, will always blame the artist, and how could it be otherwise? But I am convinced that in certain cases the blame for an artist's bad art can lie with society, and that in what concerns art there cannot be, and should not be, a relationship between the artist and society as of an inferior to a superior, but one of equality.

In a speech made in 1937, Mao Tse Tung defined the task of art as follows: Whatever its level, it should work for the people and only for the people. Fair enough; but who is to tell art *in what way* it should work for the people? Obviously not the people themselves as, for historical reasons, they may well be unaware of what is in their interests, but the rulers who are the depositories and administrators of the dominant ideology. And here precisely lies the weak spot in the marshalling of Communist art. Because the Communist ideology, in its authoritarianism, is often led to confuse what is in the people's interest with what is in the rulers' interest and moreover, at least for the time being, it does not seem to be in a position to work out an æsthetic system of its own (this includes that of socialist realism) capable of withstanding the pressure of events, one that does not end up diminished and distorted by the utilitarian requirements of dictatorship and war, and thus reduced to the function of a mere instrument of control. In such conditions art, instead of working for the people and only for the people, might well become cut off from the people.

The primary demand that should be made of party art is that it should not seem to be 'party'—if for no other reason than that birds will not let themselves be caught unless the nets are well concealed.

We have nothing against socialist realism or any other æsthetic system derived from Marxism, but we are not at all convinced when this or any other similar system becomes the official æsthetic of a powerful State which owns all the publishers, all the newspapers and reviews, all the museums, all the concert halls, all the film studios and all the theatres. Were art allowed all the autonomy indispensable to it, socialist realism would triumph and then decay (following the law that regulates all things human), and its place would be taken by another more suitable æsthetic in a quite spontaneous way through the discussions and the work of artists. But when socialist realism or any other similar æsthetic becomes an affair of the State, we have grounds for fearing that it will obey the rules that govern all affairs of State, that is, it will become an affair of bureaucracy, of regulations, of infringements, of conformity, of controls and authority. And this cannot fail to lead to a serious limitation of that very autonomy, however relative it be, that we have already declared as indispensable to art.

Do not delude yourselves that things have changed. When prehistoric man fixed the postures of a bison in flight on the wall of his cave he was not all that different from Balzac who, in one of his novels, described the bearing of stockbrokers at the Stock Exchange. Yet prehistoric man lived by hunting and Balzac's brokers by the game of rising and falling shares. What concerns the artist in both cases is not the why but the how. The movements of life, not the cause of those movements.

How much thought and philosophy has been expended to reach the point of stating what in antiquity would have been put in a few words—namely, 'We want an art that is useful to the State'. What distinguishes the modern world from the ancient world is its incapacity for cynicism. The ancient world was near to nature, and nature is cynical, direct, ingenuous. Whereas the modern world is far removed from nature; it is intellectualist, devious and cunning.

In one of his speeches Zhdanov says, among other things:

> The task of the honest Soviet writer is to bring into relief the new virtues of Soviet man, to show our people not only what they are today but what they will be tomorrow, to light up with a bright beam their forward march. The writer should not lag in the wake of events, he should march in

the van of the people and show them the road of their development.

There, in a nutshell, we have a definition of propaganda art. It does not represent men as they are, but as they ought to be; it does not deal with things present, but with things guaranteed to come; in other words, it does not describe the kingdom of this earth but the kingdom of heaven. This needs to be said to pinpoint the uplift aspect of this sort of art, its kinship with prophecy and prediction. But propaganda has rarely been poetry, it has always lacked the dimension of memory proper to poetry.

There is something revengeful in the purely class conception of art as Marxists see it. Artists may in the past have created a class art, but save in a few rare cases—and those mainly of inferior art—they have never done so consciously or voluntarily, whereas Marxist artists have to create class art consciously and voluntarily. On what do the proletarians want to take their revenge? For having read Homer and Shakespeare for centuries without realising that they were expressions of archaic Greek feudalism and of the English court aristocracy? Or for having been for centuries oppressed, exploited, colonised, despised and degraded? Obviously if vengeance exists they want to revenge themselves for the second reason. But what has it all to do with art?

Conformism, particularly in art, is no more than one of the many facets of decadence. It does not overcome or supplant decadence, it merely turns it upside down—leaving intact its exteriority, its expressive impotence and its abstraction. Socialist realism, in its aspect of political and social conformism, seems to be no exception to this rule. As is well known, Soviet artists were decadent, or European, until that day when, by orders from above, and overnight, they were obliged to take up socialist realism. So the change-over was not due to spontaneous development, it was imposed by authority at one blow. Indeed we could paraphrase Belli when he says that inside every living man there is a dead man, and say that inside every socialist-realist there is a dead abstract painter—who is always ready to resurrect. In this sense socialist realism has to be seen as an aspect, possibly the most sensational and certainly the most significant aspect, of universal decadentism.

I have said that classical art is the only possible positive outlet for art in a Communist régime. And indeed we cannot see where the absolute and universal objectivity to which Marxism aspires could be found except in classical art—which has always made its appearance as civilisations reached their pinnacle of maturity. For it is born at moments of perfect and deep stability, when the class in power has the illusion that it has found a final and eternal régime; that is, at moments in which an even remote revision of values seems out of the question. And may it not be Communism's maximum ambition to reach some such stability and immutability of values? But the civilisations of the past reached the stage of classicism through respect for nature, or the artist's individual style, though at times they imposed some specific ideological or religious content. But Communism is not satisfied with imposing a specific ideological content, it also wants a specific style. If it continues along this road, Communism will end up not with classical art but with the ritualistic stylisation of the Byzantines.

Marxism is a powerful instrument for recovery and renewal in the present-day world. It has been at work for almost fifty years and is partly responsible for the liquidation of the enormous passive inheritance of the last part of the nineteenth century and for the character that the taste and art of the twentieth century have been able to assume. The abandonment of Marxism in its accepted sense of diagnosis and criticism in all Communist countries can mean two things: either a development of art not unlike that of bourgeois compromise-art of the nineteenth century, or the installation of a classical-type art such as we have already indicated. But for the time being this second hypothesis remains a hypothesis as there are no signs whatsoever of work that confirms it.

The reality of the Communist revolution is not in question here. In 1917 the Communists were a handful of men; today, forty years later, the Communist flag waves over more than a third of the globe. What is in question is, after all, only a very tiny detail of that revolution, one with no great significance in view of Communist ambitions and effective conquests. For those of us who have only a partial and conditional belief in the theory of art as superstructure this detail would at most imply that in the Communist countries there were no good artists. But it is because the Communists propound the superstructure theory that they force us into thinking that in the Communist countries the lack of good artists must be attributed not to nature (for not bringing them to birth) but to the society which prevents them from expressing themselves. The Communists' answer is, 'Time will show'. To which we reply, 'Time is a gentleman and must perforce lead to the recognition of art's autonomy'.

Or again, the Communists say, We are at war, we are involved in a struggle, a crusade, and in these circumstances art is bound to be a weapon, an instrument, a means. To which we reply, You may well be right, at least as far as you yourselves are concerned, but are you not aware that your art cannot be a weapon, an instrument, a means, because it is bad art? A novel like *War and Peace* would do more for the revolution than a victorious war. But your novels are a series of lost battles. And don't go telling us that we're not in a position to judge. The form and content of art may possibly be bound up with an ideology, but not its value. And even if we restricted the standard of value to political usefulness, it would still be non-existent for the very good reason that your novels are not admired.

The problem of Communist art is closely linked with the question of the decadence of all the arts throughout the world. In the West this decadence shows itself explicitly, in the East implicitly—but in both by the crudity and childishness of the artist's métier. In view of this general decadence we cannot help wondering whether the real revolution of the modern world does not lie in the advent of a mechanical and practical, a scientific and bureaucratic, a eudemonistic and State-centralising civilisation, in which art no longer has any place at all, and of which the Communist revolution would be a mere episode. It is the Communists themselves who tell us that man is not immutable but capable of change as his social environment changes. Now among changes that may occur is the production of a dumb man who cannot sing. They tell us that in certain Pacific islands there are non-singing birds. Yet they are still birds, that fly and beget their kind as in the past.

What do the Communists usually answer to the sort of objections we have raised so far? They have a lot of answers, some very subtle and sophisticated, some simply negative. They can confute the objector point by point, or they can dismiss the question with the simple epithet, 'decadent bourgeois'. But in last analysis they do not produce the real answer and how could they? The real answer is that when Communism seizes power it does so with the determination that it shall keep it for centuries. And that in very long-distance matters such as Communism or art, time does not count. And that one, or two, or three generations of bad artists and good propagandists is a thing without the slightest importance. And that in the end art, like every other human activity, will flow through the channels Communism has dug for it. And that—finally—man is infinitely adaptable and hence so is art whereas Communism is not. Or perhaps Communism is adaptable, too, but this is a subject that can only be discussed in a few centuries' time.

Nearly all States, whether socialist or non-socialist, are more or less Machiavellian. But how can art, the most serious thing in the world, become material for Machiavellianism?

In the socialist countries the relation between the masses and 'reasons of State' is so close that there is no place for art. If ever a split occurred, art could breathe.

Before the revolution took place, critics had to give their work form in accord with the Marxist conception of structure and superstructure but since the revolution this concept has been abandoned because, as is obvious, it would lead to criticism corrosive of the society the revolution had built up. This transition and transformation reach a climax in the countries in which the revolution has not happened. In those countries critics with Marxist faith are Marxists as regards bourgeois art but conformists as regards the art of the Communist countries. An American work of art will be taken as indicative of a given social situation; not so a Soviet work of art. What are we to conclude from this? That Marxist theories are revolutionary only in one circumstance, that is in relation to bourgeois society and bourgeois art, but that they cease to be revolutionary the moment they come into contact with Communist art and society?

Yet Marxist theories on art are marvellously adapted for a diagnosis of the ills of the body social, and there can be no doubting their revolutionary force. If you apply them to the art of the Communist countries you will see that they give results in no way less valuable than those obtained when you apply them to the art of the bourgeois countries. They show, in fact, that even in the Communist countries there is a class art and that the ruling classes defend themselves through art with the methods and compromises we also find in bourgeois countries.

The socialist State, when it wants to dictate rules for artists, has its weather-eye cocked for the average level of the masses. If, to give one example, the masses read in the same way as they go to the cinema, few of the books printed today would be published. But the Communists imagine that the level of the masses will rise indefinitely. But, alas, by the time the level of the masses becomes really high, it will be necessary to look to improving the level of the artist which in the interval will have sunk extremely low.

The problem of reality for a State that claims to be in possession of the truth through its ideology can be put in very simple terms: everything that agrees with the ideology is real; everything that contradicts it is unreal or irrational or negative. In a word, the artist who displeases the State is going outside reality, a terrible adventure that so far has only been touched on by novelists of the future. The trouble is that often the artist is within reality whereas the State has gone outside it. But to call an artist back to reality, an unfavourable criticism in an official periodical is enough. Whereas, alas, nothing short of a revolution will bring a State back to reality.

As for social novels, there has never been such a persuasive one as Zola's *Germinal*. Compared with *Germinal*, socialist-realist novels seem like little stories in primers. What on earth has happened in the interval? Simply this, that the mines which in Zola's novel were in capitalistic hands have now passed into the hands of the socialist State.

A thing of beauty is a joy for ever. The poet who wrote that line plainly did not expect the joy to last for only a year, and then become sadness by orders from above.

Only in one case is there any point in letting politicians judge matters of art: when the politicians themselves are artists. There are some rare, extraordinary instances of this, and mankind preserves an imperishable memory of them, for we refer to 'the age of Leo X', or 'the age of Pericles'. But our gratitude only goes to show how much more frequent and detestable is the reverse situation. I mean when politicians lay down laws about art without either loving it or understanding it, and for reasons extraneous to art itself.

Some ideas about art are a real Procrustes' bed for the poor artist: have we got to cut off the feet or the head? Let us cut off the head and create art with our feet.

The victories in Asia have brought no solace to eastern Communism, at least so far as art is concerned. In Asia art has always been subjected to rules and norms, to State or religious laws. The testing-ground for Communist ideas about art is the West. But, alas, neither a victory of the East over the West, nor of the West over the East, would clear up the question of art. Art profits by exchanges, not by victories.

Admittedly Western art has reached a degree of disintegration which plays into Communist hands. But we must realise that this disintegration has little to do with the social factor. Rather, it is a biological factor. Communists may be able to suppress it, but not to rectify it. When biology knocks at history's door, it is not satisfied with a revolution. It needs the great migrations of peoples, invasions, the Middle Ages. And history obligingly gives it all it asks for, even if it involves making use of the Communists.

Your books are not in line with the dominant ideology, therefore we will not publish them. But I cannot stop myself writing in that way. In that case you are a traitor. Am I a traitor because I write these books, or because I can't stop myself writing them? You are a traitor because you can't stop yourself writing them.

What is the relation between Marxism and party art? If we look closely, there is none. With its brutal but healthy determinism, Marxism reveals the party character of bourgeois art, and so contributes to purifying it and liberating it whereas socialist realism tends to put things back as they were before Marxism. In other words the proletariat, though perhaps unconsciously, imitates the bourgeoisie of the worst Victorian period. One example is enough: in *David Copperfield* the scatter-brained and incompetent Micawber, in keeping with typical Victorian compromise, is packed off to Australia where for some reason he becomes an exemplary citizen. Put Central Asia in the place of Australia, and factories in the place of sheep farming, and you will get a character from some Russian novels, a character whose positive and extrinsic transformation is dictated not by an inner logic but by the writer's desire to compromise with Soviet society.

Communist critics usually contrast art for art's sake with party art. But this contrast does not really exist, for neither the one nor the other could be said to be healthy and direct expressions of a given society. Healthy and direct art is born of an enounter between society and the artist on equal terms. We find such an encounter in the classical writers of the great epochs of art. Whereas art for art's sake and propaganda art avoid the encounter, the first out of pride and the second out of a spirit of oppression. In other words they both withdraw from reality whose real needs are study, patience, humility, sincerity, sense of truth, and disinterestedness. In this sense abstract art and socialist art, which are both childish and lacking in power, are of equal value.

1953

BOCCACCIO

It has been remarked before now that while true men of action are usually embittered if reduced to impotence, inertia and incapacity, placid and dreamy men find that these things enrich and enhance the very real pleasure they derive from their imagination. It is surely not an accident that writers of adventure stories are mostly sedentary people.

Moreover these imaginative yet lazy men, these insatiable yet stationary pursuers of action, are by nature and necessity very far removed from any form of moral reflection. It is peculiar to the moralist that he cuts down the number of possible alternatives and acts resolutely and consistently within them. The moralist defends himself from the imagination as from the most dangerous of mirages, above all when the imagination plays on action that is entirely governed by the caprices of chance, action for action's sake. In fact action for action's sake, whether dreamed up or practised, requires a flexibility, a flightiness, an indifference, that do not harmonise with moral conscience.

I have always thought that Boccaccio—that placid and comfort-loving 'Giovanni of tranquillity' as he is usually portrayed to us—was in the depths of his soul, by way of compensation and perhaps of sublimation, a great lover of action. Surely he was the kind of man who cannot enjoy ease and comfort unless he imagines himself in danger and discomfort, who needs to conjure up a fantastically active life so as to be able to pursue his quiet existence in peace. One thinks of a man like Sacchetti, the pleasing domestic and provincial story-teller, as the exact opposite of Boccaccio. Sacchetti finds complete fulfilment in shrewd and effective representation. His imagination does not take him outside the confines of his own narrow world. All he wants as a story-teller is to give pleasure—his work, like his life, is calm. But consider the voluptuous delight with which Boccaccio's episodes are elaborated, enriched and decorated; the liveliness with which he presents his characters, as though jealous of them. Consider the enormous variety of his settings: at sea, in cities, woods, rooms, caves, and deserts; and the way his characters comprise all conditions, nationalities, and periods—facts which go to show that the important thing for Boccaccio was less to give pleasure and surprise than greedily to feel himself living within the widest variety of people, situations, places, and periods. His cosmopolitanism is made up of extent and quantity rather than of civilisation and education. Florence and its surroundings were too small to satisfy his thirst for action. He needed the East, France, Naples, Venice, Rome and Sicily, the ancient world and the high Middle Ages, and not only places and periods familiar to him, but those he knew of by hearsay. Most writers move within a given space and time. Where this does not happen, as with Boccaccio, it means that the process of liberation and consequent widening of vision has reached fruition. Boccaccio's uprootedness and freedom, which seem so extraordinary to anyone who knows how rare such conditions are, are the primary reason for his universality.

There have been various ways of explaining the amorality and callousness that many believe they can detect in Boccaccio's work. He has been called a sensualist, as if sensuality necessarily excluded moral conscience. His lack of severity of spirit has been ascribed to the decadence of customs, the death of medieval chivalry, the transition to the modern middle-class age, and the change from the ancient ideas of transcendentalism to the immanence of the Renaissance.

But I for my part am convinced that morality is not a thing—like fashions or other superficial characteristics—that follows in the wake of historical change. Unquestionably Boccaccio was as moral a man as Dante or Manzoni. We should not let ourselves be misled by the fact that his stories contain so many adulteries and deceptions as well as a kind of superficiality and indifference. A careful reading of the *Decameron* reveals it as a book of only moderate sensuality, and it is never, or hardly ever, that sensuality is the main subject of a story. And as for superficiality and indifference, they are only a defect when viewed extrinsically; to carry through a work of this kind they are a necessity.

Let us try to compare Flaubert and Boccaccio for a moment. Flaubert's problem was quite different. He was concerned with providing in each of his books a more or less disguised portrait of himself and hence with knowing and judging himself. Knowing and judging himself led logically to knowing and judging the world around him. In this sense moralism was as necessary for Flaubert as amoralism was for Boccaccio, as we shall see in due course. The fact that he described ordinary, normal, common things was simply a result of this undertaking. Only ordinary, normal, common things can provide the moralist with material that does not frustrate him or disperse his cohesion. The moralist needs to believe in the existence of a stable social set-up, of interests and passions that cannot evade judgement, of a serious and concrete world in which human beings bear full responsibility for their actions. The play of fortune, adventure and chance are excluded from his world, or if they find their way into it they are inexorably drawn into the framework of moral judgement. A hare-brained and adventurous fellow in a Boccaccio story would be turned by the moralist into a swindler and a criminal; adventure becomes error, sin, a trick or crime. Moreover variety serves no purpose, for one single fact scrutinised with attention is quite enough for the moralist's ambition. He does not wish to live many lives, but only one—his own. Flaubert felt the tyranny of this situation, and more than once deluded himself into thinking he could escape it. *Salammbô* is the result of one such attempt at escape. But Flaubert's spirit was not to be set free merely by being transferred into distant and mythical ages. *Salammbô* is just as heavy and narrow as *Madame Bovary*. The monstrous coherence of Flaubert's path ends up in the blind alley of *Bouvard et Pécuchet*.

Boccaccio's task was quite different. He wanted neither to judge himself nor to know himself, and still less to condemn or reform. The corruption and decadence of customs left him indifferent not because he shared in them but because they were factors that were of no use to him. Moralists are praised too often for pillorying certain vices. When we reflect that, given their temperaments, they desperately need those vices then we can see that their merit is not all that great. On the other hand Boccaccio, with his thirst for adventure, needed quite different things. First of all he needed not to be weighed down and impeded by serious or strict moral concepts, not to have continually to establish a relationship of moral judgement between himself and his characters, between himself and the world. So much for the negative side; as for the positive side, what Boccaccio needed was action pure and simple. Action of any kind, for the value of action lay in its being action pure and simple. Action of any kind, for the value of action lay in its being action, not in its being good or bad, sad or gay, imaginary or real. And when we think how infinitely beautiful and various and in all things enjoyable and desirable the world appeared to the enchanted Boccaccio, we see what a deprivation it would have seemed to him, amid such variety and wealth, to choose a little corner in which he could grow roots, to sacrifice so many possibilities to a concern for only one.

For these reasons it is vain to blame Boccaccio for not being moral, for being sceptical and superficial. It is contradictory to admire, say, the story of Andreuccio da Perugia and then blame Boccaccio for superficiality. What would have remained of Andreuccio's adventure if Boccaccio had probed into what lay behind his fecklessness and dash? The play, the lightness, the charm of those pages would have evaporated. It is useless to dwell on Boccaccio's flaw which to readers of today is a black separating gulf—the flaw of seeming to give absolution to his crime-prone and dishonest characters. We must realise that this absolution is the price paid for countless poetic events and curious magical details. Boccaccio seems to be saying to the reader: 'Let's agree once and for all that my characters are doing what they're doing for their own good reasons which it would be boring to pinpoint and evaluate. So relax; let them carry on, and let us enjoy ourselves.' A love of action that tends to precipitate action so as to enjoy it as soon as possible is, in my view, the mechanism with which Boccaccio's world operates. Notice how Boccaccio's way of telling a story is exactly the opposite to that of modern novelists. If we look at the first page of *Madame Bovary*, for instance, we certainly shall not find a statement of the book's main theme, nor the premisses from which the development logically stems, set down with conventional clarity. We shall not find, 'Madame Bovary, born in such and such a place, married to such and such a man, had such and such ambitions', and so on. Flaubert, like nearly all modern writers, does not set out to make his characters act, but to create them; and his attention is set on a reality of whose developments he himself is ignorant. This is the reason why books like his almost give us the impression of living through the events that we are reading; and, as happens in life, we do not know today what may happen tomorrow.

On the other hand Boccaccio, whose main concern is to make his characters act and act wholeheartedly without hesitation, provides us headlong at the beginning of each story with the characters and data essential to the intrigue. Then once he has cleared the ground of these, he can devote himself body and soul to the development of the action. It is this convention, this preliminary liberation of the author from the burden of the characters and their motives, that enables Boccaccio to ornament his action with such magic, sensuality and light-heartedness.

For this reason it is mistaken in my view to see Boccaccio as an erotic writer. The truth is that though most of the stories in the *Decameron* pass for love stories, Boccaccio is not very interested in love. The role of love here, as in reality, is as a mainspring of human action and once the spring has been released Boccaccio turns his attention exclusively to action. In other words love is a sub-heading for one kind of action and no more desirable as such than many other sub-headings. This becomes plain when we observe Boccaccio's ignorance about normal, emotional, psychological love; for him love has no savour unless it is adventurous, difficult, full of vicissitudes and equivocations. And Boccaccio hurries through love as he does through so many other emotions, giving it a few words at the beginning of his stories.

> Lorenzo . . . who was goodly in person and gallant . . . when Isabetta bestowed many a glance upon him and began to regard him with extraordinary favour . . . Which Lorenzo marking, he began to affect her . . . and 'twas not long before . . . they did that which each most desired . . .

This handful of words relates Isabetta's love for Lorenzo in the most exemplary love story Boccaccio has written. Boccaccio hurries through love, its birth, the people, the facts, so as to get, we feel, to what concerns him most, the famous passage about the 'pot' in which Isabetta, after burying the head of her dead lover, plants 'some roots of the goodliest basil of Salerno'. And about this pot, and the beauty of the plant and the way the brothers get to know that the pot contains the lover's head, Boccaccio spreads himself with a kind of tender cruelty. Once he has cleared the ground of the psychological and emotional data, he can, as usual, sit back and lavish all his care on the action and the objects on which it depends.

We have already said that Boccaccio's passion for action gave a subtler, keener edge to his enjoyment of his comforts as a peaceful man, a humanist and an honoured and solid citizen. And we have, in the structure of the *Decameron* itself, a reflection of a peaceful life rendered more delightful through the continual conjuring-up of exciting adventures and outlandish escapades. Indeed, the whole idea of the plague and the happy group of young people retiring to the country villa to tell stories, is significant, for the young people's safe withdrawal to the country, while the plague works havoc in the city, reflects Boccaccio's love of danger and his fascinated contemplation of the harsher, crueller things of life while safely basking in his own immunity. Moreover, we must not let ourselves be deceived by the seemingly 'historical' and 'pitiful' character of Boccaccio's plague. The plague—which he describes almost voluptuously and from a literary and æsthetic point of view, with obvious references to other plagues in books, and especially the vivid and detailed one in Thucydides—might well not have existed except as a foil to the delightful and reassuring description of the happy group in their *buen retiro*. As regards historical accuracy and pity, we should compare Boccaccio's plague with the one in Manzoni, which really is historically accurate and deeply pitiful in spite of its morbid and decadent overtones. Compare, for instance, the famous passage from Manzoni: 'A woman came down from the doorstep of one of those exits and approached the convoy . . .' with Boccaccio's cold and externalised exclamations which seem to betray not only the complacency of someone who has escaped death, but even a touch of irony:

> How many grand palaces, how many stately homes, how many splendid residences, once full of retainers, of lords, of ladies, were now left desolate of all, even to the meanest servant! How many families of historic fame, of vast ancestral domains, and wealth proverbial, found now no scion to continue the succession! How many brave men, how many fair ladies, how many gallant youths! . . .

With Manzoni, the sadistic taste for death, destruction and chastisement is genuinely outmatched by Christian compassion, whereas in Boccaccio we sense the thrill of someone far away in a pleasant place, removed from all danger, who contemplates a great calamity and speculates in a waking dream as to its details. And, in smug contrast, we have 'the little hill on the summit of which was a palace, with galleries, halls and chambers disposed around a fair and spacious court, each very fair in itself and the goodlier to see for the handsome pictures with which it was adorned'. We have the 'meadow where the grass grew green and luxuriant, nowhere being scorched by the sun'. We have the garden with its paths 'each very wide and straight as an arrow and roofed in with trellis of vines', and walled in with roses 'white and red, and jasmine'. We have the 'basin of whitest marble' rising in the middle of a lawn 'so green that it seemed almost black' and 'tables being already set and fragrant herbs and fair flowers strewn all about'. And there is the 'little lake' where 'the fish darted to and fro in multitudinous shoals', and the 'vale' where there were beds 'equipped within and without with stores of French coverlets and other bed-gear'. There is the 'little church nearby' where the group goes for 'divine service'; and the 'copse' full of 'roebucks and stags and other wild creatures as if witting that in this time of pestilence they had nought to fear from the hunter' and, indeed, all the other pleasing and peaceful things which, in the introductions, serve to offset the plague and the stirring events of the stories. In fact the calm and tranquil passages about peaceful occupations far removed from passion reflect life as Boccaccio lived it, for he was a frequenter of courts and côteries whereas the plague and the events of the stories are the longings of his imagination which helped him to luxuriate yet more in the quiet serenity of his life. That this is so is proved by the way in which he relegated the pleasures of country life to a marginal role in the book—not where they would be if they were the true source of his inspiration. Whereas Tasso, for instance, two centuries later, set such pleasures at the heart of his *Aminta*, for his life was neither calm nor pleasant and he had every reason to long for an idyllic life of luxury. If Boccaccio had confined himself to describing the calm, light-hearted life at the villa, he would have been a mere Arcadian; if he had confined himself to adventure he would have been a romantic yarn-spinner. But the combination of the villa and the stories reveals the dualism in the depths of his soul. The plague, with its horror, enhances the pleasures of the villa, just as corpses in a cemetery enrich the earth and thus nourish the flowers that grow in it. So it was a welcome, delightful plague, as contrasted with Manzoni's Christian plague, Defoe's demoralising plague, Thucydides's historical plague, and Poe's grotesque plague. But inventories of plagues in literature have been made before now, so let us return to Boccaccio.

We have no intention here of analysing all Boccaccio's stories so as to illustrate our point as to the mainspring of his inspiration. Such an analysis would be tedious and mechanical. Think of Bonaparte's book on Poe where the same procedure is applied to every story, and the same discoveries made, until near-boredom sets in. Nevertheless the first story in the *Decameron*, the one about Ser Ciapelletto, seems to me highly important and typical of a whole vein of Boccaccio's kind of narrative, so I would like to discuss it—the more so as many readers may find that that story, lacking in action and real events as it is, contradicts what has been said so far.

The tale of Ser Ciapelletto is well known and has no need to be retold. Boccaccio establishes at the outset, in his usual conventional and brisk way, the criminal and impious character of Ser Ciapelletto who is given to every form of corruption; and thence, with the help of a complicated and rather improbable sleight of hand, he puts him in a situation where he can play the saint and, from his deathbed, carry out a long and blasphemous joke at the expense of his confessor. At first sight this might seem to be a satire on the rites and credulity of priests, a highly irreverent satire and, in last analysis, an unwarranted one. But on closer inspection Boccaccio's main concern is seen to be not the satire itself but the mechanism by which it is obtained. In other words his interest is not in the things themselves but in their interplay when thrown violently together. His interest is not in priests or the Christian religion any more than in Ser Ciapelletto, it is in the development of the joke, and perhaps even more in the interplay of force and action that sets the joke in motion.

The theatre, whether classical or modern, is full of deceits and jokes. Moreover the theatre comes nearer to action than any other literary *genre*. Where there is deceit, the deceiver finds himself in a peculiar position of freedom and power in relation to the deceived. He knows he is deceiving, whereas his victim does not know he is being deceived. His freedom is unlimited so long as the deception lasts and his action, based as it is on contemplative satisfaction, is entirely gratuitous and an end in itself. Deceiving, moreover, means acting without danger, escaping the immediate consequences of action, acting from the cosy and perfectly safe ground of make-believe. It is precisely that kind of action that the lazy and easy-going Boccaccio must have enjoyed. Deception is a dream of action which has recourse to secrecy because it cannot be developed in an open way. They enjoy deceit who feel that the demands of open and brutal action are beyond their scope. In deceit cleverness has its revenge on force and all other irrational factors. Now Boccaccio's pages are full of deceits of this kind.

But we do not mean to imply that Boccaccio's own nature had leanings towards dissimulation and fraud. Indeed, if we realise that action pure and simple almost always lacks bite, and that deceit is intimately linked with the type of bourgeois and conventional lives that Boccaccio wanted to depict, then we shall see why nothing can be deduced from the frequency of the *Decameron*'s deceits as to similar characteristics in the author. Boccaccio's taste for deceit reveals, if anything, something akin to that constant longing of mankind: the longing for invisibility. Who has not dreamt at least once that he had a wand, or a powder, or some other device for making himself invisible, and, once invisible, that he had gone off to the ends of the earth to play practical jokes on important people, to escape punishment, and generally behave with perfect immunity in the most dangerous circumstance? Now the situation of the deceiver is equivalent to a kind of invisibility. The deceived does not see the deceiver as he really is, so the deceiver can act with all the freedom and consistency that he would have if he were invisible. As can be seen, it is a dream of power and action if ever there was one.

Boccaccio must often have thought about such very human kinds of revenge. In the story of the scholar and the widow, Boccaccio's description ends with a smirk of complacency as he concludes: 'Wherefore, my ladies, have a care how you mock men, and especially scholars.' Here we don't know which to admire most, the extremely self-interested admonishment or the bland way in which the writer first takes pleasure in a detailed description of one of the cruellest pranks that could ever be thought up, and then all unknowingly reproves the very vice in which he revelled only a short while before. The story itself is often marred by long-winded passages, above all in the dialogue between the scholar at the foot of the tower and the wretched, weeping widow at the top. We get a feeling that a more powerful ending would not have spoilt the tale. But once he has devised his prank, Boccaccio wants to make us wallow in it. He wants to squeeze it of its last drop of honey—in other words he wants action beyond the bounds of what is either possible or æsthetic. The tortures inflicted on the tender and lovely body of the widow are described with an excessive and cruel delight, just as the prank previously played by the widow on the scholar was excessive and cruel. Both cases, but especially the second, suggest a not entirely unconscious sadism. And what are their prolonged conversations if not moral tortures drawn out with voluptuous care? The deceit is shown up in its true colours, as action dreamed up by someone who has experienced a serious disillusion in real life, yet would be incapable of taking his revenge in such a cruel way even if the occasion presented itself. We have mentioned sadism but we certainly do not mean to imply that Boccaccio's art is sadistic. The frequent traces of sadism in Boccaccio bear witness not to a more or less decadent perversion but to the chance coming-together of his thirst for action and a healthy and normal sensuality. Such sadism is no more than an active, though excessive and uncontrolled, male instinct. Every action, by the fact that it is carried through from a given premiss to its logical conclusion and without regard for the consequences, always involves a certain degree of sadism. The premiss in the story of the scholar is revenge. And in fact the scholar is not satisfied until the woman's beautiful body is reduced to a 'half-burnt stump', and the same goes for Boccaccio. Or better, there is an air of disillusion and discontent in the story, as if Boccaccio had suddenly noticed the inadequacy of the dream and felt bitter about it, or noticed that he had indeed just been dreaming and nothing more.

The story of the scholar and the widow is really Boccaccio's autobiographical expression of his passion for action. And it is because the autobiography is ill-disguised that the revenge is so improbable and far-fetched and the story carried through with such angry determination with little regard to its absurdity or its very obvious retouches. The part about necromancy is touched up, for instance, for halfway through the story Boccaccio realises that the widow could easily make the experiment in magic in one of her villas or some other place where she could thwart the scholar's plans, so he quickly assures us that the lady's 'estate and the tower' are 'very well known' to the scholar. Then, later, good fortune sees to it that the place is not only isolated but, at that hour, 'the husbandmen had all gone from the fields by reason of the heat'. Finally, Boccaccio suddenly remembers that the maid, who is every bit as guilty from his point of view as her mistress, is emerging from the adventure unscathed, so he promptly makes her break her thigh when coming down from the fateful tower with her mistress. This is a typically sadistic forcing of effect, though entirely lacking the sensuality that usually goes with sadism. I have already said that Boccaccio betrays his feelings at the end. But even halfway through the story we have him exclaiming, 'Ah! poor woman! poor woman! she little knew, my ladies, how rash it is to try conclusions with scholars' and he is clearly referring to himself.

But action free from any ulterior motive, action as an end in itself, action for action's sake, in a word adventure, always lies at the heart of Boccaccio's most secret aspirations. But as we have already said, this kind of action runs the risk of seeming unwarranted and hence unreal. Ariosto, another contemplative writer in love with action, remedies this drawback by means of irony; Boccaccio, less disillusioned than Ariosto, counters it with what we could call (to use an overworked term) a kind of magic realism. That is, a visionary yet concrete precision of detail, combined—within a rarefied and ineffable atmosphere—with an extraordinary sense of the coincidences offered by reality itself at the moment of narration. I have said that this magic realism enables Boccaccio to avoid the pitfall of unreality peculiar to adventure. But perhaps it would be more accurate to say that this magic derives precisely from his indifference to the ethical factor, from the scepticism which people still insist on seeing as one of the defects of Boccaccio's art. For what is a dream, where magic seems at home, if not a reality from which all rational, practical, moral and intellectual elements have been banished, and in which the fantasies of the unconscious are expressed? For moralists reality tends to demand a judgement and thus it harmonises realistically with characters and events. But for adventure-dreamers reality is just as ineffable and mysterious as the places, objects and people that we caress with our deepest instincts when we are asleep. The surrealists, in their researches, have sometimes isolated and blown up details in old pictures and thereby revealed the magical and metaphysical character of many of these details—which have a lucid incoherence unknown to the modern impressionists and realists. This is because, like Boccaccio, the old masters often dreamed and dreams are fertile ground for analogies and enigmas. When seen through a magnifying glass, some of Boccaccio's backgrounds, places and notations become arcane and suggestive, like the tiny *natures mortes*, corners of landscapes, and background-figures of some of our fourteenth-, fifteenth- and sixteenth-century painters. Action, pure action, without intended meaning or ethics, gains depth, lucidity and mystery from those details that no amount of serious moral intention could give it.

An outstanding example of this blending of magic detail with passion for action is provided by the story of Andreuccio of Perugia. Here, moreover, the thirst for adventure is overt and total. There are none of those erotic elements that at first sight may seem to be inseparable from Boccaccio's art. Andreuccio is a young man, nothing else; we know nothing about him except that he came to Naples to buy horses. In a word, Andreuccio lies entirely within the action, and from the action he derives if not his character, at least his consistency; apart from the action he has no features, no character, no psychology. The starting-point of the tale is the intrigue initiated by the Neapolitan prostitute for Andreuccio's undoing. Without involving himself too far in the probability of the story of a sister lost and found, Boccaccio immediately enters into a compulsive, dreamy atmosphere which is truly magical. We have the 'curtained bed', with 'dresses in plenty, hanging on pegs' in the prostitute's house; we have 'the narrow blind alley' into which the unfortunate Andreuccio falls; we have the 'fellow with the black and matted beard . . . yawning and rubbing his eyes as if he had just been roused from his bed, or at any rate from deep sleep'; we have those two thieves who, on hearing Andreuccio's story, exclaim, 'Of a surety, 'twas in the house of Scarabone Buttafuoco'; and, finally, we have the cathedral in which the archbishop has been buried, the cathedral where—though not described—we seem to see the tall shadowy nave, the vast paved floor dimly shining, the massive brown groups of pillars and columns and, at the end, all twinkling with candles, the altar with the prelate's sarcophagus. Andreuccio enters the tomb and there the thieves leave him. Shut up in the tomb with a dead man, he is in an anguishing situation almost worthy of Poe. But the church echoes with footsteps, other thieves come along (and, incidentally, how many thieves there are in Boccaccio!—but in a world of humanists, merchants and courtiers, the criminal world is the only one that *acts*), the lid is raised from the tomb and the anguish evaporates. And now the point is, what does it matter if Andreuccio, the honest merchant, becomes a thief and a desecrator of tombs; what does it matter if later (as Boccaccio tells us, not without ingenuousness) his companions congratulate him and help him make away with the stolen goods—granted that the writer has borne us through the adventure in one breath?

A passion for adventure in quantity—like someone who wants to appease his hunger at all costs and to whom eating the same food matters little—can be found in the story of the Sultan of Babylonia's daughter. Here, too, the magic of the detail makes up for the monotony of the series of rapes. The ship, with only women aboard, that 'swiftly sails the sea before the storm' and then runs aground on the sand, and Pericone riding on horseback along the devastated beach after the storm, are like pictures from Ariosto. But the subsequent murder of the Prince of Morea takes place in surroundings and circumstances suggestive of Elizabethan drama.

> The palace was close by the sea, but at a considerable altitude above it, and the window through which the prince's body was thrown looked over some houses which, being sapped by the sea, had become ruinous, and were rarely or never visited by a soul.

From that window the prince looks out, 'bare to the skin', to 'enjoy a light breeze' and, as we would add, to contemplate those melancholy surfbeaten ruins under the moonlight. The murderer, Ciuriaci, comes up behind him, stabs him, and throws his body into the ruins. Ciuriaci is strangled in his turn by one of his companions, 'with a halter brought with him for the purpose', and then is thrown down onto the prince's body. This is behaviour of Machiavellian and Renaissance atrocity. Meanwhile the lovely woman sleeps on unawares and half-naked in her bed before the open window. The Duke of Athens, having strangled Ciuriaci, takes a light and

> gently uncovered her person as she lay fast asleep; and surveyed her from head to foot to his no small satisfaction . . . his passion waxed beyond measure, and reckless of his recent crime and of the blood which still stained his hands, he got forthwith into bed.

The crime is discovered in a strange and terrifying way. 'An idiot roaming about the ruins where lay the corpses of the prince and Ciuriaci drew the latter by the halter and went off dragging it after him . . .' This is only one episode of the story but quite sufficient to provide material for a tragedy by Webster or Marlowe.

Or we have the tale of Riccardo de Chinzica, with the great Mediterranean sea, scoured by gallant pirates such as Paganino da Monaco; with those two boats plying along the coast in the heat of the day, one bearing the unfortunate judge, the other the beautiful wife and her maids. Paganino's castle is not described;

but like Andreuccio's cathedral we seem to see it high on that rocky and beflowered coast. Paganino and Riccardo's wife send the poor judge back in disgrace. If Boccaccio had been the middle-class townee writer that he has often been called, this simple turn of events could well have happened within the four walls of a house. But Boccaccio, with his passion for adventure, and perhaps to counterbalance the dry-as-dust judge with his sedentary life, brings in Pisa and Monaco, the sea and the corsair—things that introduce a distant and legendary atmosphere to a not very unusual plot. In passing it is worth noting that the sea always evokes a deep and passionate response in Boccaccio, as if its huge vastness and eternal variety alone could satisfy his greed for freedom and action.

But it was not only in space that Boccaccio sought scope for his passion for action; he sought it also in time. I have always considered historical novels and stories an absurdity unless history, instead of presenting itself to the author as a kind of *place d'armes* in which time (to take the words of the imaginary seventeenth-century writer of the Introduction to *The Betrothed*) passes the years in review and draws them up in battle array, unless history brings the years back to the surface of memory like some ancestral recollection, or poetic longing, or nostalgia. Boccaccio, though he lived in a time that no one could suspect of historicism—between the Middle Ages which rejected history in the name of theological immobility, and the Renaissance which was equally foreign to the spirit of history owing to its Plutarchian cult of the personality—Boccaccio must nevertheless have had a mythical and obscure sense of the almost legendary past of the high Middle Ages and the Lombard invaders, if only transmitted by oral tradition and family memories. Apart from other stories where the period is uncertain and wrapped, as it were, in the darkness of a magic long-ago (such as the ones about Tancredi, Prince of Salerno; Nastagio degli Onesti, and Alibech in the desert of the Thebaid), we find a sense of a Lombardic and barbarous Middle Ages in King Agilulf and Queen Teodolinda, told out as it is in the stained glass of a cathedral, and there is also some kind of prenatal memory present as if someone were recounting things neither invented nor heard but experienced in another life. The Italian groom belonging to the oppressed race who is in love with the Lombard Queen, risks death to lie with her and, this achieved, spends his life remembering those minutes of royal love, is a very complex figure in whom are blended the passion for action and a sort of nostalgia for a dark barbaric era that lacked the light of art or culture yet fostered strong whole-hearted passions, like the protagonist's for King Agilulf's wife. There are plenty of kings and queens in Boccaccio, but these two are the only ones that achieve social relief and concreteness, contrasted as they are with the low-born groom. Agilulf and Teodolinda, we feel, reign barbarously by right of conquest over an enslaved people. The groom has no hope and is content just to be near the queen, tending the horses. But this timid fetishism does not satisfy his passion indefinitely. When desire gains over prudence, he decides to risk his life and try to possess the queen. As usual, once the decision is taken, and the plot formulated, Boccaccio hurtles into the action—which, as he proceeds, is deepened and enriched by the background details.

The attentive reader is sure to remember the place in which the groom's adventure occurs. This is King Agilulf's palace, probably a rough castle of wood with square palisaded towers like the ones Agilulf's ancestors built in the clearings of the northern forests, a fitting setting for a king who at night goes to seek his wife wrapped in a great mantle and carrying a 'lighted torch' in one hand and a wand in the other. It is also a fitting setting for the groom who disguises himself as the king and, making the 'drowsy' chambermaid open the doors to him, lies down silently beside the queen in the darkness. Basically it is the same kind of deception as in many another licentious story, but the remote period, the place, the palace that seems to have emerged from a Germanic saga and the royal atmosphere, confer a poetic quality on what elsewhere might be a mere diversion or joke. Once the deception is discovered, the king makes straight for the place where he imagines his unknown rival to be.

This is the 'long dormitory' above the horses' stables—words charged with evocations of feudal servitude. Here in different beds 'well-nigh all' the kings' household sleeps. 'Well-nigh all', for the Lombard kings had no courts, the king being a feudal man like everyone else. His peers were not in the palace but in other castles scattered across Italy; in the royal palace there dwelt only the members of the royal family, and the family's servants. We imagine the 'long dormitory' as narrow and low with pallets for all (or 'well-nigh all') the servants stretching as far as the eye can see under a beamed ceiling. The king enters the corridor, walks slowly along the row of beds, and feels the heart of each sleeper with his hand. Note how this deep deathlike sleep of all the servants, worn out by the day's toil, is in accord with the image of the long dormitory. The king cuts a tuft of hair from the head of the one whose heart seems to him agitated. But the groom, outwitting the king, cuts a similar tuft from the heads of all his companions. So the next day, when the king sees all the family servants partially shorn, he has to admit defeat from his unknown rival.

I have gone into this story at length because it seems to me one of the best in the *Decameron* and one in which the passion for action seems to attain the highest level of articulation and depth. Moreover, with its homely human tone and gay deceit, it marks the transition of Boccaccio's art from the stories we might call 'lucky' (that is those in which the vicissitudes lead to a happy ending in a clear and light-hearted atmosphere) to stories we might call 'unlucky', where the adventures have a tragic ending. Our traditional image of Boccaccio depends mainly on the first type, and especially on those stories with erotic and comic plots. But it is a partial image and takes less than half Boccaccio into account. In fact Boccaccio felt equally deeply about happiness and unhappiness, and this because they are the two faces of Chance, the only god who survives the disappearance of all others and still shines brightly in the serene sky of the *Decameron*. For Boccaccio chance plays the part of fate in Greek tragedies but we owe his love of chance not to cynicism but, like everything else, to his taste for action and adventure. For what is chance in Boccaccio's stories but the expression of a devoted passion for the manifold in life? All who put their trust in chance put their trust in life as in a river with multiple currents to which we should abandon ourselves in the knowledge that they will ultimately lead somewhere. Chance, moreover, allows every action to be its own self-justification as it occurs. Hence the freedom, the variety, the beauty of all actions without exception, their grafting not onto a dull and limited moral world but onto the most charming and colourful of æsthetic worlds. Chance and mischance are beautiful alike, to be caressed and wondered at with feelings of lascivious desire. All ends up in beauty.

It is perhaps this æstheticism of adventure over which the two faces of chance preside that lies behind the beauty of the stories we have called 'unlucky' for they are among the most beautiful and the most characteristic of his art (contrary to the tradition about Boccaccio as a typical licentious story-teller). They are scattered throughout the book, but one whole day is devoted to those whose loves have unhappy endings. Boccaccio participates in these sad stories with the feelings we detected in him in his treatment of the plague—with the voluptuous, dreamy caressing of tragic action by someone far removed from any such situation in fact. This may not be much, but it is enough to prevent Boccaccio from falling into the flatness and grossness of many writers who have ventured on similar themes, such as Giraldi and Bandello. It is this attitude that gives the 'unlucky' stories their enchanted air of dark immovable fate and at the same time their flavour of legend. They are stories from which, owing to the remoteness of the matter treated, all pity has vanished, and all that remains is naked action charged with mystery.

We have already spoken of Isabetta and the pot of basil. But consider the ruthlessness with which Boccaccio drags the two lovers to death in the story of Tancredi, Prince of Salerno. The grotto with an opening 'all but choked with the brambles and plants that grew about it', the room in the princely palace communicating with the grotto—these closely recall the window and the ruins by the sea in the murder of the Prince of Morea: a secret, melodramatic, melancholy place, a setting well suited to ill-starred loves. Tancredi's 'tender love' for his daughter whom he cannot bring himself to give in marriage, has the odour of incest, and his words to her when he discovers the affair with the page, his lamentations and the revenge he carries out on young Guiscardo, suggest a lover rather than a father. Ghismonda's long speeches remind us of the widow and the scholar: a complacent drawing-out of a situation already decided.

At first we expect Friar Alberto (in the next story) to be the protagonist of a tale that is all laughter. But that unfortunate lover, having taken flight into the Grand Canal without wings, and been dragged into the Piazza San Marco disguised as a 'wild man' and exposed to the mockery of the crowd, is punished for his sensuality not according to some moral concept, as the conclusion 'God grant that so it may betide all his likes' might suggest, but simply because Boccaccio enjoys the improbable and picturesque prank.

> Today we hold a revel, wherein folk lead others about in various disguises; as, one man will present a bear, another a wild man, and so forth; and then in the piazza of San Marco there is a hunt, which done, the revel is ended.

It is an animated and detailed picture, worthy of Bellini or Carpaccio. The same sought-out cruelty is apparent in the story where the King of Tunisia's daughter, after a naval battle, is bled to death and slaughtered before her lover's eyes in spite of all her tears and entreaties. Then there is the story of Girolamo, Salvestra's lover, who, in his sorrow at not being able to possess her, 'gathering up into one thought the love he had so long borne her, and the harshness with which she now requited it, and his ruined hopes, resolved to live no longer and in a convulsion, without a word, and with fists clenched, expired by her side.' Here, first, is the admirable invention of a suicide both highly unusual and well suited for producing the effects that follow: the husband getting up in the night and carrying the young lover's body into the doorway of the house; the wife, at her husband's instigation, going to church for the young man's funeral and dying in the same surprising and mysterious way. Boccaccio shows an equally inventive spirit and taste for unusual situations in the story of Pasquino who, in an extraordinary garden on a trip to the country, eats and drinks and chats happily, then rubs his teeth with a leaf from the fatal sage bush and dies. Extraordinary garden, I said; and indeed, like Agilulf's palace and Andreuccio's cathedral, it is one of those Boccaccian settings that evoke a whole vision by virtue of a single detail, in this case the sage bush. The young man who takes the sage leaf and rubs his teeth with it, 'saying that sage was an excellent cleanser', evokes the laziness and languid wellbeing that come with a successful outing. But in addition the sage bush conjures up the whole garden, a place we imagine to be outside the walls, uncultivated yet full of trees, flowers and grass while the 'toad of prodigious dimensions' discovered beneath the bush adds a note of horror and latent threat.

We have not mentioned the many other stories in no way inferior to these, and perhaps more typically Boccaccian—erotic stories, country ones, ones about nuns and priests, and simple anecdotes. This is because they are too well known to need quotation and also because of our conviction that the comic and licentious vein which has made Boccaccio famous is spectacular rather than characteristic, typical rather than deep. Though Boccaccio had a gay, carnal sense of life, the heart of his inspiration lay elsewhere, in his passion for action, in the delight he derived from imagining he was active, in his taste for adventure. As proof of this, note how, when this taste is absent, Boccaccio runs the risk of becoming no more than an inventor of piquant and witty anecdotes.

The fact that it is chance that lies behind the vicissitudes of the stories and not a high moral consciousness or system of thought, in no way proves that Boccaccio was a lazy or frivolous writer. Chance, that deceptive and enigmatic goddess, puts the more lovable and younger human faculties to the test first and foremost. Faith in chance is a prerogative of the young, of all those whose vitality has not yet been stultified and put at the service of some idea or interest. Boccaccio, who was young in spirit, trusted in chance out of excess of imagination and vitality rather than scepticism and frivolity. And after all, to oust all the dull ghosts from heaven and put in their place the blindfold goddess at her wheel means removing the grey monochrome of normality from the world and acknowledging its boundless richness and variety. Such chance, such interplay of agile and free forces is unknown to us, alas, and what we often mistake for dull and sinister chance is a destiny that is inscrutable but no less logical and pitiless for that.

1955

ROMAN WALKS

THE FIRST date in Stendhal's *Promenades dans Rome* is August 3, 1827. So it is roughly a hundred and thirty years since the day Stendhal entered the *ville éternelle* for the sixth time. The title *Promenades dans Rome* is a very accurate one for they are real walks in the course of which Stendhal provided detailed yet casual, exhaustive yet highly personal descriptions of the capital of the Papal States, for the use of the French 'happy few' who would follow in his footsteps. So we are dealing with a kind of Baedeker, written with real Stendhalian scrupulousness, which includes a complete catalogue of antiquities and papal monuments as well as reflections and comments on the nobility and the people, on customs and practices, and on the political and social situation. So when we re-read the *Promenades dans Rome* we Romans feel compelled to ask: how much of Stendhal's Rome has survived? Or, if you like: if Stendhal came back to Rome today what would he find changed and what unchanged?

We may as well say at the outset that most of the important changes in Rome have taken place in the last thirty years. The Rome D'Annunzio described in his novel *Il Piacere*, for instance, was still Stendhal's Rome, both vast and narrow, where society was composed of foreigners, nobility, a tradition-bound populace, and a restricted middle class of traders and middle-men.

And in the years around 1920 Rome was still more or less D'Annunzio's Rome, with only a few changes. Someone once told me that when he got in a *carozzella* round about 1920 and gave an address in via Paisiello, the driver said indignantly, 'What, do you live in the dark forest?' Today via Paisiello is near via

Veneto, one of the centres of the modern city. But in 1920 there were still cornfields round via Paisiello, and gardens and country farmsteads. And as regards Roman society, in 1920 there were, in addition to the usual nobles and the foreigners from the embassies and consulates, perhaps some building speculators and mill owners living in the small beflowered villas round about via Po and the Villa Borghese and dressed English-fashion. But that was all.

So Stendhal's Rome lasted almost up to our own time. It received its first blow under Fascism, with the clearances and rhetorical isolation of classical monuments, the construction of whole new quarters for state employees, and the so-called 'suburbs' for the poor. It is receiving its second blow today with the Demo-Christian government which is transforming the bureaucratic, religious and political capital into an Italian and cosmopolitan metropolis. What, then, remains of Stendhal's Rome? Leaving to one side the monuments, museums and churches which, except for the above-mentioned clearances and isolations, have remained the same, let us see how Stendhalian is society, the people—in short, the inhabitants of Rome.

Let us take, for instance, the nobility that Stendhal is always describing in the *Promenades*. True, the salons in which Cardinals could be seen in conversation with beautiful ladies, foreigners or Romans, no longer exist, but the mentality Stendhal was so fond of, the class psychology, has undergone very few changes.

Around 1927, exactly a century after Stendhal's stay in Rome, I knew a man who, though unaware of it, carried on the egotistical, *salonnard* and 'artistic' tradition of civilisation as Stendhal described it. This man—I shall refer to him as M.T., was a millionaire and middle class. A snob, he rubbed up against the aristocracy and managed to obtain free entry into the choicest aristocratic salons and exclusive circles. M.T. was convinced that the culmination of intellectual life lay in praising Raphael and Michelangelo to the skies, collecting Dresden china and Indian bronzes, taking an interest in Buddhism and spiritualism, and buying the latest Prix Goncourts and the latest pornographic best sellers of post-war Italian literature. His life was completely idle, but the endless women with whom he wove extremely complicated adulteries, as well as dinners, lunches, races, stock exchange reports and society gossip, gave him an enormous amount to do. His conversation was that of a Stendhalian *homme d'esprit*—a blend of anecdotes, unfinished sentences, and allusions both discreet and malicious. When Fascism came to power, M.T. discovered that the Fascists were intolerable boors, so became anti-Fascist. His anti-Fascism consisted in going the rounds of the salons and repeating 'the latest', that is the latest anti-Fascist joke, to noble ladies with perhaps an occasional Fascist under-secretary or minister in social mood thrown in. M.T. would have been thoroughly shocked if anyone had told him that anti-Fascism involved something more than repeating jokes—such as, for instance, subscribing to advanced political ideas that might have committed him to sacrificing a hundredth part of his enormous inheritance. There we have Stendhal's *homme d'esprit* living and flourishing a century after Stendhal's journey to Rome. Yet how things had changed! What in 1827 seemed to Stendhal no more than light, amusing and fascinating, had become by 1927 stale and rancid like a dish served too late. M.T., though unaware of it, was a ghost.

This ghostlike, out-of-date quality is still a characteristic of the whole of the Roman nobility precisely because it has remained much the same as a century ago, and has preserved, as well as its possessions, the old ideas on ethics, art, politics, and its own social importance. It so happens that this kind of dogged and decrepit conservatism has retained picturesque aspects even to-day. Stendhal would have taken great relish in the Roman princess who, a little while ago, had Botticelli's famous *Derelitta* in her bedroom, on the floor, and facing the wall. And the women of the Roman nobility would certainly not cut a poor figure if confronted with their predecessors of 1827. Today, as in Stendhal's time, they are extremely beautiful, elegant, and ignorant, and are kept busy all day long with love affairs and gossip.

And what about the common people whose energy was so much admired by Stendhal? Well, this famous energy, which Stendhal contrasted with the artificiality of French society, has not vanished either. As Stendhal noted, and as anyone today can see, the people of Trastevere are still fat yet passionate young men, phlegmatic yet hot-tempered, their blood quickly going to their heads, at least as regards words. True, there are no longer, as in Stendhal's time, two knifings a day, but then there have been the outbreaks of violence and the neo-realist excesses of the last war. Stendhal talks with mixed horror and near-admiration of the lynching of poor Basseville by the Roman mob: exaggerations of 'energy', yet as such praised. But in recent times the lynching of the governor of the Regina Coeli prison, the affair of the hunchback of Quarticciolo, and the banditry in the poor 'suburbs' have displayed the same qualities of collective and brigand-like 'energy'. Today, of course, we have no Monti to sing of Basseville in magnificent hendecasyllables devoid of the faintest trace of conviction or emotion, but the equally noncommittal photographs in the press tell more clearly and better than hendecasyllables the story of 'energy', or rather of violence, raw libertarianism and latent brigandage.

And what of the superabundance of miracles that Stendhal gently and lightly mocked? We need only to go to Tre Fontane and visit the grotto in which the Madonna appeared to Cornacchiola, the tramdriver, in the form of a pretty girl munching American chewing-gum (the words of an eyewitness), to admit, with Stendhal, that modern Italy is still full of '*crucifixes qui parlent*', '*Madones qui se fâchent*', and '*anges qui chantent les litanies en procession*'. As Stendhal notes, and as we can still see for ourselves, '*le peuple de la campagne est tellement imbu de catholicisme qu'à ses yeux rien dans la nature se fait sans miracle*'.

Stendhal's Rome was the propulsive centre of a universal Church and the capital of a State of herdsmen and shepherds. After 1870 it became the capital of the Kingdom, subsequently the Republic, of Italy. But the Church is still here, and more so than ever, and the herdsmen and shepherds have never left. As in the time of Stendhal, so today, the Roman *cuisine* is one for shepherds and herdsmen, based on heavy *abbacchio** with potatoes from the oven, on *spaghetti alla amatriciana*† with lard and sheep-cheese, on *coda della vaccina* (or *alla buttera*),‡ on *rigatoni con la pagliata*,§ that is to say flavoured with the intestines of a newborn calf, and on other similarly indelicate tit-bits. And the countryside round Rome is still for the herdsmen and shepherds despite the thousands of cars that visit it on Sundays and holidays. True, the Pontine Marshes have gone, with the malaria and the buffaloes with their great crescent horns, whose passage served to dredge the blocked canals. Gone, too, are the brigands who in Stendhal's time took to the wilds. But, except in the familiar Castelli (and here with reserves) and at Ostia and Fregene, the atmosphere has remained singularly unchanged—with a desert stretching to within a few kilometres of Rome, an incredibly rough and primitive yet homely hospitality, picturesque and near-black villages perched on Corot-like tufa crowned with oaks in which one cannot even find an egg or a sandwich, and old medieval papal homesteads, blackened with smoke, that seem like little fortresses. And the Roman idea of night-life is still that of herdsmen and shepherds; a heavy, solemn dinner at the *osteria*, with neon lighting, sawdust under one's feet, one's coat on and one's hat on one's head (if it is winter), a couple of litres of execrable Frascati wine, a round of cards, and so to bed. There are no more sheep and buffaloes to be taken out at dawn, but the idea under the surface is always the same—there must be early bed so as to be early to pasture. Today, as in Stendhal's time, Rome is the only capital in Europe that has no night-life and is almost a desert after midnight. Of course Stendhal tells us about

* Young lamb.

† Spaghetti seasoned with onion, bacon, tomato, sheep-cheese.

‡ Cowstail.

§ Pasta cut in short, wide, tubular, grooved pieces; with the upper part of the intestines of milk-fed calves. The dish is seasoned with fat bacon, onion, celery and parsley, with some wine and tomato sauce. [Translator's Notes.]

the Roman politics of his time. His barber from Trastevere, '*fort gros quoique fort jeune*', as usual '*bouillant d'énergie*', views the government '*comme un être puissant, heureux et méchant, avec lequel il est indispensable d'avoir certains rapports*'. With each ghastly event he relates, the barber adds his comment: 'What do you expect, noble sir, we are under the priests.' I do not think a modern barber in Trastevere would speak very differently, at most he would use the language of the left-wing parties instead of that of anti-clericalism. Romans like Stendhal's barber say today, 'Full stomach doesn't believe in empty stomach', or 'Big-moustache* must come', but the tone is always the same, an 'energetic' protest tempered by ancestral scepticism. Moreover, if Stendhal came back today I do not think he would be particularly surprised or disconcerted by the novelties superimposed on the Rome of his time in the last thirty or forty years: the world of the cinema that revolves round via Veneto and the big hotels, the American-style lanes of Monti Parioli, the 'suburbs', the great political parties and their bureaucracies, the anonymous quarters of the Umberto period and the twentieth-century quarters of the lesser white-collar workers. For no more than in Stendhal's time has novelty in modern Rome succeeded in transforming, or making an impression on, or in any way modifying, the unalterable core of Roman 'indifference'. As in 1827, so today, everything that is done and happens in Rome, happens and is done without any real participation on the part of the people, or rather without any of that immediate, contingent and momentary participation that lies behind the civic spirit of the great European capitals. With the people of Rome, participation is conditioned and restricted by a deep, yet at the same time discouraging (at least as regards political effects), sense of eternity; hence the all-embracing unreality of life in Rome, which is like a magnificent stage for performing tragedy, comedy, farce, or plain drama, without it making any difference.

Centuries of traffic with the Church, that is, with an institution

* *Baffone*, big moustache the popular name for Stalin. [Translator's Note.]

outside time and space, has in the end succeeded in putting a film of incredulity between the Romans and reality. A Roman old enough to have been born when Porta Pia was stormed, might exclaim, 'Now you can see how right the people of those days were who refused to have any truck with the Kingdom of Italy. The House of Savoy has come and gone. And here we are sitting in front of our half-litre of wine just as we did a century ago.' As he is convinced that he is in an eternal city where all things are transient, the Roman is always more of a spectator than an actor, and his participation has always consisted in watching and trying to understand, then booing or clapping as the case may be, then going home to the womb of his family which is eternal too. The latest of these Roman spectacles which began with clapping and ended with booing was the twenty years of Fascism, but Roman 'energy', which basically is a sort of irritation or exasperation born of laziness, only awoke when the Fascists and the Nazis had 'kicked' pretty well everyone 'in the arse'; or, put in another way, only when the hidings that the actors had been giving one another on the stage began to fall on the spectators as well.

So can we say that the twenty years of black Fascism were the last Stendhalian epoch in Italy? In a negative way, yes.

Stendhal was a liberal, but a great lover of the anachronistic absurdities and incongruities of the elderly and kindly tyrannies, and in his books he described an Italy that was not all that different in some of its aspects from the Italy of Fascism. He would have had no great difficulty in finding all the elements that went to make up the *Chartreuse de Parme*—the absolute governments that were unwarlike and corrupting, the secret police without a secret, the lampoons, the fanatical clerical ferocities, the persecution of the intellectuals, the opposition in salons, and conspiracies in attics—in the Rome of 1927, though they existed side by side with other more serious and at times terrifying aspects, which his singular capacity for lightening even tragedy would have found a way of ignoring, or at least of reducing to traits of local colour. At most he would have found that the

Fascists were boring, an unpardonable crime in his eyes. And this is not said to accuse Stendhal of being reactionary; it was the Italy he described with so much enjoyment that was reactionary, not the man who described it. It is said because the chief characteristic of the Stendhalian spirit lies precisely in introducing a sense of play and fluidity into even the most ponderous and hidebound of situations. Stendhal's description of Rome in his *Promenades* should be put side by side with the one Belli bequeathed to us in his *Sonnets*. Stendhal's Rome and Belli's Rome are like two sides of the same coin—Stendhal's aristocratic, libertine, European and illuministic; Belli's, local, Catholic, popular and dialect-speaking. The *Promenades* end with the election of Pope Pius VIII; the *Sonnets* begin with the same election.

Belli helps us to grasp, among other things, how Stendhal's infatuation with the 'energy' of Trastevere was no mere product of an æsthete's taste for the exotic; the robust, terse dialect of the *Sonnets* is there to prove that in the main Stendhal's vision was true. Possibly Stendhal's 'energetic' Rome, with its catalogue of antiquities as background, is more like Pinelli than Belli but Stendhal and Belli have in common a realism lacking in Pinelli's stylisation. Of course Stendhal, as a liberal European, had no means of seeing the motives of such a reactionary and energetic situation as the Roman one from within (he was satisfied if he found material for amusement and enchantment) but this is why Belli is useful and helps us to realise the acuteness of Stendhal's observations; Belli is the very voice of the 'energy' that Stendhal saw from the outside and could not help admiring.

In the *Promenades* Stendhal notes, for instance,

> *Cette nuit il y a eu deux assassinats. Un boucher presque enfant a poignardé son rival, jeune homme de vingt-quatre ans et fort beau, ajoute le fils de mon voisin qui me fait ce récit: 'Mais ils étaient tous deux, ajoute-t-il, du quartier de Monti (des Monts); ce sont des gens terribles . . .' L'autre assassinat a eu lieu près de Saint Pierre parmi les*

> *Trastévérins; c'est aussi un mauvais quartier, dit-on; superbe à mes yeux; il y a de 'l'énergie', c'est à dire la qualité qui manque le plus au dixneuvième siècle . . .*

and we can turn straight away to Belli's sonnets, the one entitled *L'Adducazione*, and grasp the psychology lying behind this 'energy'; or the one entitled *Chi cerca trova*, and see energy in action from within. I would particularly like to quote the last three lines of this second sonnet which, as Giorgio Vigolo points out in his commentary, has an energy almost worthy of Dante himself. A man is face to face with his enemy:

> *M'impostai cor un sercio e nun me mossi*
> *je feci fà tre antri passi e ar quarto*
> *lo pres' in fronte e je scricchiorno l'ossi.*

> I placed myself with a stone in my hand and I did not budge
> I let him take three more steps, and on the fourth step
> I caught him on the forehead and his bones cracked.
>
> [TRANSLATOR]

When we turn from energy to Papal government we find Stendhal and Belli quite inseparable: each casts light on the other, one portrays the greatness and the other the poverty of the Papal power. It is enough here to recall the election of Pope Pius VIII with which the *Promenades* end and the *Sonnets* begin.

Stendhal, a foreigner who sees things from the outside, observes:

> *Francois Xavier Castiglione est né à Cingoli, petite ville de la Marche d 'Ancône, le 20 November 1761; il fut d'abord évêque de Cesène par Pie VII; ce fut à cette occasion que ce Pape dit, 'Il viendra après'. Bientôt on sentit qu'il fallait un homme instruit pour la place de grand penitencier car la tradition des usages était interrompue et le Cardinal Castiglione fut nommé uniquement à cause de sa profonde science.*

And here we have what Belli said about the same Pope Castiglione, the man of *profonde science.*

Che fior de Papa, creeno. Accidenti.
Co' rispetto de lui pare er cacamme.
Bella galanteria da tate e mamme
Pe' fa bobò a li fiji impertinenti.

Ha un erpete pe' tutto, nun tié denti.
È guercio, je strascineno le gamme;
Spennola da una parte e bugiaramme
Si arriva a fa la pacchia a li parenti.

Guarda lí che figura da vienicce
A fa da Crist' in terra cazzo matto
Imbottito de carne de sarcicce
Disse bene la serva de l'orefice
Quando lo vedde in chiesa: uhm. Cianno fatto
Un gran brutto strucchione de Pontefice.

What flowers of Popes they create. Damn!
With due respect to him he looks like the Rabbi.
Delicious morsel for fathers and mothers
To scare disrespectful children.

He has rash all over, he has no teeth,
He is one-eyed, he drags his legs;
He is lop-sided and bugger me
If he has time to make his relations rich.

Look what a figure to come
And be our Christ on earth! mad simpleton
Stuffed with sausage-meat
The maidservant of the jeweller was right to say
When she saw him in the church: They have
  chosen for us
A really ugly old nag of a Pope.

[TRANSLATOR]

Besides its description of the new Pope seen through the eyes of a man in the street, this sonnet seems to me the symbolic description of the decrepit and anachronostic temporal power. It was written on April 1, 1829.

Stendhal left Rome on the 24th of the same month.

Italy as described by Stendhal, a rose at the root of the evils to which Belli gave the most ferocious and ruthless expression, was beginning to melt away.

Italy as awoken by the liberalism of Napoleon and (why not?) of Stendhal, was on the point of birth.

1956

NOTES ON THE NOVEL

THE ORIGINS of the essay-type, or ideological, novel seem to lie in a crisis in the relationship between the author and reality. The nineteenth-century novelist had no doubt that he was describing objective reality even when he distorted it or transfigured it—the distortions or transfigurations being attributed to mere differences in 'style', or in verbal technique. Hence the nineteenth-century novelist's realism was in a sense scientific, not only because he often stole ground-plans and terminology from the natural sciences, but also because he viewed reality in terms of study, research and investigation. Think of all the notebooks, the exact observations, the research in archives and libraries, the inquiries and *reportages* that lie behind the work of writers like Balzac, Flaubert or Zola.

The third person used in nineteenth-century novels often resembles the third person in natural history describing the habits and characteristics of mammals, reptiles and insects. It is a perfectly objective third person owing to the minute reconstruction of the surroundings and laws conditioning it and it seems to presuppose the existence of unchanging or ever recurring situations in psychology and society. Such confidence in the unchanging and stable nature of reality largely depended on the unchanging and stable nature of European society in the nineteenth century. For even the changes and developments that a novelist could not help noting did not distort society in any way—they were rather like the changes and developments that occur in nature, which nevertheless remains stable and unchanging.

This conception collapsed in two ways, one involving form, the other content. On the one hand 'style' slowly emerged as something more than the total of the technique of words, as something, that is, that could be viewed as reality, and more, as the only possible reality (in view of the fact that so-called objective reality varied according to variations of 'style'). On the other hand events in politics, war and society between 1870 and 1945 introduced a violent movement of disintegration and revolution into the social world that until then had seemed stable and unchanging.

The nineteenth-century novelist had believed in the existence of a language and a reality that were common and universal; now the novelist suddenly found himself confronted with the relativism of language and reality. It is from that time that we must date the impossibility of writing novels in the third person except by disguising the autobiographical 'I' in a way false to science and objectivity; and from that time, too, that the novel has become 'fragmentary', if by that we understand the non-existence of a common language and the impossibility of an unchanging relationship between the author and reality. It follows that we no longer have one reality and one language, but as many realities and languages as we have novelists and these realities and languages are no longer acceptable for their universality so much as for their organisation and articulation which, be it understood, sets out from a basis of unreality or, if you prefer, from a lack of relationship between the novelist and reality.

The various worlds of contemporary relativism, therefore, are conventions to an extreme degree and can be compared with very solid constructions built on fog. With such purely subjective constructions obviously the best novelist is one who, whatever else he may lack, displays the greatest amount of vitality. To this new touchstone of value we may well owe the existence of enormous and in some ways shapeless works such as those of Proust and Joyce, both of whom are characterised by a fundamental distrust and disbelief in an objective reality. In the case of Joyce's *Ulysses*, besides its large number of other meanings, we find an almost polemical intention of showing the relativity of styles and hence of objective realities. But side by side with their 'vitalistic' ambition to give us all 'reality', Joyce and Proust already display the essayist's attempt to order this reality according to the plans of an ideology, of whatever kind. Why ideology? Because even when it almost seems a piece of useless sophistry as in Proust, or is superfluous and literary as in Joyce, it will in either case have the appearance of re-establishing the language of reason which is universal in its own right, and hence of re-establishing a relationship of some kind between the narrator and reality.

2

When people talk about the crisis in the novel, they are really talking about the crisis in the nineteenth-century novel. Valéry said that it seemed to him impossible to write, 'The Marquise closed the door'. And he was right. By this time it was already impossible to write or read that statement. In other words, the principal reason for the death of the nineteenth-century novel was its endeavour to compete with the civil register, photography, journalism and scientific inquiry. The efficiency of these as means of documentation and testimony has made the novel, with its fictions and conventions, pointless and boring.

The objection may be raised at this point that the novel is, nevertheless, a work of poetry, and that there is nothing to stop the novelist from continuing to create poetry with the very means used by photographers, journalists and men of science in their inquiries. But this objection does not stand, for whenever a poetical form or tempo becomes accessible to the professionals, the novelist abandons it in favour of another more suitable and difficult one. Every time the representation of reality declines into a convention, it makes a move upwards to where convention cannot follow it.

The flight from mechanisation and ready-made formulas is characteristic of all the arts and of all really creative activities in general. At the time when Flaubert wrote 'The Marquise closed the door', the phrase was charged with expressive freshness, revolutionary novelty and deeply felt reality. Fifty years later it had become a purely verbal mechanism lacking all plastic quality, accessible to all and good for all. So in last analysis, when dealing with the ideological or essay-type novel as contrasted with the naturalist novel, it will be necessary to act as with a competition or examination and reduce the number of competitors by standards of thought that only a few can satisfy. A century ago it needed a genius to write, 'The Marquise closed the door', today nothing less will be needed to work out an ideological plan capable of holding up the framework of the novel.

3

But at this point we would like to examine the nature of the novelist's thought. Obviously a philosopher is not a novelist, and usually philosophers write very bad novels. However contradictory this may seem, the novelist's thought springs not from his mind but from his sensibility. Like oil lying at a great depth which has to be sought by boring, there lies deep down below the factual reality expressed in the phrase, 'The Marquise closed the door', the theme the phrase implies. In other words, every discovery made by the sensibility brings with it a discovery in theme, though the novelist may be unaware of it.

For instance we know what Balzac's themes were because we have at our disposal the necessary critical and historical perspective, but it is not certain that Balzac himself knew precisely what they were. An author's awareness of his themes, and their articulation and organisation into an ideology, are characteristics of the essay-type novel. We have already explained why this only happens at a determined moment in the development of the novel. The novelist does not feel the need to descend as deep down as his themes until the poetic design in naturalistic representation has degenerated into a mechanism.

But not everyone can track down the theme lying beneath the act, the character and the situation; besides special faculties of reflection and analysis, the digging operation requires the moral and intellectual experience of a preliminary devaluation of objective reality. But the themes that can subsequently be organised into an ideology will nevertheless remain, so to speak, incarnate with poetic sensibility, a thing that does not and cannot happen with systematised thought, thought purely interested in rational and direct expression. So the novelist's thought consists in the total of the themes underlying the surface of the actual narration as brought to light and put together again, rather like the fragments of a long-buried statue. From this it will derive an ambiguous and contradictory quality which will give the ideology a hypothetical character, putting it beyond the reach of exhaustive and precise definition.

We only need to quote the example of Dostoievsky, the father of the ideological novel. It would be impossible to outline Dostoievsky's ideology in a systematic and coherent way: he is at once a Christian and a Nietzschean, a humanitarian and an aristocrat, a revolutionary and a reactionary. This ambiguous and contradictory quality is well contrived for allowing for poetry, that point at which all contradictions fuse and from which all contradictions depart.

4

Dostoievsky often gives an impression of arbitrariness and inconsequence, for not only is his ideology ambiguous and contradictory but his relationship with his ideology is ambiguous and contradictory too. Indeed in plain words we could say that sometimes Dostoievsky himself does not know what he wants. But take a step beyond Dostoievsky's formula, and we have the novelist who has purified his ideology to the point of finished, systematic clarity.

The novel, then, will show us a double face—on the one side

a narrative order that seems to have reference to a rigorous ideology, on the other an ideology that seems to require a well-defined factual narrative. In other words, the allegorical or metaphorical novel. This novel seems well suited to represent a world like ours, in which the human person is no longer the measure of all things, and the necessity of interpreting and expressing collective feelings favours the creation of comprehensive formulas. Metaphor in this case is nothing but the practical devaluation of objective reality considered as chaotic and meaningless, in favour of a more current and significant, even if abstract, image.

Consider for example *The Golden Ass* of Apuleius. In that novel of decadence we feel the presence of the masses as much in the incoherence, slightness and fragmentariness of the characters as in the grandiose ideology. Without the ideology *The Golden Ass* would be a series of delightful anecdotes; without the anecdotes it would be a mysteriosophical hypothesis. The force of that novel lies in the perfect fusion of the metaphor, in the fact that the anecdotes have been ordered according to the order of the hypothesis and the hypothesis has been prevented from causing a single violation of the probability and naturalness of the anecdotes.

Of course what the allegorical novel requires before all else is that the novelist should view his allegory in a poetical way, in other words that his approach should be not so much intellectual as æsthetic and emotional. It implies an intention towards the ideology that is constant and practical, as towards something to be lived and experienced rather than merely shown in the abstract. To steal Marx's formula we could say that in this case the novelist's ideology should not only reflect reality but change it into its own image and likeness. In this way the allegorical or metaphorical novel is the novel in which the ideology has given meaning and order to a reality which would otherwise be meaningless and chaotic, or, in other words, as we have said, it has changed it. So this is the moment at which, always following Marx, philosophy should descend from heaven to earth and show its capacity to modify the conditions of objective reality.

5

Nevertheless the essay-type novel is always dependent on the novelist's capacity so to behave that the ideology does not contradict, but confirms, the naturalness of the action. Now that confirmation is of a purely historical nature. In other words, the essay-type novel presupposes an active ideology—one that, without too much difficulty, can be viewed as an ideology capable of realisation in the real and contemporary world. The strength of the essay-type novel lies in offering a possible image that is as ideological as it is factual. A defunct ideology, or at least a forced and out-of-date one, will never seem adequate to support and justify the context of the narrative.

Such is the case with Manzoni's *The Betrothed* which is constantly in danger of being judged as a work of propaganda rather than of metaphor. In other words the reader ought to be able to feel that the ideology could be adapted to his own life and that it is one of the many hypotheses to which he can have recourse without falling into the absurd and the abstract; in a word that it is historical. This very capacity of the ideology to create not only the story of the novel but also history without other qualifications is the proof that its quality is metaphorical and not only abstract and conceptual.

The essay-type novel should thus provide a possible image of life ordered in a given ideological direction. The greater and wider this possibility, the more poetic the novel. Hence it is up to the novelist to dig his own ideology out of themes underlying his own direct experience and not from cultural and religious traditions. From history in fact, and not history already past.

6

It is interesting to note how in work such as Kafka's—who in many ways is the heir to Dostoievsky's narrative tradition—the ideology remains an allusion and a presentiment. Kafka's procedure seems to be to create a precise metaphor and then subtract the ideological part from it and transcribe only its factual part, thereby generating a feeling of absurdity and metaphysical mystery. Probably this subtraction never happened, at least not consciously, instead there was Kafka's obstinate conviction that everything had a meaning though he was unable to tell us what it was.

Yet we feel this conviction so constantly and with such force that at times we ourselves feel obliged to formulate the ideology that Kafka left unclarified. Hence the conjectures—all right and all wrong—as to Kafka's meanings; hence, too, their ahistoricism. For precise and explicit ideology is always historical, but an ideology presented in the form of a metaphysical void seems to imply that history does not exist. It takes no account of its existence owing to the fact that man is incapable of creating it but can only anticipate its dark and threatening presence.

So Kafka's work, among many other things (for instance a prophetic description of Hitler's Germany, of racism and the concentration camps) is the last flower of European decadentism. Its masterly and exemplary method can be retained, but not its meanings which are all ahistorical precisely because conjectural. Nevertheless Kafka's work is very valuable as a symptom; it displays the exhaustion of the naturalist formula and sets down the need for an ideology to support and guide narration.

7

By its very nature, the nineteenth-century novel was bound to reach the point of freeing itself from plot and character, as both are superfluous and incongruous in a scientific representation of objective reality. Plot and character become difficult if not impossible as the study of surroundings and social definitions gains ground, for surroundings and social definitions reduce man to the civil register level in which everything is known, foreseen, and conventional. So in the nineteenth century plot and character gradually came to be rejected as belonging to the *roman feuilleton* and were viewed as spurious and melodramatic elements. Surely, as science itself shows us, there is no plot in nature outside the simple one of the birth, growth and death of living forms, nor any characters outside those that sum up and incarnate the species and categories. Little by little plot and character disappeared from books and impressionism triumphed in all the arts. As regards the narrative art, the name of Maupassant is example enough.

But in fact there are two kinds of plot and character: the civil register and well-assembled machine kind, and the kind where plot and character are expressions of the dramatic interweaving of the themes. Detective literature is a good example of the first kind. Plot and character are defined and set in motion by mechanically calculated interests and passions, rigidly consistent in themselves though starting out from a quite unreal convention—something like a parlour game. Whereas in the case where the novelist has been able to retrace the themes beneath the surface of event and situation, plot and character become something quite different. The characters become themes expressed and articulated in psychology and action; the plot becomes dialectical struggles between these themes. For example, the character of Hamlet is the Hamlet theme; the plot of Hamlet's tragedy is the dialectical conflict which occurs when the Hamlet theme comes into conflict with the other themes, those of the Queen, Ophelia, Polonius, the Ghost, and so on.

So we should view the increasing repudiation of, and contempt for, character and plot in good literature today as a last echo of the old naturalistic-impressionistic quarrel. The novel-as-essay is bound to take up the question of plot and character where it was abandoned and provide a new solution.

8

We shall now turn our attention to the difference between the metaphorical novel and the propaganda novel. As we have said, the themes lie deep down under the surface of the action and situation, rather as oil lies in geological caverns under the surface of the earth. Now the writer of propaganda novels is rather like someone who secretly stores up oil bought in a shop so as to be able to say that he has struck oil and sell his land at a profit.

The propaganda novel uses ideologies not born of the genuine poetical ground of individual sensibility, but borrowed ready-made from the society in which the writer happens to live. To use another simile: the metaphorical novelist is like a gardener who rears real plants equipped with stalks and roots, while the propaganda novelist is like someone who sticks rootless plants into the soil which wither the next day. Propaganda obliges the novelist to manufacture characters and plots which attract him not by deep sympathy and sensibility, but for the practical reason of justifying the propaganda which in its turn he has accepted for similarly practical reasons.

In other words the propaganda novel, whether Catholic or socialist-realist or anything else, is the opposite of the metaphorical novel. In the latter the ideology lies in the living essence of the action, whereas in the former it is the dead essence of dead action superimposed on living action whose essence is not revealed to us. Hence rises a dichotomy between the ideology and the action, just as might happen in a charade in which everyone dresses up in clothes that are not their own, and one feels the falseness of the make-up without being able to guess which clothes they should be wearing or usually do wear.

What for instance is the real theme of Renzo Tramaglino in *The Betrothed*? Manzoni would like us to believe that it is Providence's never-failing help to those who entrust themselves to her care. But in this case the Catholic ideology seems to be superimposed on a character of a very different nature and our inclination is to see Renzo in terms of the theme of a frightened and powerless lower-class group subjected to an absolute State and Counter-Reformation religion. Whereas even if we allow for the ambiguities and contradictions that are of the nature of poetry, it is impossible to detect in Julien Sorel a theme other than what Stendhal wanted to suggest; if anything, we will maintain that Julien Sorel says more to us than Stendhal intended to say through him. In a word the characters in propaganda novels often say the contrary of what their authors intended them to say, whereas the characters in metaphorical novels say more.

But a literature that we need to read *à rebours*, against the light, as with false banknotes that lack the prescribed watermark, is bad literature. By paradoxical irony it is the Church and the State that are the biggest manufacturers and distributors of this false and counterfeit poetical currency.

1956

THE SHORT STORY AND THE NOVEL

A DEFINITION of the short story as a distinct and autonomous literary *genre*, with its own special rules and laws, may well be impossible, for, among other things, the short story has an even wider sweep than the novel. It extends from the French-style *récit*, or long short story, whose characters and situations are almost those of a novel, down to the prose-poem, the sketch and the lyrical fragment. Yet when we attempt to make a rough definition of the short story we cannot help considering it in relation to its big brother, rather than in isolation: the short story is not a novel. When thus contrasted with the novel some constant characteristics do appear, and though they lack the character of laws and cannot be quoted as rules, they explain how the short story does in fact constitute a *genre* in its own right and has nothing to do with the novel or any other narrative composition of similar length.

Meanwhile it is worth noting that short story writers, accustomed as they are to expressing themselves within the limits and in accord with the rules of the *genre* however badly defined these may be, find it very difficult to write really good novels. Consider, for example, the two greatest short story writers of the end of the nineteenth century, Maupassant and Chekhov. These have both left us enormous collections of short stories which give an incomparable picture of the life in France and Russia of their time. Quantitively speaking, Maupassant's world is wider and more varied than the world of Flaubert, his contemporary; Chekhov's more so than Dostoievsky's, his immediate predecessor. Indeed, all things considered, we can say that while Maupassant and Chekhov so to speak exhaust the variety of situations and characters of the society of their time, Flaubert and Dostoievsky are rather like those solitary birds that restlessly and loyally repeat the same significant cry. In the last analysis all they did was to write the same novel over and over again, with the same situations and the same characters.

Some centuries earlier Boccaccio, the greatest short story writer of all time, exhibited a similar variety and richness as compared with Dante. If we only had *The Divine Comedy* with its static Gothic figures carved in *bas relief* round and round the monument of the poem, we should certainly know much less than we do about the life of Florence and Italy and the Middle Ages in general. Whereas Boccaccio's depiction of it is incomparable. Unlike *The Divine Comedy*, the *Decameron* presents everything in function of a complete illustration of this life, with no end in view other than that of extolling its richness and variety.

But when Maupassant and Chekhov tried their hand at novels or even *récits* they were far less gifted and convincing than with the short story. Some of Chekhov's novel-like stories, and Maupassant's *Bel Ami*, make us think less of novels than of blown-up, lengthened and watered-down short stories—rather as some frescoes by modern painters are really no more than easel paintings enlarged out of all proportion. In Chekhov's and Maupassant's novels and long short stories we feel the lack of that something that makes a novel, even a bad novel, a novel. Chekhov dilutes his concentrated lyrical feeling with superfluous plots lacking intrinsic necessity, while Maupassant gives us a series of disjointed pictures, seen through a telescope, and only held together by the presence of the protagonist. Indeed it is noteworthy that the very qualities that made these two great as short story writers become defects as soon as they tackle the novel. Someone may point out that we are dealing with different techniques, and Chekhov and Maupassant failed to master the technique of the novel. But this does not solve the problem, it merely states it differently. Technique is the form taken by the writer's inspiration and personality. Chekhov's and Maupassant's technique is unsuited to the novel because they could only say what they wanted to say in the short story, and not vice versa. So we are back where we started from. What is the outstanding distinction between the novel and the short story?

The principal and fundamental difference lies in the ground-plan or structure of the narrative. Of course all sorts of novels are being written, and will go on being written, with a variety of bizarre and experimental structures—which seems to give the lie to the validity of what we have just said. Nevertheless the classical novelists, those whose works have created the *genre*—men like Flaubert, Dostoievsky, Stendhal, Tolstoy, and later Proust, Joyce and Mann—go to prove that some common characteristics do exist in spite of this. The most important of these is what we could call ideology, that is the skeleton of the theme from which the flesh of the story takes its form. In other words the novel has a bone structure holding it together from top to toe, whereas the short story is, so to speak, boneless. Naturally the novel's ideology is not precise, preconstituted, or reducible to a thesis, just as the skeleton is not introduced into the human body by force when we are adults but has grown along with the body's other parts. It is this ideology that differentiates a novel from a short story and, conversely, it is the absence of bone structure that makes a short story not a novel. It is the ideology, however imprecise and contradictory it may be, with all the contradictions that are to be found in life itself (the novelist is not a philosopher, but a witness), that begets the things that make a novel a novel.

The first of these is what is usually called plot, or the changing succession of events that constitute the story of the novel. It can sometimes happen that the plot is an end in itself, but this is never the case with good novelists; suffice it to say that this obtains most often in detective stories where mechanical device plays the major part. With good novelists, real novelists, the plot is nothing but the sum total of the ideological themes as they conflict and merge with each other in their various ways. So the plot is made up not only of intuitions of feelings (as in the short story) but primarily of ideas expressed poetically but well defined.

The plot, for example, of *Crime and Punishment* is made up of the criss-cross, the contrast, the clash and the conflicting claims of the various ideological themes presented to us by the author from the first page: the theme of Raskolnikoff, the theme of Sonia, the theme of Svidrigailoff, the theme of Marmeladoff, the theme of the judge Porphyry, and so on. All these characters are autonomous and entirely human, but they are also ideas and it is not difficult to extract from them the ideological meanings they carry, a thing it would be quite impossible to do with the characters in a short story by Chekhov or Maupassant. The plot of *Crime and Punishment* is born of these themes embodied in characters, in other words from the grandiose ground-plan of this exemplary novel which enables Dostoievsky to proceed for five hundred pages without ever giving the impression that he is either spinning out or watering down events—the impression that we get in Chekhov's longer stories and in Maupassant's novel. The twists and turns of the plot, its surprises, its contradictions, its *coups de scène*, even its *deus ex machinas*, are never due to extrinsic interventions by the author or to what we could call the inexhaustible resources of life, but to the dialectical and necessary development of the ideological themes. From one point of view nothing could be more misleading than to say that the novel competes with the civil register. It would be more accurate to say this of the short story which passes in review a large variety of characters who have individual characteristics only. The truth is that many novels compete, not with the civil register, but with a philosophical treatise or a moral essay.

Besides the plot, the quality of the characters, too, stems from the presence or absence of ideology. Andreuccio da Perugia, Boule de Suif, the boy of the steppe, are short story characters; Raskolnikoff, Julien Sorel, Madame Bovary, Prince Andrey, Bloom, Proust's 'Je', and the protagonist of Mann's *Doktor Faust* are novel characters. Those familiar with the short stories and novels in which the above-mentioned characters operate cannot fail to perceive the difference between the first group and the second. The first are caught at a particular moment, within narrow limits of time and space, and act in function of a determined event which forms the object of the short story. Whereas the second have a long, ample and tortuous development that unites biographical with ideological data, and they move in a time and space that are both real and abstract, immanent and transcendent. Characters in short stories are the product of lyrical intuitions, Those in novels are symbols. Obviously a character from a novel could never be compressed within the narrow confines of a short story, just as a character from a short story could never be drawn out to the dimensions of a novel without an alteration in his nature.

So the short story is distinguished from the novel in the following ways: non-ideological characters of whom we get foreshortened and tangential glimpses in accord with the needs of an action limited in time and place; a very simple plot, even non-existent in some short stories—when they become prose poems—and in any case one that gets its complexity from life and not from the orchestration of some kind of ideology; psychology in function of facts, not of ideas; technical procedures intended to provide in synthesis what, in the novel, needs long and extended analysis.

Of course all this has little to do with the principal qualities of the short story—I mean that indefinable and inexpressible charm of narration experienced both by the writer and the reader. An exceedingly complex charm, deriving from a literary art which is unquestionably purer, more essential, more lyrical, more concentrated and more absolute than that of the novel. Whereas, by way of compensation, the novel provides a deeper, more complex, more dialectical, more polyhedric and more metaphysical representation of reality than the short story.

So, while the short story comes near to being a lyric, the novel, as we have said, is more likely to rub shoulders with the essay or the philosophical treatise.

1958

ANSWERS TO NINE QUESTIONS ON THE NOVEL

1. Do you think the novel is in crisis as a literary *genre*, or only insofar as it participates in the more general crisis of all the arts?

The novel is not in crisis as a literary *genre*. The techniques of fiction have always been in crisis, that is, in evolution, and the fact that novels today are very different from those of a century or two ago would seem to show that the novel is still in full development. Comparison with the epic poem is not convincing, because the epic poem died precisely through lack of developments and crises; it became fossilised in unchangeable and conventional forms. Anyway, the epic poem lasted for more than two thousand years, and the novel, in the form we know, is scarcely three hundred years old.

But it is certain that the novel participates in the more general crisis of all the arts. Put succinctly, this crisis concerns the relationship between the artist and reality. The Marxists find it easy to point to the crisis between the artist and reality and say that it reflects the alienation of man in the capitalist system. Yet, alas, the Soviet novel and Soviet art in general seem to reflect an analogous and perhaps even greater alienation—but with this difference, that western art recognises the existence of the crisis and expresses it in appropriate ways (as, for example, in music with twelve-tone composition and in painting with abstract art) whereas Soviet art pretends to ignore it.

For these reasons we should probably trace back the crisis between the artist and reality to more distant and subtle causes. One of these is undoubtedly the industrial civilisation in which both capitalist and communist countries participate in equal measure. It is probable that the crisis in the arts is partly due to the peculiar character of industrial civilisation, which has of its very nature an incurable tendency to substitute industrial products for artistic products, either directly by means of substitutes, or indirectly by destroying the surroundings and psychological conditions favourable to artistic creation. For if one views art as a very high form of artisanate (and to a certain extent this is so, just as any artisanate is a modest form of art), it will immediately be seen that art, like the work of the artisan, has been given a death blow by industrial civilisation as regards all products destined for the consumption of the masses—products that industrial civilisation is in a position to provide better and more rapidly than the arts.

The substitutes with which industrial civilisation proposes to replace the novel are plentiful. First of all the cinema, then television, then mass-produced literature such as newspapers, glossy magazines, cartoons and digests. The cinema, like the television, has encroached enormously onto the novel's field, perhaps for ever. To itemise the various ways in which this has been done would be pointless, as they are so well known. Better to say what still remains to the novel, what the cinema cameras will never be able to express and represent owing to the crude and inadequate means at their disposal. Obviously the cinema will never be able to say what Proust said, to take one example. And the significance of this is that it automatically condemns the novel to an enormously restricted readership and enormously restricted subject-matter. In other words the novel, having for several centuries enjoyed the position of being the most popular vehicle for fiction, is now obliged by events to become a product for the few, rather like the theatre.

But these are, so to speak, external aspects of the problem. A more crucial aspect is that the cinema and the television have robbed the novel of the objective representation of reality. Or at least the pseudo-objective and naturalist representation which, from the point of view of the consumer, comes to the same thing. And it is a great deal; indeed it would be almost everything if the novel were to continue to be what it was in the last century.

2. There is a great deal of talk about the essay-type novel. Do you think it is destined to supersede the novel of pure representation or the behaviourist novel? In other words, will Musil supplant Hemingway?

Curiously enough the essay-type novel has nothing in common with the nineteenth-century novel *à thèse*. The essay-type novel is a product of the evolution of the technique of fiction, or, more precisely, of the impossibility and improbability of the third person which today is being increasingly replaced by the first person. This substitution in the recent history of the novel is an indication of the way in which the general crisis in the arts, or the crisis in the relationship between the artist and reality, has hit fiction. For the third person took objective representation and the belief in the existence of the object for granted, a belief shared by both writer and reader. But as the relationship with reality reached a state of crisis, and reality itself became obscure, problematical and difficult to grasp, then the third person was seen to be a convention; that is, it inhibited the illusion and delight of representation in the novel. For conventions are only tolerable when founded on something deep and real. The convention by which nineteenth-century novelists said, 'He thought', was based on a scale of values that allowed for belief in the existence of objective reality. Once this scale of values collapsed, to say 'He thought' seemed an empty and intolerable convention. Hence the need to replace it with 'I thought', for this answers exactly to current conceptions of reality, a conception which sees reality as something whose existence one does not know about, or at any rate as something that exists for each man individually and without prejudice to other entirely different realities.

But the first person is a vehicle that allows for an indefinite widening and deepening of the novel. For while it is very difficult, and anyway artificial, and often boring, to make a third person character say more than the scope of his actions permits, and above all to make him say it without implying an indiscreet intervention by the author, it is very easy and entirely legitimate for a first person character to give himself over to reflections, reasonings and the rest. The third person only allows for the immediate, dramatic representation of the object; the first person allows for analysing him, taking him to pieces, and in certain cases doing without him entirely. But to analyse an object and take it to pieces instead of representing it immediately and dramatically, involves writing an essay, or at least merging an essay with representation. It is for this reason that first person novels often have some sort of resemblance to essays, and readers who can find all the immediate and dramatic representation they want at the cinema, demand more and more that the novel should be an essay, a mediated reflex, an indirect representation.

Oddly enough the novels that most resemble essays are novels of memory, those in which the first person character recalls events in the past. And one can immediately see why: because the material of memory-novels is inevitably arranged in accord with an ideal and ideological time, and not in accord with the naturalistic time of direct and dramatic representation. This ideal or ideological time requires a continuous intervention of reflection, a continuous comment of reason. From this point of view we could say that *À la Recherche* is just one enormous essay.

3. The French school to which Butor, Robbe-Grillet, Natalie Sarraute and others belong proclaims that the novel has at last turned its back on psychology, and that what we need now is to make objects talk and keep to a purely visual reality. What is your opinion?

Robbe-Grillet and the others in France who aim at a visual novel, that is to say a novel in which nothing can be challenged and everything is secure because based on the surest of our senses, sight, would in last analysis favour a dehumanised novel, or one restored to the virgin and terrifying objectivity that may have existed before man appeared on earth. In fact Robbe-Grillet has said,

> It is illegitimate and arbitrary to refer to a smiling sea because the sea has no mouth and hence cannot smile; it is a human characteristic and we are attributing a human character to the sea, or, in other words, using a metaphor. Whereas it is legitimate to refer to 'the blue sea', because that is what it is, and we see it to be blue.

Our first answer to this is that a follower of Dalton would see the sea as another colour. But in addition, the very fact of giving a vast expanse of water the name of sea is equivalent to humanising it, for the fact of indicating an object by a word involves withdrawing it from the anonymous objectivity of the prehuman and extra-human world and incorporating it into the human world. In other words the word 'sea' is only objective in appearance; in reality it humanises, that is subjectivises, the object precisely because it names it. So at most the method only allows for allotting limits to the humanising process, such as not allowing us to forget that the sea has properties and characteristics which are not human.

Hence the proposal for visuality, or for the reduction of reality to what sight perceives, can only have value as a symptom and in polemics. For the rest, even sight selects, that is, expresses judgement. And if we do not wish to select, then ten thousand pages will not be enough to describe even a room.

4. You will have noticed that modern novels are being written more and more in the first person and less and less in the third, and that the first person tends increasingly to be the voice of the author himself (whereas the 'I' in *Moll Flanders*, for instance, is equivalent to the third person). Do you think there could ever be

a return to the purely objective novel of the nineteenth century type? Or do you think the objective novel is no longer possible?

For the answer to this question see the answer to question 2.

5. What do you think of socialist realism in fiction?

Socialist realism is a State and authoritarian attempt to resolve the crisis in the arts along the lines of a State and authoritarian ideology. There can be no worse theoretician of art than the State, and there can be no worse artist than anyone who tries to apply State theories. And this is not only because State theories about art are erroneous (a defence could be put up for the idea of socialist realism) but more because the State by its very nature can, in last analysis, only have in mind the interest of the State, in this case propaganda art. But the main value of socialist realism is that it is a symptom of a situation that confronts us everywhere alike. The solution proposed with abstract art in the West is equivalent to that of socialist realism in the East. But as we have already said, Western solutions have one great advantage over Eastern ones—they are more positive precisely because they are more negative, in other words they recognise the crisis and make it a point of departure instead of suppressing it and claiming to be unaware of it.

6. The problem of language in the novel is primarily a problem of the writer's relation with the reality of his narrative. Do you think language should be transparent like limpid water, in the depths of which all objects can be distinguished? In other words do you believe the novelist ought to let things speak for themselves? Or do you believe the novelist ought to be first and foremost a writer, even a showy writer?

This is a difficult question to answer. As regards what will last,

I feel inclined to say that novelists who let things speak for themselves are more likely to be read in the future than those mainly preoccupied with 'writing' and style—and this for the very good reason that a writer's style, even more than his personality, reflects the taste and fashion of his period, which are perishable things. On the other hand, precisely because he reflects the taste and fashion of his period, the novelist who is a stylist is often more appreciated by his contemporaries than the novelist who lets things speak for themselves. Of course these two ways of writing are not mere matters of form, they are determined by deep and original ways of feeling and for this reason it is impossible to say what should or should not be done. As always in these cases, there is a 'classical' solution which reconciles the two opposites, that of letting things speak for themselves while treating them in a literary and stylistic way. But it has never been possible to define what is 'classical' in advance. The only way of defining it is to attribute moral significance to the word.

7. What do you think of the use of dialect in the novel? Do you think that everything can be said in dialect, or in an idiom akin to dialect? Or do you think that the literary language is the only language of culture and that dialect has very clearly-defined limits?

The use of dialect in Italy always has some sort of link with a crisis in the cultivated language and hence in the ruling class. It is not by chance that the three greatest Italian dialect writers, Goldoni, Porta and Belli, wrote in or around the years of the French Revolution, for the Italian ruling classes were utterly unprepared for the Revolution and were subsequently hostile to it. The use of dialect at that period showed that the cultivated language, which had reached an extreme degree of rarefication and aridity, was incapable of expressing the new realities taking shape in Europe. Similarly, the use of dialect during the last few years is an indication of the crisis in the cultivated language, and the class speaking it, since the Fascist disaster. All the reasons, whether implicit or explicit, for which contemporary writers adopt dialect have to do with this crisis. Some adopt dialect so as to have a firmer hold on reality, above all on popular or provincial reality—the main significance of their distrust of the cultivated language being literary and philological. Others adopt dialect from feelings of sympathy with the humanity of the people and aversion for the ruling classes—their distrust of the cultivated language being thus more social and political than philological. Both groups point to the presence of a serious gulf between the Italian ruling class and culture, between the intellectuals and the bourgeoisie. Obviously the cultivated language is the idiom of culture and dialect the idiom of necessity, but it could be said that nowadays—as often happens with us—necessity and culture are one and the same thing, and hence that the use of dialect is justified and legitimate even from the cultural point of view. Which amounts to saying that in Italy the ruling class is incapable of culture, just as culture has no possibility of imposing its laws on the ruling class.

8. Do you believe in the possibility of a historical and national novel? One, that is, which in some way represents the recent or not so recent achievements of Italy? In other words, do you consider it possible to reconstruct happenings and destinies that go beyond the individual, and are outside their 'historical' time?

I would like to answer this question by asking others. Is it still possible to believe in History? Can national histories still exist in Europe? And what *is* the history of Italy, teeming as it is with defeats that are victories, and victories that are defeats, with the Risorgimento turning into Fascism, with the Church, which was chased out of the door at Porta Pia, coming in at the window with the Concordat and with Italian society willing to sell its soul to the devil only to be able to survive physically between

Communism and the Atlantic Pact? And again, is it not significant that in the greatest historical novel written in Italy, *The Betrothed*, history has no weight and is subject to Providence? And that in *The Leopard*—our latest attempt at a historical novel—history is denied?

9. Who are your favourite novelists, and why?

My favourite novelists are the ones who empty out their bag and say everything they have to say right to the end without regard for the conformisms of their own or future times. My special preference goes to the 'comic' novelists of all ages: Petronius Arbiter, Apuleius, Rabelais, Cervantes, Gogol and so on.

1959

ALESSANDRO MANZONI, OR THE HYPOTHESIS OF A CATHOLIC REALISM

THIS IS not meant to be a preface to *The Betrothed* so much as a few reflective notes concerning a particular aspect of Manzoni's masterpiece. At the origin of these notes lie the faint uneasiness that some of the characters arouse in us and the novel's actuality at the present moment of Italy's history. The uneasiness and the actuality have an obvious link, for the characters that arouse our uneasiness are the very ones that make Manzoni actual—using the word 'actual' in its practical sense; of course *The Betrothed* will always retain the eternal actuality of poetry whatever contingent situations may arise. To put it better: after the Risorgimento, Italian criticism was in the best possible position for extolling Manzoni's great art while justifying, if not ignoring entirely, the aspect that perplexes us today. Of course in Italy at that time there was no likelihood of a Catholic restoration—quite the reverse. But today things are different, and having been for almost a century one of the great books of our literature, *The Betrothed* is now well on its way to becoming a mirror of contemporary Italy (which would have astounded its author). For it is a fact that Manzoni's novel reflects an Italy which, with a few inessential modifications, could be the Italy of today. The religion of *The Betrothed* has many affinities with the religion of contemporary Italy; the society Manzoni described is not all that different from our own; the vices he condemned and the virtues he highlighted are the very vices that afflict us and the very virtues that are encouraged in us now. Moreover the collapse of the Risorgimento, which was swept away with much else by the disaster of Fascism, brought with it the downfall of many of the differences that could have existed between contemporary Italy and the Italy of *The Betrothed.* So Italians today can hardly be expected to look on Manzoni with a spirit of detachment. It has always been difficult to judge oneself.

Add to all this the debt of gratitude our literature owes to Manzoni who, with Verga, is the founder of the modern Italian novel, and it will be easy to see why the question of Manzoni's art of propaganda has never really been raised. True, in the past there has been talk of the art of oratory in connection with *The Betrothed*, but in a way more or less in line with tradition—that is, distinguishing oratory from poetry and taking it in its old humanistic and didactic sense. As far as we know, no one has ever perceived that Manzoni's art of propaganda, viewed either as to its means or its ends, has nothing whatever to do with the old art of oratory, however generically we understand it, or that it originates in an entirely modern concept, namely the totalitarian one, which is no longer content with traditional oratory (too obvious and limited to be effective), but aims at making propaganda by means of poetry itself, or pure representation and this alone. In other words, Manzoni's art of propaganda in many respects anticipates the ways and means of the art of propaganda as the moderns understand it, that is, the writers of the school of socialist realism. From the outset this school, too, saw the traditional art of oratory as inadequate. It aimed not at the cynicism of fine writing, but at the authenticity and sincerity—however rough—of poetry, as being the only guarantee both of the author's sincerity and of the ideology's infallibility. In a similar way modern totalitarianism, not content with the formal submission that satisfied the older tyrannies, demands real faith or the identification of the writer's conscience with the ideology. Of course Manzoni did not aim at this result, but he achieved it all the same when, though in different circumstances, he found himself facing similar problems. So, a century before socialist realism, we have in *The Betrothed* what, for convenience, we might call an attempt at Catholic realism. And if anyone finds the comparison too bold, we need only recall the common ground of social and political conservatism in which both socialist realism and Catholic realism grew. For socialist realism and Catholic realism are the æsthetic products *par excellence* of conservatism. And if, as we shall show, Manzoni's Catholic realism made—luckily for us—many concessions to decadentism, whereas socialist realism, alas, makes none, this is at least partly due to the fact that the conservatism of a society of recent formation such as the Soviet is bound to be more intransigent than that of a society of long duration such as the Italian. But in both cases conservatism and the art of propaganda justify and uphold one another at the expense of the only really revolutionary force that exists in literature: poetry.

The first observation we should make about *The Betrothed* is that it is the most ambitious and complete book that has been written about real Italian life since *The Divine Comedy*. More than Boccaccio who was not concerned with plumbing the depths of things, more than Machiavelli who was a poet of politics, no more than Dante, perhaps, but no less, Manzoni sought to represent the whole Italian world from top to bottom, from the humble to the powerful, from the simplicity of popular commonsense to the sublimity of religion. Naturally Manzoni's ambition was not overt; indeed his attempt to resolve highly complex and difficult problems and to depict a large variety of happenings suggests rather that it was the spontaneous and inevitable product of a universal mind. And yet we should note here that while the poetic results of Dante's poem exceed his ambition, as it were, and thus nullify it, in *The Betrothed* the results, though remarkable, are less than the ambition, and thus we cannot let ourselves ignore it. When compared with *The Divine Comedy*, which seems wholly inspired and poetic even in its didactic parts, *The Betrothed* presents large areas in which the poetry fails, though it cannot be said that it is replaced by oratory. Manzoni intended these areas to be just as poetic as the others, perhaps even more so, but in fact—in spite of himself and without realising it—he anticipated in them what we have defined as an attempt at Catholic realism.

If we want to distinguish the inspired parts in Manzoni's masterpiece from the propaganda parts, we must ask ourselves the well-worn question: Why did Manzoni write a historical novel? In our view the underlying motive which made Manzoni write a novel about an episode in the seventeenth century rather than an episode in his own time can easily be found if we consider the most obvious aspect of *The Betrothed*: the preponderant, massive, indeed excessive, almost obsessive importance given to religion in the novel. This aspect is especially obvious if seen through Italian eyes, but it is no less so if we compare *The Betrothed* with other nineteenth-century masterpieces that were almost contemporary with Manzoni's novel: *Madame Bovary, La Chartreuse de Parme, War and Peace, The Pickwick Papers, Vanity Fair, Le Père Goriot*, and so on. If we could measure out the dosage of religion, whether Catholic or otherwise, in the contents of the sum total of the above-mentioned novels, it would not come to more than five per cent whereas it would jump to a good ninety-five per cent in *The Betrothed*. Yet the authors of these other novels were involved in the same political and social reality as Manzoni, that of European society after the French Revolution. We repeat: in *The Betrothed* the importance of religion is inordinate and obsessive and in no way corresponds to the real condition of Italian and European society in the nineteenth century and this excessive importance explains why Manzoni had recourse to a historical novel. After all he was not a small-scale romantic realist like Scott but a great moral and social realist like Stendhal, and could easily have chosen as subject an episode in contemporary life. But in fact Manzoni's ambition was not only to represent the whole of Italian reality on a huge scale, but to force this reality—without distorting or amputating it in any unnatural way—into the ideological framework of Catholicism. In other words, as we have already pointed out, over a century before socialist realism was thought of, Manzoni raised, in his own way, the problem of a comparable

Catholic realism—that is, of a novel which, with only poetry as means, should achieve a complete identification of the reality represented with the prevailing ideology, or with the ideology he would like to prevail.

Now let us suppose for a moment, however bizarre the supposition may seem, that a Soviet Manzoni took it into his head to tell the story, according to the socialist realist method, of an episode that occurred in the age of the Tsars. Naturally he would avail himself of all the resources of his literary craft to conceal the problems inherent in forcing the reality of the past into the ideology of the present. But our imaginary Soviet Manzoni knows perfectly well that he cannot get out of his difficulties by his literary craft alone, that is with the art of oratory; he knows that much more is expected of him, nothing less than poetry. In other words he knows that he should not apply socialist realism in an extrinsic way but should show that he has found it at the very heart of things, that is, in things that happened decades or even centuries before the revolution. But as he looks at these things more closely he will find they are rebellious, refractory, and extraneous to socialist realism and after a few unsuccessful attempts he will abandon the enterprise and return to the present, that is to say to the familiar circumstances and personalities of five-year plans.

Now just as our Soviet Manzoni is unable, without obvious constraint, to force the reality of the past into the ideological framework of the present, so the real Manzoni was unable, without the same constraint, to force the reality of the present into the ideological framework of the past. We have already pointed out the difference, or rather the abyss, that cuts off *The Betrothed* from the typical nineteenth-century novel. A similar abyss separated Manzoni, as a convinced Catholic, from his own age, inasmuch as his own age, his present, did not permit him to write a novel that was both Catholic and universal. But Manzoni wanted to write a novel in which Catholicism and reality were identical, in which the forces hostile to Catholicism could not claim to be positive either historically or æsthetically, in which propaganda was poetry and poetry was propaganda. So he had to turn his back on his own age and dig into the past for a more propitious moment in history. But which? With a sure instinct he passed over the Middle Ages which had inspired the play *Adelchi*, as they were too far away and different from modern times, and instead chose the seventeenth century when, with the Counter Reformation, Catholicism had attained an appearance of universality for the last time. The seventeenth century was not too far away, at least to some of the more conservative circles of old Milan, as we can see from the poetry of Carlo Porta who had no ambition to make propaganda but confined himself to describing his own age. So to set the novel in the seventeenth century involved no outright invention of characters and situations (as with Scott and other 'historical' novelists), but rather a tracing-back of present characters and situations to their counterparts in the past. So, to sum up: Manzoni chose the past for the same motives for which modern Soviet writers choose the present, and, in the past, he chose the seventeenth century because then, for the last time, Catholicism informed all Italian life just as today Communism informs Soviet life.

At this point someone may ask why Manzoni was not the writer he could have been had he accepted himself and his own time as they really were and not as the Church would have had them be. A Catholic, yes, but not more Catholic than he was in reality, not more Catholic than Boccaccio, Petrarch, Ariosto, or even Dante, and, anyway, sufficiently sure of his own Catholicism not to feel the need to flaunt it. A writer, in brief, to whom the formulation of Catholic realism, or the art of propaganda, did not appear as a necessity and a duty; a writer content to depict the reality of his own time as it was and not as he would have it be. But whoever asks this is forgetting that Manzoni's Catholic realism, like the socialist realism of the Soviets today, was born, and affirmed itself, in opposition to other ways of feeling and representation that carried every bit as much conviction if not more. Manzoni built up his Catholic realism piece by piece in opposition to the illuminism that lay in himself and all around him. Had there been no enemy against whom Manzoni had to defend himself, had the world around him been Catholic through and through like Dante Alighieri's world, with no cracks and no exceptions, then Catholic realism would never have been born. Manzoni would have been like Dante, simply a writer of his own age. We call Manzoni a Catholic writer, but it would never enter our heads to say the same of Dante. Hence in Manzoni's case the word Catholic implies precisely the artistic, and hence historical, limitation peculiar to all propaganda art. Catholic realism, like socialist realism, is born of an aspiration to universality that reality denies, of a totalitarian impulse that is not confirmed by the facts.

We have spoken of the massive, excessive, obsessive importance of religion in Manzoni's masterpiece. This is apparent not only in the number of characters in *The Betrothed* who belong to the clergy—that is, in the clerical character that Manzoni wanted to give Lombard society in the seventeenth century, one certainly not borne out by reality—but also, if we look at the book from the point of view of style, in the language used by the characters which on every possible and impossible occasion forms a continual refrain of pious invocations, giving the impression that seventeenth-century Italians were like Jews in the bronze age. This plethora of religious references is not due to a systematic exposition of Christian doctrine, as with Dante where it appears as something organic, necessary and inseparable from the events. On the contrary, except for the sermons of Cardinal Borromeo, Father Felice and Father Cristoforo, which are pretty modest in concept, this plethora—examined from the point of view of style, and above all in the dialogue—is entirely exclamatory, totally lacking in dramatic necessity and necessity of characterisation. One gets the feeling that it is due not to the tranquil faith of a Christian who knows he has no need to flaunt his faith, but to the anxiety of a convert fearful of not being able to convince himself and his readers that nothing happens save under the aegis of Providence, as though any event that does not seem linked with

Providence in some way contradicts it—which, psychologically, is a characteristically totalitarian preoccupation. So the importance of religion in *The Betrothed* is excessive precisely because it is unsure and betrays an insufficiency rather than a superabundance of inner conviction. Of course Manzoni was religious in spirit (he was religious in an outstandingly genuine way, as we shall see), but probably he was not religious in the manner of Catholic realism, for instance in the manner of Giovanni Papini (to take a well-known example), the manner needed for the art of propaganda. We feel this to be the highest praise possible of Manzoni's religion.

It is, as we know, a delicate point. We shall try to explain our view by a metaphor. Manzoni's masterpiece could be compared to a geological stratification. The first stratum—the one that leaps to the eye and is, in our view, the most superficial—is the art of propaganda fed by a strenuous will to conform and adhere to the Catholic interpretation of life. It is at this level that Catholic realism grows in all its profuse vegetation, like a plant with enormous leaves and tiny roots. The second layer is Manzoni's political and social sensibility which is a phenomenon in its own right and unique in the whole history of Italian literature. To this layer belong all the typical scenes—consistently felicitous with a thread of subtle humour running through them—in which Manzoni illustrates the society of the time; dialogues like the one between the Count Uncle and the Father Provincial, complete scenes like the meal in Don Rodrigo's house, descriptions of ceremonies such as Gertrude's reception or where Cristoforo appears in the presence of the brother of the man he has killed. Finally deep down and further removed is the third layer, that of the genuine, if often obscure, religious and non-religious feelings of the real Manzoni, of the poet Manzoni, of the Manzoni who, besides being a great writer, was also a specific man belonging to a specific society at a specific moment in history. This third layer, speaking broadly and without going into too much detail, can be described by the overall term of Manzoni the decadent, understanding this last word as modern, and giving it a psychological, moral and social significance rather than a literary one. It is to Manzoni's decadentism that we owe the poetry of *The Betrothed*. It will be noted that Manzoni the decadent is the very opposite of Manzoni the Catholic realist—or rather, is the other side of the coin, and it is this that explains and justifies Manzoni's propagandist zeal.

So we find ourselves dealing with a composite novel whose formal perfection is not enough to mask the co-existence of its two parts—the propaganda one, which is never, or only rarely, poetry, and the poetic one which is not propaganda, or is less so than the author would like. If we begin with the first, we will note that the clue to the paucity of inspiration and the purely cerebral procedure is provided by Manzoni's relative inability to fulfil the primary task of Catholic realism—that is, of creating for didactic and propagandist ends absolutely negative and absolutely positive characters, and describing how the former turn into the latter. In other words, and to use Manzoni's terminology, of creating real 'scoundrels' and real 'saints', and describing the transformation, through religious conversion, of scoundrels into saints. This inability, which we shall examine in detail, is very odd in an author like Manzoni who was so obsessed by religion, or holiness, and who was also a convert, that is informed by direct experience in the ways in which the indifferent man and the sinner can be changed into the opposite. Religious conversion, or the transmutation of values, is at the centre of Manzoni's life and the fairly obvious mainspring of all his work. Now, by a curious contradiction, conversion itself is the weak point of *The Betrothed*, the place at which intimate inspiration gives way to the expediencies of Catholic realism. So that if we wanted to understand what conversion is, and how and why it happens, we would have to look to other books, St Augustine's *Confessions* for example, and look elsewhere, too, for Manzoni's poetry.

As we have said, Catholic realism, like socialist realism, is primarily based on the contrast between negative characters and positive characters, and the conversion of the first into the second. In *The Betrothed* the negative characters, taken in order of importance, are: Don Rodrigo, the Unnamed (up to his conversion), Cristoforo (also up to his conversion), Attilio, Egidio, and finally Griso, Nibbio and the other cut-throats. We do not include Gertrude and Don Abbondio among the negative characters because, as we shall see, they do not belong even indirectly to Catholic realism. The first observation we have to make is that Manzoni's negative characters all belong to the category of those in power, to the ruling class, as we should say today. The second observation is that they are not really wicked (except for Egidio of whom we shall speak later) but are given to stupidity or empty and unjustified violence, and this is not because Manzoni wanted it this way—it was in spite of himself or through inadequate portrayal. Thus the wickedness of Manzoni's negative characters has something abstract about it, it is stated, not portrayed, affirmed, nor proved, and on closer inspection we see that this abstraction derives directly from the conservative prejudices of Catholic realism. For we are left with the impression that if, instead of the criterion of religion, Manzoni had had recourse to some other more modern criterion—such as consideration of the social factor—for defining and judging his wicked characters, these, as if by magic, would have found an inner justification for their behaviour. But Manzoni was unable to transfer judgement from the religious plane to the social plane precisely because of his conservatism, the fact that he himself belonged to the same class as the 'scoundrels' he was accusing. So all he did was to point out the evil, but not its origin. He came very near to doing what our modern conservatives do when faced with the Sicilian Mafia: they punish the agents, but take care not to denounce those who give the orders.

If we look at an artist like Flaubert, who was not at all revolutionary but much freer than Manzoni, we see how the wicked character, Homais, who represents petit-bourgeois philistinism, is really wicked and not, like Don Rodrigo, merely stupid. And this because, in the scale of values of Flaubert's book, bourgeois philistinism is truly and intrinsically evil and poetically felt as such by the author. Anyway, it is not at all difficult to create negative and positive characters—even the authors of thrillers can do that. But to do it properly one has to be armed with a poetically valid moral criterion which is not possible in propaganda art, for it substitutes for real good and evil—as the writer would feel them if he let his own temperament take over—the extrinsic and sermonising good and evil of a given society or belief. With the curious result that characters that seem negative to simple common sense are projected as positive, and vice versa, as, for instance, happens with Soviet socialist realism whose positive characters often become odious owing to their endless good example, whereas the negative ones arouse our sympathy because they seem to escape from the general conformity.

When we take a close look at the negative characters of *The Betrothed* we find that the main reason for their inadequacy is that Manzoni never bothers to explain why and how they are wicked. Don Rodrigo takes a fancy for Lucia, so it seems, owing to that form of lust we could call feudal, in that it comes of idleness and privilege. But about this form of lust, so typical and frequent both in seventeenth-century and eighteenth-century Italian society, Manzoni tells us absolutely nothing. We hear Don Rodrigo talking about Lucia for the first time when he says, 'Let's make a bet on it,' to his cousin Attilio. In other words when Manzoni has already substituted for the obvious motive of the lust that of a Spanish-style point of honour, and has turned this into the pivot of a gigantic machination which, as it lacks any deep justification, ends up out of all proportion with its aim. Now we would not expect a direct and explicit description of Don Rodrigo's passion for Lucia, a thing inappropriate to the atmosphere of *The Betrothed*; we would have been satisfied with an allusion in a few words such as portray the similar passion of Gertrude. As this allusion is lacking, Don Rodrigo does not emerge as a wicked man, nor even as a man with a misplaced sense of honour, but only—to use the affectionate term of his uncle, the Count—as a 'bad boy'. To be sure Manzoni did not share this indulgent estimate, but as he was either unwilling or unable to trace back the wickedness to its true cause, he ends up by endorsing it even against his will. This goes to confirm what we have already said about the inadequacy of religion as a criterion for dealing with characters and situations in the modern world.

We shall never know how and why Don Rodrigo became wicked. Manzoni leaves us equally in the dark as to how or why the Unnamed fell into the depths of iniquity in which we find him when Don Rodrigo turns to him for help. True, as compared with Don Rodrigo's wickedness which is handed to us as a piece of information beyond discussion, the Unnamed's wickedness is allotted a lengthier treatment. But if we compare the two chapters that recount Gertrude's story with the few pages devoted to the Unnamed, we realise that Manzoni had no intention of really telling us about this sinister personality. In the few pages in question there is not a single precise fact or characteristic, much less any unfolding of an inclination or a passion; everything is exceedingly vague and generalised. Manzoni, who elsewhere pursues the analysis of the human heart to extraordinary depths, here hovers on the surface with curious reticence and embarrassment. Even the happy invention of the appellation 'the Unnamed' is more than a stroke of sombre coloration but refers to the near-impossibility of defining the man. Why is he called the Unnamed? Are we to lay the blame on Francesco Rivola and Giuseppe Ripamonti who had good practical reasons for not mentioning the name, or on Manzoni who does not name his character because he has failed to give him recognisable features? Anyway it is symptomatic that quotations from the two abovementioned chroniclers are repeated by Manzoni without comment either serious or ironical, as also happens with public proclamations or quotations about the 'anointers'—precisely as proof that they can take the place of the detailed and realistic analysis which we had every right to expect given the importance of the character. We are left with the impression that Manzoni is saying to us, 'He was a wicked man, even his contemporaries said so, so what more can I add?' Whereas it seems obvious that the Unnamed's wickedness, like Don Rodrigo's, is the immediate and typical product of a given society and this is what gave it its form. After rushing through the earlier facts about the Unnamed, Manzoni hurries on to his conversion—an event that would have required deep preparation in view of its enormous significance in the novel's economy.

As for Cristoforo, Manzoni's aim is to make him out to be a man of a violent temper—before his conversion, that is. But alas, we see Cristoforo not as a violent man but as an impulsive one, which is quite another matter: violence is an incorrigible passion of the spirit, impulsiveness is a graduation of action. Cristoforo's real passion, seen in black and white, is really of a social kind that nowadays we should call inferiority complex. But was Manzoni aware that Cristoforo's conversion seems due, not to spiritual travail, but to a kind of haughty inversion of his inferiority complex which initially urges him to assert himself by violence, and then prompts him to do the same by humility? No, Manzoni's intention seems to be to portray a fundamentally good but violent, misled man. From this unresolved relationship between author and character comes our dissatisfaction with the figure of Cristoforo, alike before and after his conversion.

Given these premisses and the failure to provide motives for, or reconstruct, the Unnamed's wickedness and Cristoforo's violence, it is hardly surprising that the conversions of these two characters—that is, their metamorphosis from 'scoundrels' into 'saints'—are not at all convincing. Of the two conversions, the one least unacceptable, though only faintly inspired by really religious feelings, seems to be Cristoforo's. Manzoni presents it for us as a social fact rather than a religious one. Its suddenness seems motivated not so much by a sudden illumination as by the practical necessity in which Cristoforo finds himself—that of extricating himself as rapidly as possible from the vicious circle in which he is caught. For all its Counter-Reformation and baroque characteristics, Cristoforo's conversion, then, seems plausible if not admirable. And the scene of Cristoforo's voluntary self-humiliation before the relatives of the man he has killed is a very fine and mannered picture in the style of similar seventeenth-century scenes in the story of the Nun of Monza.

As for the conversion of the Unnamed, from our point of view it is the weakest point of the whole novel, whereas it should have been the strongest—for surely the conversion of a 'scoundrel' into a 'saint' is the biggest test and focal centre of Catholic realism. What is the aim of propaganda art? To convert unbelievers. In what way? By showing them why and how they should be converted. Now, if we read St Augustine's *Confessions*—a book which treats of conversion clearly and simply and within the range of the most uninitiated reader—we feel an almost contagious sense of the irresistibility of conversion whereas the episode of the Unnamed's conversion leaves us at most lukewarm. The Unnamed, once nameless in his wickedness, has become nameless in his goodness. He is a character without a face; he moves over from generalised wickedness to didactic goodness. And the extraordinary thing is that many critics consider the Unnamed's 'night', as it is called, to be among Manzoni's best passages. Any such judgement can only bear witness to a pretty limited experience of the religious act. The truth is that the Unnamed's crisis follows no inner logic proper to him and to him alone, and nor could it, for—as we have said—the psychological situation existing before the crisis was never deeply explored. But the Unnamed's crisis does follow, and point by point, the rules of Catholic realism. Manzoni deliberately turns his back on his own invaluable experience as a convert, which would have served him well in describing a situation in some respects similar, and clings with great logic but little penetration to the portrayal of the ideal conversion of an exemplary 'scoundrel' into an equally exemplary 'saint'. Already before the conversion, the potentially strong scene between the Unnamed and Lucia is in fact surprisingly weak, lacking light and shade and all those contrasts needed to suggest the presence of two psychologies and two distinct and opposing outlooks on life. In this scene the real weakling is the Unnamed, in spite of his angry grimaces straight from a puppet show; he is weak because he is not really wicked, not because wickedness itself is weakness. The really strong character is Lucia, but her strength flounders in a vacuum precisely because the Unnamed's wickedness is not there. Consequently once the Unnamed is by himself, his conversion is coldly and skilfully presented to us, step by step, until he reaches the rock-bottom of his crisis—the temptation to suicide. From this point, starting out with his recollection of Lucia's words, 'God forgives so many things for one work of mercy'—a very precise phrase which indicates not only the cost but the profit of the imminent conversion—the Unnamed begins climbing up the slope again, step by step, until the meeting with Cardinal Borromeo. We have said that his conversion is coldly and skilfully graded; we should now add that it is precisely this shrewd and impersonal gradation that betrays its edifying and didactic character. For it is not the conversion of an individual person—indeed how could it be as the Unnamed himself does not exist?—but a typical conversion, the conversion of everyone and no one, in other words conversion according to Catholic realism. Every bit of it is propaganda, technique, literature, without a single genuine moment—at the very place where Manzoni could most easily have moved us, had he so wished. Yet even here we cannot speak of the art of oratory, for, just like the socialist realist writers, Manzoni intended not to make propaganda but poetry; that is, he intended to give us a poetic reality effectively inspired by Catholicism. He failed; he had to rely on his superb literary technique. Never mind, he is a poet here as elsewhere, even if elsewhere he succeeds in his intention, and here he fails.

It is surely no accident that the absolutely positive character in *The Betrothed*, Cardinal Borromeo, comes up against the absolutely negative one, the Unnamed. It is no accident because the Unnamed, as we have said, is a character created by Catholic realism, so a saint such as the Cardinal, made of the same propagandist material, would obviously be the person to receive him on his conversion. What can we say about the Cardinal? He stands in the centre of the novel like a baroque statue under a gold and marble canopy at the heart of the Counter-Reformation Church; or like a figure by a mannerist painter, all eyes up to heaven, hands joined, halo and ecstasy, upright before a background of stormy clouds and shafts of light. It is a great stylised painting, admirable in its complete and perfect literariness, amusing and interesting if looked on as a sheer product of talent without regard to the meaning Manzoni wants to attribute to it. To be sure the Cardinal expresses himself very well. Even Manzoni grows aware of it and issues his warning at the beginning of Chapter XXVI:

> ... and to tell the truth, even we, sitting with our manuscript in front of us, and a pen in our hands, even we, I say, feel a certain reluctance to proceed. We find something rather strange in this proposal, with so little effort, of a series of such admirable precepts of heroism and charity, of keen solicitude for others, and of unlimited sacrifice of self. But reflecting that these things were said by one who actually practised them, we will forge bravely ahead.

But while this warning note is a proof of Manzoni's artistic awareness, it cannot—and how could it?—modify the Cardinal's fundamentally propagandist character. And let it here be noted, *à propos* of Manzoni's famous irony that can be glimpsed even in the above quotation, that while it is always deep and beguiling in the truly realist parts of the novel, it seems inadequate, if not positively non-existent, in the Catholic realist parts. The absolutely negative characters such as Don Rodrigo or the Unnamed are taken as seriously as the absolutely positive figures such as Cardinal Borromeo and Father Cristoforo. And this because Manzoni's irony serves always to indicate a complete command of the material; it is inseparable from his poetry. Where it is lacking or inadequate, we guess that Manzoni is operating within fine writing which by its very nature is refractory to irony.

Another of the positive characters of Catholic realism is Cristoforo after his conversion. We have had to divide him into two distinct figures for the purposes of what we are trying to prove. He closely resembles Cardinal Borromeo, the more so as he is shown us in similar situations to the Cardinal's (compare the dialogues between Father Cristoforo and Don Rodrigo, and

Cardinal Borromeo and Don Abbondio), and it would be easy to put the friar's sermons into the Cardinal's mouth, and vice versa. But Cristoforo is less of a success artistically than the Cardinal for his action spreads through the whole book and displays the immobility of oratory, whereas the Cardinal is restricted to a short and circumscribed episode. Father Cristoforo is the character with whom Manzoni's Catholic realism has least happy results. The simile with which Chapter VII begins,

> Fra Cristoforo arrived with the air of an able general who has lost an important battle through no fault of his own and goes hurrying off, distressed but not discouraged, worried but not overwhelmed, in haste but not in flight, to reinforce points that are hard pressed, rally his troops, and give out fresh orders . . .

is ugly and almost ridiculous in a way rare in Manzoni, who is possibly second only to Dante for beauty, originality, and apposite imagery. It serves to measure the icy exteriority into which the man who created Don Abbondio or Gertrude falls when he begins applying the rules of Catholic realism. Would Father Cristoforo have been different without Catholic realism? No, he would not have been different, he would simply have disappeared from the novel, for he owes his existence to a kind of subtraction Manzoni made from the character of Renzo in the interests of Catholic realism. In other words Father Cristoforo either preaches sermons, that is, does nothing, or else does the things that Renzo should have done had his character been exploited to the full. It is he who confronts Don Rodrigo instead of Renzo, he makes the Christian reproaches to Renzo that Renzo should have made to himself, he takes on his shoulders part of the persecution in fact destined for Renzo. He is an intermediary in a cowl, superfluous like all intermediaries, who allows Manzoni to leave nothing to the personal initiative of his hero, and to correct his conduct with literary precepts whenever necessary. He is Renzo's conscience, confiscated for the Church's benefit and embodied in a churchman. This is not to deny at all that in seventeenth-century Lombardy such situations could have occurred, of two innocent victims of persecution putting themselves under the protection of a friar. Let us say that the character of Father Cristoforo reveals the smoothness of propaganda rather than the ruggedness of reality.

So far we have been discussing Manzoni's Catholic realism, and seeking to explain the failure of the religious propaganda understood by Manzoni in a thoroughly modern sense—that is to say not as oratory but as poetry, and the only possible poetry. We have said that the clue to the abstract nature of Catholic realism lies in the conversions of Cristoforo and the Unnamed—that is to say in the transformation, by means of religion, of negative characters into positive characters. Now we have to add that when it comes to representing corruption, and corrupt characters, Manzoni excels. What is corruption? It is the exact opposite of conversion. In conversion the character proceeds from bad to good, in corruption from good to bad. It is the transformation of a positive character, or one at least potentially positive, into a negative character. Moreover Manzoni excels when it comes to depicting what we should call public corruption. This consists in society passing from a state of normality to one of abnormality, from a state of order to one of disorder, from a state of prosperity to one of abject poverty. Incidentally, we must note that Manzoni, who expends so much effort on depicting conversion, or the transit from evil to good in the individual, never dealt with the public equivalent to conversion, that is revolution. Or rather he dealt with it in the episode of the hunger riots in which both Renzo and the crowd are inspired by unreservedly revolutionary feelings; but it is typical of Manzoni's conservatism that the whole episode is interpreted in terms of its opposite, in terms of the corruption of a previous state which was positive only because it was the *status quo*.

So when we are dealing with Manzoni's excellence in describing private and public corruption, it is hardly necessary to emphasise the complete success of the character of Don Abbondio, the character of a man slowly and deeply corrupted by fear. Who is Don Abbondio? If Providence is the chief protagonist of *The Betrothed*, then Don Abbondio is her opposite, the one who not only does not perform miracles, but does not even do what he could or should do like other men. In this way, besides being the opponent of Providence, he is—like all those who do not do their duty—its very justification. Don Abbondio refuses to marry Renzo and Lucia because he is afraid; Providence intervenes in the shape of the flea that bites a plague-ridden rat and so transmits the plague to Don Rodrigo. Don Abbondio believes in nothing, not even in Providence. So great is his unbelief that he will not agree to perform the wedding until it is mathematically certain that the plague, which has already carried away several hundreds of thousands of Milanese, has also made away with Don Rodrigo. For Don Abbondio is not a wicked man but a corrupt man, and his corruption in a corrupt society is looked on with indulgence even by those who are not corrupt. Like the thieves in Butler's *Erewhon*, he is a sick man who deserves compassion rather than hatred.

At the beginning of the novel Don Abbondio is presented to us as a man aware of where good lies and even inclined to perform it. Upright even, an important trait. In other words so far Don Abbondio has done nothing outrageous. Manzoni brings out what could be called the positive side of Don Abbondio in strong relief, so that, later on, the negative effect of Don Rodrigo's injunction will stand out all the more sharply in its corruption. This corruption is a sickness of soul. But Manzoni underlines its diseased nature by the fever that strikes Don Abbondio immediately after his meeting with the cut-throats, a fever that persists throughout the novel and ends only with the death of Don Rodrigo. Thus we have the story of Don Abbondio whereas we do not have the story of Don Rodrigo. But we have it because Don Abbondio is not wicked—though he does evil—but only corrupt, because Manzoni unloads Don Abbondio's guilt onto Don Rodrigo though, as we have seen, telling us nothing whatever as to how Don Rodrigo became the wicked man he is. Thus

Don Abbondio's corruption remains rather in mid-air, as it does to Don Abbondio himself, as something that can be forgiven because attributed to remote causes and obscured by a whole number of distant responsibilities. That is to say we find ourselves on the ambiguous soil of corruption, not on the clear unequivocal soil of wickedness.

Don Abbondio's character has been compared to Sancho Panza. But this is not really exact because in *The Betrothed* there is no Don Quixote to act as a foil to Don Abbondio's cowardice and make it comic; Cardinal Borromeo is the opposite of a Don Quixote, and so Don Abbondio's conscience has to do without the salutary stimulus of Don Quixote. True, he seems to be aware of his wrongdoing for a moment during his interview with the Cardinal, but only for a moment. When the plague is over and he meets Renzo again, he is just as cautious as ever—'You want to ruin yourself, and you want to ruin me.' It is the moment to say that Don Abbondio is the perfect exponent of a particularly Italian kind of corruption, which, for want of a better word, we shall call historical. In Italy one is always coming across men of every class, profession or status, powerful or humble, famous or unknown, intelligent or stupid, old or young, rich or poor, who display a fear of speaking their minds, of offending some authority or other, of taking down their defences, of compromising themselves, of letting themselves go and saying what they think about whatever it may be. At first one is tempted to attribute this to some particular self-interest that might explain, if not excuse, it. But more often than not, no such interest exists. All that exists is fear, fear without any immediate or apparent cause, and coupled with fear, and just as strong, the liking for a quiet life. And as there is no immediate cause we feel almost obliged to delve back to a distant, indirect, ancestral and historical one, so that we think, We must blame the Counter-Reformation, foreign governments, Italian tyrannies, heaven knows what, for this man having water in his veins instead of blood. Don Abbondio's character is living and immortal because he is the very embodiment of a national corruption so ancient that by now it seems second nature.

Don Abbondio is corrupted by the fear instilled in him by Don Rodrigo's cut-throats, whereas Gertrude is corrupted by the suggestion implanted in her by her father and the society to which she belongs. The story of the Nun of Monza has always been praised as one of the finest parts of *The Betrothed*, and with reason. It is not by chance, we might add, that it is the story of a long and tortuous corruption, the transformation of an innocent person into a wicked one, followed step by step with a wonderful, realistic and inventive capacity that we would look for in vain in the descriptions of the conversions, or transformations of wicked characters into good ones. For instance we know nothing of the childhood of the Unnamed; whereas we first meet Gertrude when she is 'still hidden in her mother's womb'. The progressive metamorphosis of the innocent baby into a desperate liar, then a faithless nun, then an adulteress, and finally a criminal, is as strong as anything that has ever been written on the subject of corruption. If we compare the story of Gertrude with the similar one in Diderot's *La Réligieuse*, we feel we are comparing a deep well of black, still water with a swift, clear stream. For whereas Diderot knows the causes of the corruption and points them out for us, Manzoni—as in the case of Don Abbondio—prefers silence. For Diderot the catharsis takes place outside the novel as result of the pending Revolution that the author seems to be forecasting in every line he writes. For Manzoni, the conservative and Catholic, the only possible catharsis is æsthetic, and very remarkable it is, but a catharsis that is only æsthetic is peculiar to decadentism. Even the rottenness in the State of Denmark is purified in a practical way with the blast of trumpets, after the bloody supper, heralding the arrival of Fortinbras. But Gertrude's corruption is a 'fine' corruption, a mysterious, dark corruption, without cause and seemingly without effect; begotten of an ambiguously historical and social destiny, it is lost in the silence and shadow of the Church.

At all events, this decadent Manzoni is at the peak of his powers. In the story of Gertrude (unlike the story of the Unnamed) there is no moment of abstraction, nothing is stated without being shown, or said without being illustrated. This time we have a close series of pictures pressing one after the other—things, objects, situations, characters. Here Manzoni is not content to play the impartial historian, as when he summarised the Unnamed's criminal career in a few pages. From the outset he establishes a strong subjective relationship with the figure of Gertrude, a relationship composed both of sorrowful pity and refined cruelty. So we are utterly astonished to find Benedetto Croce maintaining that the 'method' used in constructing the successful characters in *The Betrothed* is the same as that used in constructing the characters that belong to Catholic realism. For ourselves, we are not going to discuss method, for we have no idea what it means in connection with poetry, but rather the greater or less relationship between the artist and his material. A lively and complex relationship runs between Manzoni and Don Abbondio and Gertrude; whereas between Manzoni and the Unnamed there is little or no relationship, unless we are to use the word relationship about the instrumental relationship between a propaganda writer and his prefabricated and didactic material.

Strange to say the total wickedness that Manzoni was unable to portray in Don Rodrigo (silly rather than wicked) or the Unnamed (quite unreal), he is able to describe in a few lines and with perfect felicity in telling the story of Gertrude's corruption. For here we have Don Egidio, a wicked man, wickeder than Don Rodrigo or the Unnamed because, unlike them, he has motives for his wickedness, and the very modern motives of sadism and sacrilegious lust at that.

> Our manuscript calls him Egidio without mentioning his family name. This fellow had noticed Gertrude from a little window that overlooked a courtyard in the wing of her appartments as she sometimes idly passed or strolled there; and *attracted, rather than alarmed, by the dangers and impiety of the undertaking*, one day ventured to address her. The wretched woman replied.

The provision of a brief, but deeply psychological, motive for

Egidio's behaviour is entirely lacking in the case of Don Rodrigo, and we shall never know why or how he took a fancy to Lucia; and this is because Don Rodrigo is a wicked man without roots, in function of Catholic realism, whereas Egidio is a wicked man who is justified, a functionary of the corruption for which, as we have seen, Manzoni had a special feeling. But in the course of the story of Gertrude, Manzoni paints good as well as bad. Here, for instance, we have a few lines that are worth all the edifying eloquence of Cardinal Borromeo:

> One might think that Gertrude would be drawn to other nuns who had not taken part in those intrigues, who liked her as a companion without having wanted her as one, and who showed by their pious, busy and cheerful example how one could not only live, but be happy, there . . . She might have been less against them had she known or guessed that the few black balls found in the box which had decided her acceptance had been put there by them.

Here the goodness is real, deep and mysterious, not the merely preached and mannered goodness of the Cardinal or Father Cristoforo. And as with Egidio's wickedness, we must note that the goodness, too, exists in function of corruption, gets its justification from corruption and is the counterweight to corruption.

To be sure the picture changes when we turn from private to public corruption. There are no more gloomy, narrow, individual destinies, like the episode of the Nun of Monza, nor ruthless caricatures as with Don Abbondio, but collective disasters and tragedies with history as background. Yet if we look closely we see that the procedure is the same. Manzoni begins by showing us the normal, positive, upright condition which is destined to be corrupted: the Duchy of Milan before the war, the city of Milan before the plague. Thereupon, with cruel precision, he notes down the first symptom of corruption, the tiny cloud in the clear sky out of which the storm will develop—the political and military punctilio of the King of Spain that will lead to German troops passing through the Valtellina, and Lovati's entry into

Milan—the soldier who introduces the plague. Thereafter, slowly and powerfully and very gradually, he describes the progress of the corruption and its final overflowing. As we have said, the procedure is the one he follows when describing private corruption, and now we should add that what in private corruption is psychological in public corruption becomes physical and material. Gertrude's degradation has its counterpart in the diffusion of the plague in Milan; and it is with the same almost clinical complacency that Manzoni notes both the increasing disintegration of the Nun of Monza and the increasing havoc of the plague. Though unquestionably the episode of Gertrude, for all its strength, stands out less in our minds, and has less importance, than the part devoted to the plague.

It is not difficult to find the reason for the domination of the plague, which, together with the gentle landscapes and certain specific emotions, forms the principal characteristic of Manzoni's singular world. The reason is that a plague is absolute corruption, corruption generalised to cover the particular: with its swellings and fevers and blight of the whole body it is the symbol of all that is unwholesome and disintegrated; and with its mysterious and irresistible way of spreading it is the very image of moral evil against which no defence is possible. So, unique among all writers in all ages for having made a plague one of the principal subjects of his novel, Manzoni (by using the general to cover the particular) is *the* painter of disease or corruption. But there are plagues and plagues; the plague in *The Betrothed*, unlike the plagues in Boccaccio and Defoe, owes its fame to the fact that Manzoni really feels it as a primarily moral phenomenon—rather like the seven plagues of Egypt in the Old Testament. So when he is describing the plague Manzoni feels, so to speak, in his element, in a metaphysical and universal corruption that spares nothing and no one. As in the part devoted to the Nun of Monza, so here in the plague, Manzoni reaches the peak of his art—for instance with the famous incident when the mother hands over her dead child to the *monatti* or corpse-bearers, or the episode of Don Rodrigo. The truth is that corruption inspires the decadent

Manzoni every bit as much as conversion weakens and deflates his expressive powers.

The plague, then, as we have said, is corruption *par excellence*. But in *The Betrothed* there are other forms of public corruption, described with the same power, the same slowly mounting drama, the same satisfaction: the episode of the shortages that lead up to the bread riots; that of the war which culminates in the sacking and devastation of the villages invaded by the troops; the one concerning justice, centred round Renzo's arrest, and even earlier in the scene between Renzo and 'Tangle-Weaver', the lawyer. An underlying idea can be seen running like a thread through all these episodes of public corruption. Man can do nothing against evil; evil has to work itself out to the bitter end: then Providence will take charge in its inscrutable manner so as to save those individuals or societies worthy of salvation. Which means we are up against a pessimism of the conservative kind that harmonises well with decadentism, or the delighted and apathetic contemplation of that evil which is judged to be beyond remedy. This explains why, in *The Betrothed*, the descriptions of social unrest have a close resemblance to those of the plague. Manzoni, who is conservative because he is decadent and decadent because he is conservative, has no belief in palingenesis and rebirth. He interprets social unrest in terms of sterile and disorderly tremors in sick organisms incapable of cure.

Now let us take a further step forward. As we have said, corruption signifies the opposite process to the process of conversion. In conversion you go from evil to good; in corruption you go from good to evil. But in corruption there is also something else; corruption can last indefinitely and become chronic. At times the progress of corruption is so gradual that it passes unobserved. Men, societies, nations, grow corrupt slowly—by stages so imperceptible that they do not observe them. Moreover the corrupt man, the corrupt society, the corrupt nation, do not want—owing to their conservatism—to reform, so they end up by accepting their corruption. Now, for all Manzoni's moralism, it is precisely this that we notice in *The Betrothed*. Corruption, though described with such power, originality and depth, is given no cathartic outlet; it stagnates in the book rather as it stagnates in Italian life, whether yesterday or today. Don Abbondio is corrupted by fear and so he remains to the end; Gertrude is corrupted by lying and cannot escape; Milanese society, for all 'the great broom' of the plague, remained corrupt; and men like Tangle-Weaver and Don Rodrigo and Attilio, who have been carried away by the plague, will be replaced, we feel, by others equally overbearing and dishonest. The point is not that we would like to see these people change their characters, or Milanese society undergo radical reform, it is rather that the make-up of both characters and society excludes any ideal element, that is, any real awareness of corruption. To take a single example: Chichikov, the hero of Gogol's *Dead Souls*, is every bit as corrupt as Don Abbondio, even more so. Yet Chichikov has a semblance of awareness of evil, and it is this that allows him to be a protagonist. Whereas Don Abbondio gets no further than being anything but a huge caricature.

So the stuffy atmosphere of *The Betrothed*, which Tommaso Scalvini attributed to 'a temple that covers the faithful and the altar', is not due to religion (in *The Divine Comedy*, too, we find ourselves in a temple, and yet we can breathe there as deeply as we like), but to Manzoni's conservatism which, like all conservatisms, is decadent and fascinated by corruption, yet incapable of finding a solution on any but the æsthetic plane. *The Betrothed* is a nineteenth-century villa, not a temple, and the air we breathe there is not dogma but social conservatism. This decadent conservatism, or conservative decadence, leads directly, as we have already noted, to Catholic realism, or the attempt to overcome corruption by means of propaganda.

But like all conservatives who are disinterested and in good faith, Manzoni nursed in his heart the dream of a different life, a life incorrupt, pure, simple and outside history—in other words, harmless and in keeping with his conservatism. It is in this dream, as we see it, and not in Catholic realism, that we find the ideal counterbalance to corruption. This dream is expressed in the figures of the two main characters and in the world they represent.

We have kept Renzo and Lucia to the last because they are the finest and most original figures in *The Betrothed*, and also the key to Manzoni's conception of life, society and religion. Unlike Gertrude, these two characters have not been reconstituted from history, in the manner of an essay; we see them through what they do, like Don Rodrigo and the Unnamed. But, unlike Don Rodrigo and the Unnamed, they are alive and real. For the wickedness of Don Rodrigo and the Unnamed are cerebral, whereas Renzo and Lucia have qualities and defects that are intuited by sympathy. What are these qualities and defects? Lucia is gentle, sweet, discreet, bashful and reserved; yet at times affected, obstinate, peasantlike, and inclined to take pleasure in work too much following a kind of stereotyped perfection. Renzo is frank, honest, brave, full of good sense and energy; but also at times stupid, rash and violent. As we can see from the sum of these qualities and defects, Manzoni wanted to portray two peasant figures whom he had probably had the opportunity of observing at length in real life before re-creating them in art—doubtless in the country round Lake Como itself. Manzoni's social sensitiveness, which was so subtle and quick, can be appreciated yet again in these two characters in whom we see all the attributes of a lower social rank yet without that detachment and sense of superiority that often accompany portraits of the kind. Manzoni managed to look on Renzo and Lucia with real affection; the well-known remark at the end of Chapter XV—'that name for which we too feel some affection and reverence'—was not a literary device but the plain and simple truth. Affection of this kind was new and original. In Manzoni's time, as in ours for that matter, to have two working people as the hero and heroine of a novel demanded a not inconsiderable qualitative leap, and a powerful capacity for idealisation. We can judge of the novelty of Manzoni's affection for Renzo and Lucia when we consider that we had to wait for Verga to find another Italian writer who turned a brotherly eye towards the ordinary people.

Manzoni has gathered around Renzo and Lucia, as around two modest but truly venerated idols, all the things he loves in his heart, all the things he contrasts with the society of Gertrude, Don Rodrigo and the Count Uncle. That is to say, with his own society, and in general with society as borne out by history. For to Manzoni history seems nothing but corruption; and Renzo and Lucia are not corrupt precisely because they are outside history. The equation, history = corruption, antihistory = purity, is especially easy to observe in those places where Manzoni puts one of his two main protagonists, who are pure and outside history, face to face with a character who is corrupt because he belongs to history: Renzo and Tangle-Weaver, Renzo and Don Abbondio, Renzo and Ferrer, and, even more, Lucia and Gertrude. In the meeting between these last two we find the fundamental contrast of *The Betrothed* in all its force and significance. On one side there is the country girl who 'blushes and hangs her head', on the other the lustful and criminal young abbess whose portrait is among the finest and the most powerful in the whole novel. At last Gertrude is confronted not by a secondary character but by her opposite. When we compare the brief but real meeting between Lucia and Gertrude with the meeting that is all eloquence and mannerism between Lucia and the Unnamed, we can see that the real contrast between good and evil in *The Betrothed* is not the contrast between the holiness of religion and the impiety of the wicked—along the lines of Catholic realism—but between the natural purity of people and the corruption of history and the classes that make history.

In any case Renzo and Lucia act as catalysts, and everything that Manzoni loved and cherished gathers spontaneously around them. Manzoni described horrors and terrors every bit as much as Poe, if not more, and with a sensibility not all that different. Yet when we use the word 'Manzonian' we imply something very different from the macabre and the terrifying; we imply something gentle, sweet, idyllic, homely, affectionate; something recalling Virgil and Petrarch—that very something which, in the novel, we know as Renzo and Lucia. It is to them that we owe his famous passage of goodbye to the mountains and the flight towards the river Adda; to them we owe his paintings of Lombard landscapes, his loveliest metaphors and images, his poetic passages of family intimacy; to them we owe all that was truly religious in Manzoni—not the religion of Catholic realism along the lines of Father Cristoforo and Cardinal Borromeo, but his own religion, which was, after all, the religion of his hero and heroine. Manzoni's character as creator of Renzo and Lucia—either because it is more positive and lovable than his character as creator of Gertrude and the plague, or else because it corresponds more closely to the Italian sensibility—has finally prevailed over all the alternatives, so much so that it has become almost proverbial and has strengthened Manzoni's public image (incomplete, to say the least) as an educationalist and a faithful and peaceful mirror of the Christian and middle-class virtues of the nineteenth century.

So when we define and explain Renzo and Lucia, we are really defining and explaining Manzoni's ideal world, with the qualities of his decadent sensibility and the rather narrow boundaries of his upper-class conservatism. Who are Renzo and Lucia? They are two working-class people. Their life is extremely simple because they are poor and because they live in a little country village with only a few houses, a mere hamlet. So we have the first ideal: poor, simple country life, not to say primitive and needy country life. Life with no public duties, that is; no civic responsibilities, no political ambitions, no financial cares, in fact none of the headaches of the city-dweller. Life fined down to the bone: work, the family.

But in the little hamlet, the small cluster of houses in which Renzo and Lucia live, there is a church. Renzo and Lucia are religious. Hence, in addition to poor, simple country life, there is also the ideal of a religion that expresses this life directly. It has been said too often that the background of Manzoni's religion was Jansenist; perhaps it was so in his life, but in *The Betrothed* there is nothing to show it. In fact Renzo's and Lucia's religion —which is also the religion of Manzoni, the cultivated and intellectual aristocrat—has much closer links with the parish than the library and is as far removed from learning as is possible. It is the religion of two uneducated people who can neither read nor write; the religion, as we have said, of humble people, and of two such humble people as Renzo and Lucia. It is a religion of the heart rather than of the head, of feeling rather than of reason. A religion, incidentally, that is very modern; the only one, indeed, that is still felt and practised today in a sincere and whole-hearted way by the Catholic masses of the world.

In order to become acquainted with the religion of *The Betrothed* we need only compare it with the religion of Dante Alighieri—keeping strictly to its æsthetic results. In *The Divine Comedy* religion penetrates everywhere and is nowhere imposed. There is no line of demarcation between religion and culture, politics, society, *mores*. In *The Betrothed*, on the other hand, religion seems to be the almost exclusive inheritance of humble (that is, uneducated) people; whenever Manzoni turns to describing the ruling (that is, the educated) classes, religion disappears and one gets the impression that it has never existed. Renzo's and Lucia's religion (that is, Manzoni's religion) has for long lost all relationship with learning. The result is that politics (the Thirty Years War, Don Gonsalvo of Corduba, Ambrogio Spinola), learning (the caricature of Don Ferrante) and history as a whole, all fall an easy prey to Manzoni's corrosive irony. With an author of less artistic stature than Manzoni, less reflective, less deep, less complicated, the caricature of Don Ferrante, or the discussion of the Thirty Years War, would have a purely reactionary ring. And this not because Don Ferrante's learning was not a hotch-potch of superstition and mistaken ideas and the politics of the Thirty Years War was not to a great extent absurd, but because Manzoni seems to conclude from this that all learning and all politics are equally misleading and unnecessary. Manzoni makes fun of Don Ferrante because he studied erroneous and misleading books, and does not seem to realise that after all Don Ferrante was a respectable person precisely because he read and studied, even if the books were false and misleading. Similarly, when Manzoni pulls the Thirty Years War to pieces he does not seem to realise that that war was simply a reflection of the war of ideas that was tearing Europe apart at that time and was to end with the rise and establishment of the Reformation countries on the ruins of the Spanish Empire. Assuredly, however, these things could not have the slightest importance as seen through the eyes of two poor little peasants; and especially as seen through the spectacles of their simple religion.

We must remark at this point that the ideal of the poor and simple life, of ignorance, and the religion of the heart, is nevertheless not so extreme and thus revolutionary in Manzoni as, for instance, the fundamentalist and uncompromising evangelism of Tolstoy. Tolstoy, as everyone knows, wanted to live out his ideal to its end, to the point of himself becoming a peasant and working in the fields; whereas Manzoni, as is equally well known, for all his sincere sympathy for humble people, did not himself become humble but spent his life as a shrewd and astute administrator of his property. In reality, as we have said, Manzoni's ideal has narrow limits imposed by his conservatism. It is the ideal of the good master who looks benevolently on the simple people who work for him, treats them with affection and humanity, but never for a moment forgets that he is the master. The ideal, in Manzoni's own words, of the marquis heir of Don Rodrigo who was humble enough to set himself below Renzo and Lucia but not to be on an equality with them. This ideal is made perfectly innocuous as being maintained with great firmness within the limits of a given society—the society Manzoni himself belonged to.

This paternalistic and patronal limitation can be detected in all those places in *The Betrothed* where Renzo and Lucia—or Agnese or the other humble people—are on the scene, by an extremely light, almost imperceptible, yet firm and exact, nuance of upper-class detachment; but above all those passages where Manzoni's affection is tempered with indulgent irony. It is typical of his complicated psychology that after he has made fun of Don Ferrante's learning, Manzoni makes use of the same learning to make fun gracefully of poor Renzo who is the very opposite of Don Ferrante and has no learning whatsoever. It is Manzoni's way of circumscribing his own ideal and making it harmless; a typically paternalistic way based on the superiority of better education. All the part about Renzo on the road and in the inn after the hunger riots shows a masterly play of this indulgent, yet strongly restrictive, irony of the good master who sees one of his peasants having a drink too many and talking a whole lot of nonsense about things he does not understand and are above his head. Here, and in similar places, the Manzoni who idealises humble people is interrupted by the Manzoni who sees them as they are, naturally in terms of his experience as a master.

Here—to put it frankly—we come to one of Manzoni's most disconcerting sides. And we are all the more perplexed because it is a side closely bound up with Renzo and Lucia, with the two people who are the finest and most original in the book. Critics have often said that the best parts of *The Betrothed* are those that treat of humble characters or Manzoni's feelings of sympathy towards them. And we have already pointed out just how much we agree with this judgement. But there is humility and humility. There is Christian humility which is a universal virtue common to rich and poor alike, and there is servile humility, social, inferior humility which is special to the poor and the outcome of age-long oppression and humiliation. Now we in no wise deny that Manzoni intended to extol that first kind of humility in the characters of Renzo, Lucia, Agnese, and the rest of his plebeian characters, but we only wish that he had not confused it with the second kind of humility which is also present, alas, and in greater quantity than poetic truth would require.

The fact is that we continually find, side by side with expressions of Christian humility in the talk of the characters in *The Betrothed*, phrases that seem to confirm their condition of inferiority, of subjection, of obscurity. Agnese says, 'For us poor people the wool seems more tangled...' (Chapter III); Renzo says, 'We poor people can't talk...' (Chapter III); and Renzo again, 'With someone who really helps the poor . . .' (Chapter III); Agnese, 'And we poor people can't understand everything' (Chapter IV); and again Agnese, 'But you'll forgive me if I speak badly, because we're decent folk' (Chapter IX); Lucia, 'We poor women . . .' (Chapter IX); Renzo, 'How glad he was to find himself with poor people' (Chapter XIV); Renzo, 'And sleep like a poor boy . . .' (Chapter XIV); Renzo, 'The words a poor boy says . . .' (Chapter XIV); Renzo, 'They want to muddle up a poor boy who hasn't studied' (Chapter XVI); Renzo, ' . . . Tie down a poor boy' (Chapter XVI); Lucia, 'The master [that is to say the Unnamed who has kidnapped her] promised it to me. He said, "Tomorrow morning". Where is the master?' (Chapter XXIV); the tailor, 'A gentleman of that sort, like a parish priest' (Chapter XXIV); Agnese, 'You don't need much to make the poor seem rascals' (Chapter XXIX) and so on, in many other places. These are the phrases that made Gramsci say that 'the aristocratic character of Manzoni's Catholicism can be detected in amused "pity" towards his working-class figures'. From these phrases it would seem as though Manzoni was at pains to put his humble characters 'in their place' through their own lips; they are indications of the attitude he is always attributing to those characters. What exactly is that attitude? It can easily be summed up: an attitude of resigned subjection, of almost complacent inferiority, of submissiveness beyond discussion. It is the attitude of plebeians totally bereft of pride if not of dignity, literally prostrate before the powerful. Yet what a set of powerful people they are! For one of the most curious and significant of Manzoni's traits is this: that he makes his humble people full of respect for the powerful, while making the powerful totally unworthy of their respect.

Still in connection with Manzoni's attitude to the humble, we could recall the episode of Cardinal Borromeo's visit to the tailor's house where Agnese and Lucia have been taken in. The anecdote is full of grace, a picture typical of a kind at which Manzoni excelled, as giving scope for all his kindly and subtle humour. The Cardinal visits the two women at the tailor's—a good man, according to Manzoni, if rather infatuated, and with the speech he wants to address to the Cardinal firmly in his mind: but when he actually finds himself in the Cardinal's presence he gets all flustered and can only come out with an idiotic 'Just think of it . . .'. As we have said, the incident is very charming and told with great elegance; but when we look at it more closely we cannot fail to note the way in which the humility of the humble man and the power of the powerful man are, so to speak, rubbed in and confirmed. In other words the story underlines the tailor's subjection before the Cardinal and endows him not only with social, but also with moral and intellectual inferiority. Now we are all well aware that it is not very illuminating to compare Manzoni with such a different writer as Boccaccio. But we can hardly resist the temptation to recall, in contrast to the tale of Manzoni's tailor, the story in the *Decameron* which tells of Cisti, the baker, who in a similar situation puts a man of power to shame with a sharp phrase; or the one about King Agilulf's groom who feels so little inferior to the King himself that he manages, by an ingenious trick, to sleep with the Queen. Why make such a comparison? Because while Manzoni seems almost to take pleasure in corroborating that poor people are also inferior, Boccaccio has no fear of showing us the hard core of human equality within the multicoloured shell of social importance. Probably the servitude of the common people was greater in Boccaccio's time than in Manzoni's, five centuries later. But there was more democratic spirit in Boccaccio than Manzoni.

So Catholic realism does not stop at preaching a mannered religion, it also presents us with a social world in its own image and likeness. And it is Catholic realism, speaking through Renzo, that dictates the moral at the end of *The Betrothed*: 'I have learnt not to get involved in riots . . . and not to make speeches in the street.' A moral that is certainly not Christian. Jesus never learnt not to get into riots and not to make speeches in the street. He threw himself into riots, and preached in the streets; and the rest is known.

*

At this point we will be asked why on earth we chose Manzoni so as to speak of Catholic realism, or rather of socialist realism—or the art of propaganda as it is understood today. Our answer is that we chose Manzoni precisely because he is so great an artist. The propaganda art of modern artists is so inferior that there is always a danger of being told that the fault lies not with the propaganda but with the inborn mediocrity of the artists. But with Manzoni we have one of the greatest artists of all time; and yet, for all the resources of his genius—which indeed are infinite when compared with those of socialist realist writers—the art of propaganda as carried out in the modern way, that is to say not with the procedures of eloquence but with poetic portrayal, produces in him the very same effects.

It may be objected that there are no novelists without an ideology, and that thus all novelists in some way practise the art of propaganda in the modern, that is the poetic, way. But we distinguish between the novelists whose ideology is an original creation of their own, lacking an even indirect relationship with political, social and religious situations, and those who, for whatever reason, accept the pre-existing ideology of some institution or party or society or religion. And they accept it not so much because it lies within the reality they are describing (which could partly explain why they accept it) as because they would like it to do so. Stendhal's heroic ideology, Dostoievsky's Christian-decadent ideology—to take two examples—are original creations of those two writers; it would be difficult indeed to imagine a real world governed in practice by either ideology. But Manzoni's Catholic realist ideology, or the socialist realism of the Soviet writers, have nothing original about them, they are the orthodox ideologies of a religion such as the Catholic one, or of a political party such as the Communist one; and alas, it is only too easy to imagine a world governed in practice by either of these. The difference is substantial. Stendhal and Dostoievsky put their ideologies before us in a disinterested way, as they would put a landscape before us; whereas Manzoni and the socialist realist writers try to impose it on us. The obscure uneasiness we spoke of at the beginning thus comes from a suspicion that we are being 'got at'.

So these notes have no other intention than to defend poetry, beginning with Manzoni's poetry. Please do not tell us that poetry does not need defending. It is in fact more threatened today than ever before. For in our time totalitarianism no longer demands decent oratory, it demands poetry. Whereas Manzoni has shown us in his masterpiece (if unknowingly) that anti-historical totalitarianism cannot produce other than propaganda art; and propaganda art, being outside history, is not poetry.

1960

EROTICISM IN LITERATURE

Eroticism in modern literature has no resemblance to eroticism in pagan literature nor to eroticism in the literatures that followed it, though if there are any resemblances at all these are to the former rather than the latter. But there is the difference that in pagan literature eroticism has all the innocence, brutality and cohesion of a nature not yet divided and turned against itself by the Christian sense of sin, whereas eroticism in modern literature is bound to take the Christian experience into account. In other words, eroticism in modern literature derives not from a situation of nature, but from a process of liberation from pre-existent prohibitions and taboos. With the pagans, freedom was an unconscious, simple fact, whereas with the moderns it has been reclaimed, rediscovered, rewon. In compensation eroticism in modern literature has, or should have, the character proper to subjects that neither shock nor draw undue attention to themselves—that are, in short, normal if we understand normal to mean the transformation of the sexual act into something scientifically known and poetically valid, and therefore insignificant from the ethical point of view.

The result of this is, or should be, that for the first time since the pagan literatures sex is becoming material for poetry without the need for recourse to the props of symbols or the disguises of metaphor. Today, for the first time for many centuries, the sexual act can be represented directly, explicitly, realistically and poetically in a literary work, whenever the work itself makes this necessary. At this point someone will ask: but *is* it necessary to talk about the sexual act and, if so, when? My answer is that it is not always necessary to talk about the sexual act, just as it is not always necessary to talk about social questions or adventures in Africa, but that, as the prohibitions and taboos that stood in its way no longer exist today, to pass it over in silence when it *is* necessary is no longer, as it once was, a moral question but an inadequacy of expression. To take an example: the contemporary writer who does not speak of the sexual act when the subject-matter of his book requires it, is behaving like the citizen who refrains from talking about politics in a democratic régime because the dictatorship that preceded it forbade him to do so. Of course, let me repeat, it is not always necessary to talk about the sexual act; but it is necessary to talk about it when—to make a play on words—it is necessary.

Our objector now asks why on earth it seems so often necessary to talk about the sexual act in modern literature. To this we answer very simply that in the modern world sex is synonymous with love, and who could deny that love is a very common subject in the literatures of all times and places?

But how in the world, someone else will say, has love been transformed into sex in modern literature; in other words how has it lost the indirect, metaphorical and idealised character that it had in the past, to end up as identified with the sexual act? There are many reasons for this identification, the principal one being, as we have already pointed out, the collapse of the prohibitions and taboos that only too frequently and artificially lay at the root of the false idealisations of eroticism.

These taboos and prohibitions were only in appearance of Christian origin; in reality Christianity confined itself to counselling chastity. Probably the taboos and prohibitions were the outcome of a slow social involution, an involution not unlike the one that can be observed in, for instance, class relationships in some Western societies.

However, the collapse of these taboos and prohibitions has been caused mainly by what is called depth psychology, or psychoanalysis and the related psychological sciences. The discoveries of psychoanalysis have had a crucial result in two ways: they have broken down the taboos, and have raised the sexual act from the ignominy into which the taboos had cast it, and have reinstated it among the few ways of expression and communion available to man.

The sexual act in modern literature is, or should be, neither diabolical temptation, as with the medieval ascetics, nor an almost gastronomical pleasure as with the eighteenth-century bourgeoisie, but as it shows itself when we manage to separate it both from moralistic horror and vulgar hedonism: an act of insertion into a cosmic and superhuman order. Seen in this way the sexual act is effectively something higher, more mysterious, and more complete than love, especially if love is interpreted as the simple physico-sentimental relationship between man and woman.

1961

NOTHING AMEN

A SIGNIFICANT feature of modern American literature is the inability of many of the writers to get beyond the world of their adolescence and youth, so as to add to it and develop it. The American writer often starts off splendidly, with courage, candour, curiosity, a sense of adventure, and a thirst for experience. But unfortunately a maximum charge of vitality is matched by a minimum of cultural equipment. In other words, faith in life is accompanied by a lack of faith in the resources of culture, which the American writer sees as cramping and weighing down the immediacy and authenticity of direct experience. Naturally this attitude is also a fact of culture, though of a minor, degraded and anti-humanistic culture.

As a consequence of his lack of faith in culture, the American writer for the most part confines himself to recounting the story of his youth. For him it is an inspirational capital that must be spent without delay and without thinking about profitable investments to assure him a tranquil old age. Metaphor apart, in the United States literary careers such as those of Thomas Mann or André Gide—who went on developing a train of writing begun fifty years earlier up to the last days of their life—are rare. After he has made his début with a couple of books, the American writer tends to restrict himself to re-writing them, and so increasingly falls into imitating himself and his own particular mannerisms. That is, he seems incapable of developing his themes by gradually dropping the worn-out and decaying parts and bringing the vigorous and lasting ones to leaf and flower. If we wanted to trace the writer back to the civilisation to which he belongs, we could almost say that despite himself the American writer imitates the standardised industrial production that is the dominant characteristic of his country's economy. He sets out from a prototype designed when he was young, and spends the rest of his life turning out a standardised production based on the blueprint of his original prototype. What is the explanation of this unfortunate development? Let us point out at the outset that writers in the past, such as Emily Dickinson and Herman Melville, went on writing in an original and fresh way right up to their death without declining into mannerism and self-imitation. So we get the impression that the modern American writer has failed to extract himself from the general alienation of society in the United States. After the deceptive freshness of youth he mirrors increasingly, in the mechanisation of his own work, the general mechanisation of the society for which he is writing.

In these observations we are aware that we have involuntarily drawn almost a portrait of Ernest Hemingway. Hemingway was our contemporary, and he met his death when he was still young, yet, precisely because of the infantile and precocious state of arrested development we have just described, his work as regards our time is as discounted and anachronistic as any, and for this same reason ranks with all that is most classical and beyond discussion.

Where did Hemingway come from? By his origins he was a 'frontiersman', that is he inherited the view of life peculiar to those American social groups that moved westwards towards the great spaces open to conquest and colonisation. Strange to say, this by and large healthy, youthful, brave and frank view of life was to reveal itself through Hemingway as related to all the most refined, tired and corrupt elucubrations of old Europe during the same period. I mean the spirit of decadence at its most superficial and exasperated level, the sort of decadence which, finding literature insufficient, was later to spread to *mores* and politics by way of D'Annunzianism and Nazism. This amounts to saying that the sporting, boisterous young man from Chicago was related, in the great family of writers, to two such different figures as D'Annunzio and Malraux. We could easily trace him back to Theodore Roosevelt who was also a great huntsman, explorer and man of action and even to Byron who swam the Hellespont, was a *carbonaro* in Italy and a patriot in Greece. Whereas with his real contemporary, Proust, Hemingway had nothing in common. We have mentioned Proust so as to situate Hemingway. The French novelist, in fact, was saved from decadentism by his faith in culture; his work is far removed from the superficial and brand new temptations to decadence of his time owing to his character as humanist and moralist. Memory is reason reclaimed, life reordered, rationality never betrayed. Proust is the last of the great European realists whereas Hemingway belongs to the irrationalist wave of men like Lawrence and Malraux.

Surely nothing could throw light on Hemingway better than a comparison with D'Annunzio and Malraux. What has Hemingway in common with these two writers? With D'Annunzio he shares the ambition of creating a myth about himself, that is to say, building himself a pedestal in his own mythological monument not only by means of literature but also, and chiefly, by a tendentious choice of modes of action—bull-fighting, big game hunting, civil war, world war, revolution. This myth of self outlives literary creativeness; the writer is already dead and embalmed, whether at Gardone or Cuba, but the man of action goes on firing off cannon or lion hunting, taking part in politics, or war. Of course the myth makes heavy demands: D'Annunzio had to live it to the bitter end, that is, until he became ridiculous and senile; Hemingway, who was more modern and less rhetorical, lived it up to a splendid suicide with a bullet from a big game rifle in the temple. Despite the undoubted sincerity of both Hemingway and D'Annunzio, what remains of such myths? Nothing, even less than nothing. They are fabricated for the masses, and the masses forget them as soon as other more up-to-date and beguiling myths arise.

The comparison with Malraux, on the other hand, involves an examination of Hemingway's themes. Malraux, in his life, is not an actor like D'Annunzio, but a terribly serious European intellectual, a sort of Parisian Raskolnikoff. So with Malraux Hemingway has in common the ambition to interpret, and live, the great modern revolutionary movements in an individualistic, super-mystical and Nietzschean key. Malraux starts off with the adventure of a theft of valuable statues in the depths of the forests of Indo-China, then passes through Stalinist Communism and ends up as one of de Gaulle's ministers. With him the parabola from decadentism to Fascist-type nationalism is complete. Hemingway, who is less coherent and rational, more artistic and voluble, stops halfway; he attempts to insert his cowboy individualism, in love with courage and death, into the Spanish revolution, fails, and withdraws in time into private life. How are we to explain the failure of both Hemingway and Malraux? It was because their idea that revolution was an adventure like any other was fundamentally mistaken. Revolution was not an adventure, though there were many adventures involved in it and it was often adventurous; it was a struggle for a ruthless order and one without imagination, as was made perfectly clear with the development of Stalinism. It was therefore not unexpected that Hemingway's Marxism, picked up by flipping through a popular handbook, evaporated as soon as could be after the unfortunate effort of *To Have and Have Not*. Yet Hemingway wrote *For Whom the Bell Tolls*, his most ambitious and careful work, whose cruel episodes and conventional characters betrayed his decadence and lack of ideas, and then re-crossed the Atlantic. Africa—*The Green Hills of Africa*—was a mere intermezzo; the return to Italy after the second world war—*Across the River and into the Trees*—a fiasco. Finally, with *The Old Man and the Sea*, a bad book if an enormous success, Hemingway seemed to reach out once more to the original motifs of American literature and his own. With *The Old Man and the Sea* he tried to write his *Moby Dick*. All he really did was to imitate himself in a painstaking, clumsy and mannered way.

His best books are far removed from our time and are really fine. They are the only ones we like and are ready to re-read. Unfalsified reality shines through them, and they have preserved intact the fascination of his infantile, one-dimensional and boisterous prose, apparently simple and ordered, in reality full of poetic ambiguity (there is no shadow of rationality in Hemingway's prose). Anyone who has tried to translate it has experienced how it falls to pieces, and one has to start again from the beginning, luminous, and always a trifle conventional; these books, written between 1920 and 1930, will live as examples of the literary idea of a whole epoch. All told they amount to two novels, *The Sun Also Rises* (*Fiesta*) and *A Farewell to Arms*, and a volume of short stories, *The First Forty-Nine Stories*. Hemingway's simplicity, or rather his lack of ideas, makes him better as a short story writer than a novelist. He was the creator of that lyrical and autobiographical way of telling stories which in Italy, after various modifications, came to be known as neo-realism.

In *A Farewell to Arms* Hemingway's inclination to create a myth of himself is blended in a natural way with his rejection of the traditional novel endowed with plot, characters, psychology and conflicts. In this novel, which relates his war experience in Italy, as in *The Sun also Rises*, which describes the sojourn of a group of Americans in Spain, and as also in *Men without Women*, a collection of stories about sport and sporting champions, Hemingway blueprinted an ethics and a type of hero of his own that he repeated in all his subsequent books: the ethics of physical courage, or the capacity or incapacity to face one's adversary without fear, the adversary being in turn a boxer, a lion, a bull, an enemy soldier, death; and a hero of American intellectual nomadism, a war correspondent, a hunter, a journalist, a traveller. Physical courage is no more than an infantile and puritan sublimation of sexual energy and it is possibly for this reason that the portraits of women in Hemingway's books are all conventional, rather like those of Kipling, another writer of physical courage with whom he has some affinities. As for the hero, at first glance he seems an energetic and adventurous Stendhalian character but in reality he is a weak-nerved man always hunting for new sensations and distractions, who acts as he drinks and drinks as he acts to conceal the nothingness inside him and around him. Hemingway's famous dialogues, even before they are literary invention, are the direct expression of this desolation of action divorced from any meaning and any justification. Their elegance is not, as many imitators have believed, a question of style but of ethics. So if it be true, as would appear, that Hemingway killed himself, it may well be worthwhile recalling his story, *A Clean, Well-lighted Place*, in which two waiters are talking on the very subject, precisely, of an old regular who had tried to kill himself a few days earlier:

> 'Last week he tried to commit suicide,' one waiter said.
> 'Why?'
> 'He was in despair.'
> 'What about?'
> 'Nothing.'
> 'How do you know it was nothing?'
> 'He has plenty of money.'

Later the old man goes away, one of the waiters goes to bed, and the other one, now alone, repeats to himself his night prayer:

> 'Our nada who art in nada, nada be thy name thy kingdom nada thy will be nada in nada as it is in nada . . .' amen.

Hemingway wrote the story when he was young and confident. But—once again following the tradition of modern American literature—he was incapable of developing or adding anything of value to his early, naïve nihilism. So it truly can be said of him that he died as he had lived.

1961

DIALOGUE ON THE PAINTING OF RENATO GUTTUSO

Do YOU like Renato Guttuso's paintings?

Yes, I do.

Why do you like them?

Heavens, what an insatiable questioner you are! I like them because I like them—there's nothing else to be said.

Are you sure there's nothing else to be said?

Quite sure. Generally speaking, I don't think there is anything to say about the arts, except perhaps literature.

Why?

Because painting, sculpture, music, all the arts except literature, appeal to our silent evaluation and appreciation. Literature prompts us to talk, yes, but only with its more logical and explicit, its least mysterious, side. Perhaps this is why art criticism, especially the kind concerned with painting, is so often presumptuous, vapid and absurd. There is really nothing to say.

So if you look at a painting, a Guttuso for instance, what should you do?

Look at it.

And then?

Look at it again.

Only look at it?

Yes, painting is to be looked at. What's odd about that?

Only looked at?

Yes, only looked at.

Tell me something about looking.

Looking is looking.

Nothing else?

Looking starts with my eyes, then rests on Guttuso's painting, examines it, observes it, goes over it from top to bottom, rests on it and then leaves it, having not so much understood as enjoyed the painting.

But what does looking look at most, or if you like, what strikes you most? Could you tell me that?

You mean you want me to make a long speech about an act of looking that scarcely lasts a second?

Yes.

Well, I'll try. But the speech will be incomplete. You can talk exhaustively about a mental operation, but not about a look.

Very well. Tell me what you can.

Well, what strikes me first when I look at one of Guttuso's paintings is the sensuality.

But Guttuso isn't a sensual painter.

You're right, he isn't. And that makes his sensuality, weighed down as it is by all the difficulties of expression it has to surmount so as to reveal itself, all the more remarkable.

Give me an example.

I don't know . . . Let's take, for instance, his *Reclining Nude*, 1940. First I would like to underline the 'disagreeable' quality of this, as of nearly all Guttuso's nudes. The same disagreeableness is apparent of course in his pictures on other subjects. But a nude is always the reality that provides the best measuring-rod for the reactions of sensuality. Guttuso's disagreeableness in *Reclining Nude*, 1940, helps to show a particular relationship between the painter and reality as a whole.

What kind of relationship?

I won't tell you, I'll leave it to the *Nude* to speak. She's a woman depicted in a moment of heavy drowsiness at an hour of the day and on a day of the year that we guess to be still and sultry. Awkwardness, disharmony, unhappiness, torpor, maturity, deformation produced by food and age, are the principal characteristics of the Nude. The face is blotched with red, and the blotches are repeated on the forearm; it is a red blotchiness the skin develops after drinking too much wine, or after skin-pressures during sleep. The years have slackened the woman's breasts, slightly distended her stomach, and thinned her legs. The outline of the buttocks is seen from below upwards, with the cold glance of a man who insists on noticing certain details even in the transports of love. The cushion on which the woman's head is resting has the greenish cold tones of some material bathed in saliva that set one's teeth on edge—tones repeated on the walls and the door, disgusting, repulsive tones. The woman is lying on a red blanket that we can guess to be of rough, coarse, cheap wool with hard folds and irksomely hot. A kitchen chair accentuates the poverty of the surroundings. Its straw has a sort of bluish tone, disagreeable because cold and shiny, and this is echoed on the door-knob. The painting's general effect is one of disagreeable intimacy, but chosen and loved precisely for that reason.

What, then, is Guttuso's relation with his material?

Haven't I already told you in my description of *Reclining Nude*, 1940?

I get an inkling, but I'd like you to be more explicit.

It's a relationship of irritation, cruelty, aggression, nausea, repugnance, attraction and repulsion, in other words a relationship of violence. Violence above all.

Why violence above all?

Look at my hand. I'm lifting it to hit you. When I'm just on the point of hitting you, I experience all the feelings of one ready to establish a relationship based on violence: repulsion, irritation, aggression, nausea and cruelty. But violence always implies a relationship of some sort with reality—at least it is better than indifference.

You mean Guttuso never experiences indifference?

He probably does—it must be his biggest temptation. But precisely because it is his biggest temptation he overcomes it with a qualitative leap in the other direction.

How would you define that in terms of expression?

It means that Guttuso reacts against the temptation of abstract painting—one that he feels very strongly and which is always with us in modern times—by means of a special kind of violence. The violence is special because it has its origin in the insidious and highly reasonable quality of the temptation.

Yes . . . ?

He overcomes indifference—which would justify abstract painting—with a shout, with gesticulation, with noise, with tumult, agitation and explosion, with, in a word, everything capable of suggesting excessive participation. Every painting by Guttuso is a kind of besieged fortress in the desert of abstraction.

So you maintain that Guttuso's violence is a defensive violence?

Yes, partly. Guttuso, in order to express himself, has to keep on crossing a frontier of repulsion, timidity, reserve, discretion, tenderness and silence—things that would draw him straight to abstract painting if he hadn't got this will to self-defence. In its good moments Guttuso's violence is an active possession of reality; in its less good moments it is eloquence. But it is always violence, first exercised on himself, then on reality.

Do you like this violence of Guttuso's?

No violence is pleasing at first sight. At the first impact we are left disconcerted, surprised, upset and repelled. But at a second stage Guttuso's common-man, even proletarian sincerity, his human frankness, his primitive simplicity win us over to him. Guttuso's violence has something warm, vital, generous and peasant-like about it. It is a Mediterranean violence, fine and sunny even if brooding. Guttuso's so-called expressionism has its origins in the fatality of the blood, of the pride, of the taste for power and cruelty that all rightly belong to the peasant and artisan society of Sicily. Hence Guttuso's many affinities with Picasso, who is another Mediterranean expressionist. The affinity with Picasso goes beyond the space-time limits of modern painting; it is rooted in a common ancestral past.

But Guttuso is more than a Sicilian and Mediterranean painter. You yourself hinted at his double nature when you said that his violence was a thing of the common people, proletarian.

Yes, indeed. Guttuso lives in the age of the two great and universal social phenomena of the modern world, the revolt of the peasant masses, and their massive urbanisation. The urbanisation is a direct outcome of the revolt.

So are we to view Guttuso as a man of our time who has felt deeply both revolt and urbanisation?

Yes. But once again, let us leave it to his painting to speak. This painter of cacti, olives and fishing boats is also the painter of, for instance, *Nature Morte with Tin Cans*, 1957. Here the proletarian Guttuso, denizen of the great industrial cities, replaces the peasant Guttuso. Here too we can see disagreeableness expressed in an almost obsessive way. Implements, irons, tools, mass-produced industrial products, tins, cans and so on take the place of wicker baskets, olives, flowers, fruit, and other products of the country. Guttuso has experienced urbanisation as a phenomenon of alienation; the former countryman is an outsider in a world of mass-produced objects that are worthless and don't last. In the morning you have a spotless tin of shining metal with a beautiful label nicely stuck on; by the evening it has become a dirty reject, mangled by the tin-opener, filthy, empty, rattling on a refuse dump in the suburbs. This feeling of the fleetingness and brutality of the world in which the proletariat lives is present in all Guttuso's pictures. Even love is not immune.

Even love?

Love is felt as something that can only be pleasant at rare intervals, during respites from stultifying labour, brutalising fatigue, wearing exhaustion. Guttuso's women are like his starving dogs or his skeleton horses. They are carcases with ample flanks and thin legs, with sunken chests and swollen stomachs, ready to yield to an embrace they endure rather than desire. For them love is a brief pain between two wearinesses, violence wrought on defenceless and resigned flesh. Such love smells of sweaty clothes, a room in the shanty towns, and working-class promiscuity. Sometimes there is cruelty and violence. For instance look at *Nude*, 1959. A woman lies prostrate on a blood-red blanket with her eyes shut and her face turned away. Her ribs and the bones of her pelvis stick out from her body. The outspread thighs are massive, then suddenly taper away into the skinny shin-bone. The pubic hair is a triangle of fiery darkness. The woman has been knocked over onto the floor; she has been thrown, she did not lie there of her own accord. But she has stayed there, her mouth half open, her eyes half closed, waiting.

Waiting for what?

For some other and final violence. But let us look at working-class violence in action. Guttuso's composition pictures mostly represent crowds grouped together by only one relationship—violence. So we get *The Flight from Etna*, 1938; *The Crucifixion*, 1940; *The Occupation of the Lands*, 1947; *The Battle of Ponte Ammiraglio*, 1952; *Portella della Ginestra*, 1952; *Beach at Night*, 1957; *Pedestrians' Passage*, 1957.

Don't you feel all these pictures are too unlike to be put under the single heading of violence?

No, because it is precisely violence that constitutes the link between his pictures. Violence between the figures in the picture, violence of the painter on the figures. Do you know what the first clue to violence is?

No.

The embarrassment, clumsiness, awkwardness, discomfort, discordance and unnaturalness of gestures and attitudes. Think a moment: supposing you do something of your own free will, without being coerced or urged to do it by anyone else, then your movements will be harmonious, co-ordinated, rational, inevitable. But if someone comes along with a push or a punch or a rifle or some other violent means, and compels you to do what he wants, then your movements will betray the disarray and disorder that go with coercion and the absence of inner necessity. Now the attitudes of the people in Guttuso's pictures are not those of men and women who want to move and know why they're moving of their own free will, but those of people who are pushed and forced to move by some external agent against their own free will. The Germans in *Gott mit Uns*, for instance, are not shooting, arresting, torturing, and threatening by their own will but by the external will of the author, that is by a violence that forces them to be violent. The peasants aren't fleeing because they want to flee, but because the author's violence makes them flee, at dead of night, half naked, and all disordered. The labourers are not occupying the land because they themselves want to occupy it but because Guttuso wants them to occupy it. Movement in Guttuso's pictures goes from the outside inwards, not from the inside outwards. Hence Guttuso's crowds are like objects thrown into confusion and borne away by a hurricane, or hurtled in all directions by an explosion. In this sense Guttuso is a real Marxist. He firmly believes that the representation of reality is not enough; he has to introduce movement and dialectical impulse into reality.

A lot has been said about Guttuso's expressionism. How do you reconcile expressionism, which is always decadent, with the Marxism you have just mentioned? Expressionism excludes the healthy and humanistic reclaiming of reality to which the Marxist method should lead.

Yet it is the only way nowadays of being figurative. Nowadays you have to be either expressionist or abstract. If we look close enough we see that the crisis in the modern world cannot possibly be expressed in painting except in these two ways of approaching the real. They are equivalent, even if unalike. Expressionism is figurative art under constant temptation by the abstract, just as abstract art is non-figurativism constantly tempted by expressionism.

I don't understand.

I'll try to explain. Expressionism is figurative only because the expressionist painter accepts the world we usually call objective, as a pretext. But nothing more than a pretext. Today real objectivity, that is to say the objectivity of one and the same conception of reality once shared by painter and viewer, no longer exists. We lack the ideology to justify it. The painter's world may differ from the viewer's to a greater or lesser degree, but the difference is there. Yet expressionism is different from abstract art because, unlike abstract art, it allows for the appeal of objects.

What does that mean?

Have you ever reflected on the fact that things have a shape, that is to say that on the surface, and to all appearances, they're made differently from how they're made inside? Take the human body, for instance; its outward shape is symmetrical, but within there is no symmetry, all the organs are arranged asymmetrically. There are two arms, two legs, two eyes, but there is only one heart situated on the left, and one liver situated on the right. The shape is verifiable through the senses, but even if it weren't we could none the less affirm that objects want to have a shape, whether verifiable or not. That is, they want to get out and exist outside the chaos within which they are born. But perhaps it would be more exact to affirm that the shape of objects can't be ignored or abolished inasmuch as it is born of the same necessity as art.

And what does that mean?

The shape of a flower is born of a necessity of nature which is only mysterious because we can't retrace the phases the flower passed through before it became a flower. The necessity that required that that chair should exist as shape is much clearer to us, and we can say with conviction to what the chair owes its shape. Now, in art objects are born from the same necessity as in nature. Just as the object is what it is because it could not be otherwise than what it is, so in art, it is representable in one way only. And this because the object demands from our senses that given representation and no other. Of course the appeal of the object can be rejected, as it is by the abstract painters. The expressionist painter, on the other hand, welcomes it. Naturally he doesn't welcome it as classicist painters did, for whom objectivity wasn't a sort of concession but an almost automatic fact; he welcomes it, as we have already said, as a pretext. Which precisely explains what you call the diminished or partial character of representation in expressionism.

Even Guttuso's expressionism?

The modern world is a world of nomads. Each artist is a world unto himself, separated from the world of others, autonomous and alone. In some of these worlds—as in some remote stars lost in sidereal space—breathing is impossible, for the elements necessary for life are lacking. In others we find ourselves more at ease. Finally there are other worlds which, though entirely subjective, give an impression of perfect objectivity. Now what we have to see is whether Guttuso, in welcoming the appeal of objects' shapes, creates a world in which it is possible to breathe or not.

And what is your opinion?

I should say that one can live very well in Guttuso's world. And here, in my view, we come to the most important point. Guttuso stops at the threshold of incommunicability and of impossiblity of life not only because of his violence but also because of the gift of humanity which lies at the root of his ideological position.

Do you mean Marxism?

Yes, Marxism. Guttuso's expressionism is corrected, integrated and rendered accessible by his fidelity to Marxist humanism. Expressionism alone would not be enough to guarantee communication; probably Guttuso would end by giving in to the temptation of abstraction. It is Marxism that saves Guttuso from the despair peculiar, for instance, to German expressionism after the first war. And again it is Marxism that stops him on the threshold of abstraction, so alluring to the modern painter. Marxism, in Guttuso, has something of the same balancing and integrating function as Christianity in Baudelaire. And perhaps art has always been made in this way: by a cross-breeding between what today we call decadentism or subjective violence, and a realistic and objective ideology.

But classical art, as you have already said, was objective by nature. The fusion between subject and object was achieved not by contrast but by identification.

True. But Giotto had twelve centuries of Christianity behind him. Guttuso has only sixty years of Marxism. Modern ideologies are on the move, they have all the characteristics of risk, experiment and gamble. They make us hope for a better world, but that world is not yet with us. In his picture Guttuso mirrors this quality of the modern ideology, incapable of inspiring contemplation because it is still entangled in the doubts, conflicts and hypotheses of action.

So Guttuso is that improbable character—the artist to whom the moment of contemplation is denied?

No, there is no art without contemplation, and in Guttuso the capacity for contemplation is at least as strong as the capacity for drama. But it will always be a contemplation *sui generis*. Take, for instance, the *Nude*, 1959. A woman is seated with one knee higher than the other, and her arms round this knee. In this picture we must look for Guttuso's contemplation in the novelty of certain colour harmonies which do away with the original naturalistic approach and replace it with unpredictable invention: the lilac of the breast, the green of the ribs, the chestnut of the arm. Only contemplation could suggest such symbolic language as this. In other pictures Guttuso aims at reclaiming the magic of the real, and we have the intricacy of the green twisting branches through which we glimpse the red, chestnut, orange and grey roofs of Velate—in the painting called *The Roof of Velate*. Guttuso's contemplation reveals one of his important characteristics, the tendency to obsession.

What do you mean by obsession?

I mean this: Guttuso fixes himself on an object in an obsessive way, like a bull with a red flag. He contemplates, if I may so put it, because he doesn't understand. Guttuso's contemplation is made up of stupefaction and relentless concentration. Why, for instance, did he paint the *Nature Morte with Tin Cans* which I mentioned earlier? Because he had contemplated these homely objects in an obsessive way, not really understanding them but, precisely for that reason, identifying himself with them.

Now you are trying to tell me that Guttuso doesn't understand what he is always representing.

In a certain sense, yes.

In what sense?

As we have already seen, practical will, ideological charge, and a tendency to eloquence are extremely strong in Guttuso. But at the same time he is an extraordinary delicate and sensitive artist.

This quality of his as an artist is shown by his obsessive, contemplative incomprehension. For all his ideology and his violence, his eloquence and his expressive frenzy, he is still a poet who, when confronted with the intimacy and the mystery of the real, pauses in astonishment, submerged in a deep and vital stupefaction.

1962

THE 'VULGARITY' OF GIUSEPPE VERDI

THERE IS something petty, tired and provincial about the Italian nineteenth century. It is a middle class century—only, unlike the French and English, the Italian middle class had no proper identity papers. It had never beheaded kings, or made a Reformation, or adored the goddess Reason; it was, and still is, a timid, cautious, narrow-minded middle class that cringed before the aristocracy and licked the boots of the clergy. True, urged on by the French Revolution and the Napoleonic wars, it made a supreme effort and managed to bring about the Risorgimento, but even the Risorgimento lacked men, made little impression on the masses, was full of humiliating contradictions, and was far behind the rest of Europe. A petty affair all in all. And there is the question of proportion. Though in any other country the Risorgimento would have been an important upheaval, in Italy, given her grandiose past, it was a mean little enterprise. The men of the Risorgimento were provincial middle class and their mixture of nationalism and liberalism produced something very weak in alcoholic content. Their romantic intoxication was a prelude to the drunken orgy of rhetoric under Fascism, and the lower-middle-class camomile-infusion under the Christian Democrats.

The truth of what has been said can be appreciated if we take a glance at the types of architecture in Italian provincial cities. Side by side with the medieval palaces in stone and iron, the gigantic buildings of the Renaissance, and the vast houses of the seventeenth and eighteenth centuries, we find little neo-classical style houses of the middle class nineteenth century—petty, cold, narrow, as though planned by art-masters from elementary schools. In these nineteenth century, middle and lower middle class houses we breathe an enclosed, guarded and withdrawn atmosphere. We feel that Italy has exchanged her grandiose vices and far from conventional virtues for a decorum in which everything, from religion to art, from ethics to literature, is reduced to the level of timid, provincial society.

Often, and above all in provincial cities not yet in the grip of the industrial revolution and its prosperity, we can come across immense and illustrious palaces that have fallen on evil days and are inhabited by artisan and working class families. These unfortunate people show up the unavoidable decay of the once-splendid buildings in which they live. And yet there is something natural in this decay and dilapidation, in the mysterious but undeniable relationship between the common people of today and the illustrious people of the past.

Whereas we feel a yawning gulf in cases where these palaces have been spruced up and restored and divided into large numbers of luxury flatlets for middle class 'artistic' people on the look-out for 'historic' surroundings. Between the middle classes and the aristocrats who once inhabited the palaces, the gulf is complete and irreparable.

Giuseppe Verdi's situation in the Italian nineteenth century is rather like the situation of those illustrious but impoverished palaces in the heart of the now bourgeois cities in our provinces. Verdi's full-blooded, passionate, robust and explosive personality, within the poor and petty Italian nineteenth century, seems almost incredible. As soon as we begin comparing Verdi with other great men of our nineteenth century we realise that he was not only an exception but an anachronism. Consider Manzoni and Leopardi, for instance. Both stemmed directly from the Italian ruling class, both belonged to the provincial aristocracy and were in positions typical of Italian society of the period. Verdi was of peasant stock. Now both Manzoni and Leopardi are artists of a stature certainly not inferior to Verdi; yet the difference is enormous. In Manzoni and Leopardi the artistic temperament, negatively speaking, drew its distinctive colouring from the prudent, provincial and timid society to which they belonged and from which they originated. In a way Manzoni accepted and expressed the pettiness of that society, whereas Leopardi rejected it. But in both, despite their stature as artists, the acceptance or rejection bore the distinctive mark of what was accepted or rejected—with Manzoni this was prudence, with Leopardi despair. Yet both Manzoni and Leopardi are 'modern' artists, that is, they fitted perfectly into the culture of their epoch. And both are artists of impeccable, strict, and aristocratic taste.

There is nothing of all this about Verdi. As by origin he was neither aristocratic nor middle class, but peasant, he had no obligation to accept or—in last analysis—reject anything. His genius is not a genius that accepts or rejects, but a genius that identifies itself and expresses itself in its own creations. Verdi's art is exuberant, explosive and passionate, and it is not represented by prudence or led astray by revolt. At its best it is upheld by the animal astuteness peculiar to the artisan. Finally, unlike Manzoni and Leopardi, Verdi is 'vulgar'.

To me it seems that this vulgarity is the most mysterious and problematic aspect of Verdi's personality. At first sight the thing seems obvious, and anyway not very interesting; for, heaven help us, some artists are not vulgar, and others, no less gifted, are. Stendhal, for instance, is never vulgar; Balzac, also a great novelist, is. But for Stendhal and Balzac we have an explanation to hand, for a deep social upheaval separated them in time, with consequent change in style. With Verdi there was no such thing for, as we have seen, Italy underwent no social upheaval comparable to the one in France and we have also seen that nineteenth century society in Italy is better expressed by Leopardi's despair and Manzoni's prudence than by the extremely rich and full-blooded 'vulgarity' of Verdi.

Nor is Verdi's vulgarity the vulgarity of the romantics, of Hugo, for instance. The resemblance is only superficial. Hugo was a real European romantic—from him the path to the decadents, to Baudelaire and Rimbaud, is an easy one; whereas Verdi's apparent romanticism leads to no similar stage of decadence. And there is another difference between Verdi and Hugo: Hugo believed in history, he believed that men's conduct changed with history, in other words that it was determined historically.

As an outcome of this belief the characters in Hugo's plays have to be Middle Ages men, or Renaissance men, before they are men at all, with the result that Hugo's plays are unreadable and unplayable nowadays. Whereas Verdi had no belief in history either as something to be reconstructed or as something to be escaped into—and this, apart from everything else, separates him off from the romantics. Though Verdi's characters are 'dressed up', they are outside history. Verdi's conception of history was immobile, static, humanistic, Plutarchian. And so his characters still interest us today, because they are first and foremost men, and only secondarily medieval men or Renaissance men.

In what, then, does Verdi's vulgarity consist? To keep the metaphor we used earlier on, with Verdi we have the illustrious and ancient palace fallen on evil days and inhabited by artisans and workers. In other words we have the humanist view of our Renaissance which was abandoned and betrayed by the Italian ruling class after the Counter-Reformation, but preserved by the common people in a decayed form of folklore. This explains the difference between Verdi and nineteenth century Italians such as Manzoni, Leopardi, Cavour and Mazzini, and his resemblance to Garibaldi who was also a man of another age, and the analogies between Verdi and Shakespeare.

I would like to pause for a moment on the analogies with Shakespeare because they give us another key to the understanding of the nature of Verdi's vulgarity. The comparison between Shakespeare and Verdi has often been made and is substantially exact. In both we find the same idea of man, the same prodigious knowledge of the human heart, the same love of life, the same wonderful capacity for splitting themselves up and disappearing behind countless characters, dismembering their autobiographies into a thousand existences and hence making them unrecognisable. Yet the comparison needs correcting on one important point: Shakespeare is never vulgar. He is not, like Verdi, a plebeian in whom the culture of a dead epoch survives as folklore; he is a man of his time and of the society of his time, like Manzoni and Leopardi. The kind of beauty he creates has nothing popular, rustic or ingenuous about it; it is an aristocratic and cultivated beauty.

Verdi's characters, therefore, are Renaissance rather than romantic. We can recognise Renaissance humanism in the complete image of man that Verdi presents. For beneath Renaissance affectation there is always respect for the whole man with his vices and his virtues, and this we would look for in vain beneath the emphasis of romanticism, for romanticism anticipates the amputated and shrunken scale of decadentism. What Verdi offers is a Plutarchian or, if it be preferred, Shakespearean idea of man and it is not his fault if he inherited this idea not from the decorous, timid and petty middle class culture of his time but from the folklore of the common people of the Po valley. Even today these people retain a full-blooded and exuberant vitality which is a reflection of old pre-Counter-Reformation Italy: we can still imagine that we are in Verdi's age. Anyone who knows the Po valley round Parma will recognise Verdi's atmosphere in the monuments, in the people and in the landscape. Verdi is a close relative of the peasants who used to know Ariosto's rhymes by heart, of the gondoliers who recited Tasso's verses. With Verdi the greatness of Italy, and the best and most typically hers that she had to give to the world, died out: that is to say, humanism. After Verdi, Italy became definitely and finally petit bourgeois.

After the comparison between Verdi and Shakespeare, we have another comparison to make, that between the Duke Valentino as described by Machiavelli in *The Prince*, and the Duke of Mantua as portrayed by Verdi in *Rigoletto*. When we look closely we see that the two characters are made of the same Renaissance stuff and are probably the finest, strongest, most complete characters ever created in Italy. But here too, as with Shakespeare and Verdi, there is a substantial difference which, yet again, can be traced back to Verdi's plebeian vulgarity.

Duke Valentino is a full-length portrait executed with incomparable vigour. He is a Renaissance man as seen by a Renaissance intellectual. In him there is no vulgarity, everything about him breathes the paradoxical, aristocratic impiety that Stendhal was to admire so much two centuries later.

The Duke of Mantua is Verdi's equivalent of Duke Valentino. But in *Rigoletto* the great political enterprises of the Borgias have become the low intrigues of a tiny Italian court, captain adventurers have turned into idle courtiers, and the hero is a provincial good-timer. Yet the degraded world of *Rigoletto* is pervaded by a breath of the Renaissance as seen with the admiration, envy, and amazement of an urbanised peasant who is out of touch with modern European civilisation and whose standard for cultural comparison is still the Renaissance. With the Duke of Mantua Verdi has given us his Duke Valentino. If Verdi had been born in the sixteenth century he would have given us the real Duke Valentino with his ravening nobility and tigerish energy. A plebeian two centuries out of date, he has given us a provincial Casanova; but if we listen carefully and analyse the stupefying vitality and subtlety of the Duke's character, we shall see that the vitality and dimensions of this Casanova are in no way inferior to Machiavelli's Valentino.

So Verdi is our plebeian, folkloristic peasant, our 'vulgar' Shakespeare. They say that Stravinsky once said he would give much of his work to have invented the notes of *La donna e mobile*. Now if this is true it confirms our comparison with Shakespeare, with the important modification about 'vulgarity' thrown in. For in their lightning association and evocative force these notes stand up to Macbeth's famous soliloquy after he has been told of Lady Macbeth's death. It would be useless to look for anything like this in the nineteenth century romantics. They aimed for such things, but never managed to create them.

We see Verdi, and will always see him, as a Renaissance man, for his knowledge of human nature goes back to the age when man still saw himself as the end, and only himself, and nothing less than himself. Folklore and vulgarity do not impair this inspiring conception born out of its time. So our return to Verdi today is based on a fundamental misunderstanding: the effort to seek out and re-evaluate his modernity. Verdi is not in any way modern; already an anachronism in the nineteenth century, he is yet more so today. His actuality is the actuality of poetry. But to speak of Verdi's revival has an odd sound, exactly like talking of Shakespeare's revival. Verdi must be considered with the respect and understanding due to phenomena of culture, which are every bit as mysterious and powerful as those of nature.

1963